Pra

Sevan Nisanyan

Prentice Hall Travel

New York • London • Toronto • Sydney • Tokyo • Singapore

THE AMERICAN EXPRESS ® TRAVEL GUIDES

Published in the United States by
Prentice Hall General Reference
A division of Simon & Schuster, Inc.
15 Columbus Circle
New York, NY 10023

PRENTICE HALL and colophon
are registered trademarks of
Simon & Schuster, Inc.

First published in the United
Kingdom by Mitchell Beazley, an
imprint of Reed Consumer Books Ltd,
Michelin House, 81 Fulham Road,
London SW3 6RB and Auckland,
Melbourne, Singapore and Toronto

Edited, designed and produced by
Castle House Press, Llantrisant
Mid Glamorgan CF7 8EU, Wales

Library of Congress Catalog
Card Number 93-084013

ISBN 0-671-86822-5

The editors thank Neil Hanson
and Alex Taylor of Lovell Johns,
David Haslam, Fred Midwood,
Sylvia Hughes-Williams and
Sally Darlington for their help and
co-operation during the preparation
of this edition. Special thanks to
Maggie Smales and Peter Jones,
without whose vigilance we might
have been Czechmated, and for their
assistance with picture reference. We
are also grateful for the materials
helpfully provided by the Čedok
office in London.

FOR THE SERIES:
Series Editor:
  David Townsend Jones
Map Editor: David Haslam
Indexer: Hilary Bird
Gazetteer: Anna Holmes
Cover design: Roger Walton Studio

FOR THIS EDITION:
Edited on desktop by:
  David Townsend Jones
Art editor: Eileen Townsend Jones
Illustrators:
  Sylvia Hughes-Williams,
  David Evans
Cover photo: Tony Stone
  Worldwide/Joe Cornish

FOR MITCHELL BEAZLEY:
Art Director: Tim Foster
Production: Katy Sawyer
Publisher: Sarah Bennison

PRODUCTION CREDITS:
Maps by Lovell Johns,
  Oxford, England
Metro map by TCS,
  Aldershot, England
Typeset in Garamond and
  News Gothic
Desktop layout in Ventura Publisher
Reproduction by M & E
  Reproductions, Essex, England
Linotronic output by Tradespools
  Limited, Frome, England

Contents

Culture, history and background

Practical information

Planning your visit

Walking tours

Sights and places of interest

Where to stay

Eating and drinking

Entertainments

Shopping

Recreation

Excursions

Maps

How to use this book

Few guidelines are needed to understand how this book works:

- For the general organization of the book, see CONTENTS on the pages preceding this one.
- Wherever appropriate, chapters and sections are arranged alphabetically, with headings appearing in **CAPITALS.**
- Often these headings are followed by location and practical information printed in *italics.*
- As you turn the pages, you will find subject headers, similar to those used in telephone directories, printed in CAPITALS in the top corner of each page.
- If you still cannot find what you need, check in the comprehensive and exhaustively cross-referenced INDEX at the back of the book.
- Following the index, a LIST OF STREET NAMES provides map references for all roads and streets mentioned in the book that fall within the areas covered by the main city maps (color maps **3** to **5**).

CROSS-REFERENCES
These are printed in SMALL CAPITALS, referring you to other sections or alphabetical entries in the book. Care has been taken to ensure that such cross-references are self-explanatory. Often, page references are also given, although their excessive use would be intrusive and ugly.

FLOORS
We use the European convention in this book: "ground floor" means the floor at ground level (called by Americans the "first floor").

METRO
Near the back of the book there is a full-page color map of the Prague metro system.

Key to symbols

☎	Telephone	◁∈	Good view
Fx	Facsimile (fax)	♿	Facilities for disabled
★	Recommended sight		people
☆	Worth a detour	👥	Conference facilities
i	Tourist information	☐	Cable TV in rooms
🎫	Entrance fee payable	≋	Swimming pool
ƒ	Guided tour	⛹	Gym/fitness facilities
♣	Special interest for	🍵	Sauna
	children	⅄	Bar
♋	Hotel	▬	Minibar in rooms
AE	American Express	⟺	Restaurant
Ⓓ	Diners Club	♪	Nightclub
ⓒ	MasterCard/Eurocard	♫	Live music
VISA	Visa	♥♪	Dancing

PRICE CATEGORIES

☐	Cheap	▥	Expensive
▢	Inexpensive	▦	Very expensive
▥	Moderately priced		

Our price categories for hotels and restaurants are explained in WHERE
TO STAY (page 125) and EATING AND DRINKING (page 134) respectively.

About the author

Sevan Nisanyan was born in Istanbul and educated at Yale (philosophy) and Columbia (politics). His exploits include stints as the boss of a large computer firm, adventurer in the Andes, political prisoner and gentleman farmer. Among his previous publications are *Insight Guide: Istanbul* and, in this series, *American Express Athens and the Classical Sites* and *American Express Vienna & Budapest*. He currently lives in Sirince, an ancient village in the Aegean hills of Turkey.

A message from the editors

Months of concentrated work were dedicated to making this edition accurate and up to date when it went to press. But time and change are forever the enemies, and between editions we are very much assisted when you, our readers, write to tell us about any changes you discover.

Please keep on writing — but please also be aware that we have no control over restaurants, or whatever, that take it into their heads, after we publish, to move, or change their telephone number, or, even worse, close down. Our authors and editors aim to exclude trendy ephemera and to recommend places that give every indication of being stable and durable. Their judgment is rarely wrong. Changes in telephone numbers are something else. We apologise for the world's telephone authorities, who seem to change their numbers like you and I change shirts.

My serious point is that we are striving to tailor the series to the very distinctive tastes and requirements of our discerning international readership, which is why your feedback is so valuable. I particularly want to thank all of you who wrote while we were preparing this edition. Time prevents our responding to most such letters, but they are all welcomed and frequently contribute to the process of preparing the next edition.

Please write to me at **Mitchell Beazley**, an imprint of Reed Illustrated Books, Michelin House, 81 Fulham Road, London SW3 6RB; or, in the US, c/o American Express Travel Guides, **Prentice Hall Travel**, 15 Columbus Circle, New York, NY 10023.

David Townsend Jones, Series Editor, American Express Travel Guides

Prague

Prague: a city in revolution

On January 1, 1993, a few days after this introduction was committed to the keyboard, Czechoslovakia — the country whose capital Prague had been, more or less, for 75 years — ceased to exist. Two years earlier, the collapse of the Czech–Slovak marriage would have been something unthinkable; in the event, Prague hardly seemed to notice. There was a ceremony in the Hradčany to hoist the flag of the new Czech Republic; a few young people protested quietly on Wenceslas Square. Others did what Praguers do best, and retreated to their favorite pub to debate grocery prices over a glass of Pilsner and a coil of smoke.

The separation was in fact a minor twist in an astonishing revolution that has rolled on like a rogue locomotive since 1989. In November 1989, one of the most thuggish and unenlightened tyrannies in Eastern Europe was toppled in ten miraculous days of near-peaceful protest in the streets of Prague. It took a banned playwright — Václav Havel — who embodied the conscience of the nation, and a retired politician — Alexander Dubček — who represented the dashed hopes of the Prague spring of 1968, to pull the plug on a dictatorship that had for almost 42 years mired the country in the mud of stagnation, fear, hypocrisy and public cynicism.

Since then, change has been everywhere. In politics: the rebirth of freedom in a land that was the model democracy of interwar Central Europe, with that special moral tinge that has always set the philosophical Czechs apart from, say, flamboyant Magyars and unruly Poles. In spirit: a president who showed up regularly in jazz clubs, and practiced roller-skates with a chief-of-staff who was a hereditary prince and a presidential adviser who used to be a rock lyricist. In the nuts and bolts of everyday life: the privatization of a state-confiscated economy at the rate of a thousand businesses a month, and the restitution of hundreds of thousands of properties — homes, medieval castles, monasteries, Picassos, shops — to owners who had been mugged out of them after 1948. In outward looks: the flood of Western goods and fashions that is washing away the shabby brown–gray patina of socialism, and a restoration fever that has begun to recover one of Europe's most beautiful historic cities from under five decades of mildew and ash.

These are difficult times for the guidebook writer, who must keep abreast of regulations, offices, shops, hotels, restaurants, galleries, cafés, street names, even countries, that sprout and vanish faster than you could fax a manuscript. Even castles and 600-year-old cathedrals are no longer quite as solid as they look: they shut down for months or years, to re-emerge unrecognizable after a face-lift, with all the predictability of Russian roulette.

For the traveler, it is an exhilarating time: the time to be there to witness the rebirth of a nation that was once one of the most civilized in Europe, and is now back to reclaim its legacy.

11

Culture, history and background

PRAGUE
Capital of the Czech Republic.
Population: 1.2 million.
Municipal area: 171 square kilometers/66 square miles.
Location: 50° 05' north, 14° 25' east.
Altitude at riverbank: 180 meters/590 feet.
Highest point: White Mountain, 383 meters/1,257 feet.
History: Settled in the 9thC; town incorporated c.1230.
Language: Czech.
Religion: Roman Catholic 83 percent, the balance being mainly Czechoslovak Church (Hussite) and Bohemian Brethren (Lutheran).

A brief history

The Czech Republic comprises the historic lands of **Bohemia** (capital: **Prague**), **Moravia** (capital: **Brno**), and a small slice of Silesia. Bohemia was an independent kingdom under the Holy Roman (German) Empire until its annexation by Austria in 1620/27. **Slovakia** (capital: **Bratislava**) formed a part of Hungary for nearly 900 years; Hungary, in turn, was under Austrian rule from the 16thC onward.

The union of the Czech lands and Slovakia was effected at the end of World War I in 1918. It disintegrated during World War II (1939–45), and again after the revolution of 1989. A communist regime held power in Czechoslovakia between 1948 and 1989.

CZECH PREHISTORY
5thC BC: The Celtic tribe of Boii settle the Bohemian basin, giving their name to the country. **1stC BC**: German tribes (Marcomanni, Quadi) in Bohemia. **6thC AD**: Immigration of Western Slavs, ancestors of Czechs and Slovaks.

c.830: The "Great Moravian Empire" brings Western Slav tribes under its rule. **863–85**: Sts Cyril and Methodius, Byzantine missionaries, evangelize Moravia, devise the glagolitic ("Cyrillic") script, and translate the Bible and liturgy into Old Church Slavonic. **907**: Moravian empire destroyed by invading Magyars.

MEDIEVAL BOHEMIA
Before 873: Czechs establish a tribal stronghold on Prague's Castle Hill, possibly as vassals of Moravia. **c.873**: Bořivoj, earliest documented

ruler of the Přemyslid dynasty, and his wife St Ludmila baptized by St Methodius, the "Apostle of the Slavs."

921–935: Good "King" Wenceslas (Václav), Bořivoj's grandson, establishes numerous churches with the aid of German missionaries. Latin replaces Slavonic liturgy. **935**: Wenceslas is murdered by his pagan brother Boleslav the Cruel. Later, Wenceslas is declared a saint.

965: First written description of Prague, in the travelogue of the Jewish merchant Ibrahim ibn Jacob. **967–999**: Boleslav the Pious, son of Boleslav the Cruel, establishes Christianity. **973**: Prague made a bishopric. Monastery of St George, first in Bohemia, established on Castle Hill. **1002**: Prince Vladivoj takes office as a vassal of the German (Holy Roman) Empire.

1125–40: Soběslav I builds a Romanesque palace in stone on Castle Hill. Market settlements below the Castle and on the opposite bank of the Vltava. **1172**: First stone bridge across the Vltava.

1212: The Sicilian Golden Bull: Ottokar (Otakar) Přemysl I recognized by the emperor as hereditary king of Bohemia. Bohemian kings are one of the seven ex officio electors of the Holy Roman Empire.

13thC: German immigration changes the ethnic, economic and cultural composition of Bohemia. Establishment of new towns. Silver deposits mined at Kutná Hora (Kuttenberg) support an economic boom. Gothic architecture introduced. **c.1230**: The Old Town of Prague (Staré město) receives its charter. The town is razed and rebuilt 3 meters (9 feet) higher to prevent flooding. **1257**: Lesser Side (Malá strana) incorporated as a separate town.

1253–78: King Ottokar (Otakar) Přemysl II acquires Austria and Styria and expands his territories from the Baltic to the Adriatic. Bohemia becomes Central Europe's dominant power. **1278**: Ottokar defeated and killed by Rudolf I of Habsburg in the Battle of Marchfeld. Austria falls to the Habsburgs. Sixty years of chaos in Bohemia. **1306**: The male line of the Přemyslids extinguished with the death of Wenceslas (Václav) III.

1310–46: John (Jan) of Luxemburg becomes king of Bohemia, devoting his energies to private adventures in various parts of Europe. **1333–78**: Under Charles (Karel, Karl) of Luxemburg, his son (joint ruler until 1346), Bohemia reaches its political and cultural peak. **1344**: Prague made an archbishopric. **1347**: New Town (Nové město) incorporated.

1348: Charles elected Holy Roman Emperor as Charles IV, with Prague as his residence. New buildings in Prague (with date construction began) — **1344**: St Vitus's Cathedral; the royal castle of Vyšehrad; **1346**: Carolinum, Central Europe's first university; Karlštejn Castle; **1357**: Charles Bridge; **1365**: Týn Church.

1378–1419: Twilight of Prague's greatness under Wenceslas IV, Charles's son. Tensions pit burghers against royalty, Czechs against Germans. **1380**: The Great Plague devastates Bohemia. **1389**: Massacre of Jews in the ghetto. **1394**: Wenceslas abducted by nobles and kept prisoner for a year. **1396**: In Bethlehem Chapel (Betlémská kaple), mass is said for the first time in Czech.

RELIGIOUS WARS
1402: Jan Hus, a popular preacher, advocates church reform. His views

find support among the Czech clergy. **1414–15**: Invited to the Council of Constance by the Pope, Hus is arrested by treachery and is burned at the stake. **1419**: Hussite radicals in the New Town storm City Hall, hurling Catholic councilmen from the window (the First Defenestration of Prague). Hussite revolution spreads through Bohemia and Moravia. **1420–31**: Five crusades sent by the Pope and the Emperor fail to defeat the Hussite army led by Jan Žižka and Prokop the Bald. **1434**: Radical Hussite party (Taborites) defeated at the Battle of Lipany. **1436**: The Compromise of Jihlava: moderate Hussites (Utraquists), supported by a majority of Czechs, gain recognition and political representation. King Sigismund allowed to enter Prague.

1437–58: Interregnum. George (Jiří) of Poděbrady, a Hussite nobleman, acts as regent. **1458–71**: George of Poděbrady becomes king of Bohemia in disputed election. Catholics elect Matthias Corvinus of Hungary counter-king. Renewal of Hussite wars. **1485**: Toleration Edict of Kutná Hora: Religious peace re-established under Vladislav II. Period of reconstruction. Golden age of Bohemian feudalism. **1526**: Vladislav's son Louis (Ludvík), king of Bohemia and Hungary, killed in battle against Turks. Ferdinand I, the Habsburg ruler of Austria, inherits his titles.

1526–1618: Tug-of-war between the Bohemian Towns and Estates (council of lords) and the Habsburg rulers who attempt to establish autocratic rule. A majority of lords and towns adopt Lutheran Protestantism. **1547**: Unsuccessful rebellion of Towns and Estates. Prague loses rights and privileges. **1556**: Ferdinand I adopts forcible Catholic policy. Jesuits summoned to Prague to conduct Catholic propaganda.

1576–1611: Rudolf II withdraws to Prague's Castle: revival of Prague's cultural life. **1609**: Rudolf grants religious liberty to Bohemia. **1611**: Rudolf deposed by the hard-line Catholic party of his brother Matthias.

1618: Protestant revolt: leaders of the Bohemian Estates throw imperial envoys from Hradčany's windows (the Second Defenestration of Prague), launching the Thirty Years' War. **1619**: Insurgents elect Frederick V of the Palatinate ("Winter King") king of Bohemia. **1620**: Army of the Catholic League defeats rebels at the Battle of the White Mountain. Frederick escapes on horseback. End of Bohemia's independent existence. **1621**: 27 leaders of the Bohemian nobility executed on Old Town Square. **1627**: The Revised Ordinance abolishes Bohemian self-rule, establishing Catholicism as sole permitted religion. Protestant properties confiscated and granted to Habsburg loyalists.

1631: Albrecht of Wallenstein, the imperial generalissimo, defeats an invading Swedish army. **1634**: Wallenstein assassinated on claims of high treason. **1648**: Swedes occupy and loot Prague's Lesser Side days before the end of the Thirty Years' War. The war leaves Bohemia in ruins: 507 out of 737 towns and as many as 28,000 out of 34,000 villages obliterated.

HABSBURG AUTOCRACY

1627–1918: Bohemia and Moravia ruled from Vienna as Austrian provinces. **1627–1740**: Jesuit dominance in politics and culture. The Baroque style in arts and architecture. **1742–44**: French and Prussian troops occupy Prague during the Seven Years' War.

1745–80: Maria Theresa creates a centralized, bureaucratic administration based in Vienna. **1780–90**: Joseph II, an Enlightened reformer, modernizes government, abolishes serfdom, expels Jesuits, dissolves monasteries and grants civic equality to Jews. German declared sole official language.

1784: The Old Town, New Town, Lesser Side, Hradčany and Vyšehrad united as one city. **1787**: Mozart's *Don Giovanni* performed in Prague to enthusiastic reception.

c.1800: Rebirth of Slav national consciousness among Czech intellectuals. **1818**: National Museum founded by Czech nationalists. **From 1820s**: Industrial revolution transforms Bohemia into one of the most densely industrialized countries in Europe. Rural immigration creates a Czech-speaking majority in Prague. **1841**: First modern bridge on the Vltava. **1845**: First railway in Prague.

1848: Nationalist revolution in Prague. Pan-Slavic Congress, led by the historian František Palacký, demands autonomy under Austrian rule. Austria regains control after street fighting. **1861**: For the first time, German members lose majority in Prague's City Hall. Palacký leads Czech delegation in Austria's newly-constituted Parliament.

1867: Austria grants Hungarian autonomy (Austro–Hungarian dual monarchy). Czechs agitate unsuccessfully for a similar compromise. Hungary's policy of Magyarization sparks nationalist awakening in Slovakia. **1882**: Prague University divided into German and Czech sections. **1886**: Ethnic crisis forces Germans to withdraw from provincial government in Bohemia.

THE CZECHOSLOVAK REPUBLIC

1914–18: World War I. The Czech nationalists Tomáš G. Masaryk (1850–1937) and Edvard Beneš (1884–1948) canvass Britain, France and USA for a postwar division of Austria–Hungary along national lines. An early supporter of Czech aspirations is US President Wilson.

1918: The Czechoslovak Republic is proclaimed in Prague (October 28), with Masaryk as President. The new state comprises the Czech lands (Bohemia and Moravia), with a Czech majority and 32 percent German minority, and Slovakia, populated by a Slovak majority and 24 percent Magyar minority.

1918–38: Ethnic issues (Czech versus Slovak, Czech versus German, Slovak versus Magyar) dominate Czechoslovak politics. **1935**: German separatists led by pro-Nazi Konrad Henlein win elections in Sudetenland, the German-populated districts of Bohemia/Moravia. **1938**: Munich Accord: Britain and France accept Hitler's demands in Czechoslovakia (September 30). Germany annexes Sudetenland (October). President Beneš leaves the country, and forms a government in exile in Britain. **1939**: Slovakia declares independence (March 14). Germany occupies remaining Czech lands, constituting the "Reichsprotectorate of Bohemia and Moravia" (March 15).

1942: Reichsprotector Reinhard Heydrich assassinated in Prague Germans annihilate the village of Lidice in retaliation. **1945**: The Prague uprising (May 5) precedes liberation by the Soviet army (May 8). Allies re-establish Czechoslovakia with Beneš as President. **1945–46**: Three million Sudeten Germans expelled from Czechoslovakia under terms of the Potsdam agreement.

1946: Communists led by Klement Gottwald receive 38 percent in elections and obtain key posts in coalition government. **1948**: Communists seize power in a coup and oust Beneš (February 25). **1948–53**: Gottwald's regime of terror: murder of Foreign Minister Jan Masaryk (son of Tomáš); the Slánský show-trial. **1953**: Gottwald dies in Moscow while attending Stalin's funeral. Relative liberalization of the regime.

1968: Alexander Dubček, a liberal, elected First Secretary of the Communist Party (January). His reforms promise "socialism with a human face," but unleash vocal opposition to the communist regime (the "Prague Spring"). Led by the Soviet Union, Warsaw Pact countries invade Czechoslovakia (August 21).

1969: Jan Palach burns himself alive on Wenceslas Square to protest against Soviet occupation (January 16). Dubček removed from office (April). **1969–89**: "Normalization" under the repressive regime of Gustáv Husák. **1977**: Dissident intellectuals publish Charter 77, a declaration of political rights.

1989: Days after the collapse of the Berlin Wall, mass demonstration in Prague (November 17) grows into a revolution. The government caves in (November 24). Václav Havel, a dissident playwright newly freed from jail, elected President of the Republic (December 29). **1990**: Civic Forum (Občanské Fórum, OF), an anti-communist coalition led by Havel, wins a landslide in free elections (June). **1991–92**: Economic reforms managed by Finance Minister Václav Klaus privatize state enterprises, restitute nationalized properties to previous owners, and abolish price and currency controls.

1992: Klaus elected Prime Minister of Czech Lands. Nationalist agitation in Slovakia led by Vladimír Mečiar. **1993**: Czechoslovak federation dissolved by agreement between Czechs and Slovaks. Havel elected President of the Czech Republic.

Rulers of Bohemia

Rulers' numbers were restarted after Bohemia became a kingdom in 1212; thus there is a **Prince** Vladislav II and a **King** Vladislav II. Later monarchs are better known by their number as **Holy Roman Emperors** (or **Emperors of Austria** after 1804), rather than as Kings of Bohemia.

The resulting numbers game can be a bit confusing. The ruler who gave his name to Prague's historic bridge, for example, was the first Charles to wear the Bohemian crown, although he is much better remembered as *Emperor* Charles IV of the Holy Roman Empire. The next Charles of Bohemia is the Sixth, because the Fifth of the imperial line never occupied the Bohemian throne.

The case of the *next* Charles (Charles I of Austria) is even more complicated: he would be numbered Seventh had history run its course more smoothly, but the Holy Roman Empire was dissolved during the Napoleonic wars, and from then on the Habsburgs had to settle for — and be numbered by — the more modest title of Emperors of Austria. Of course, he was also Charles III of Bohemia.

Přemyslids
(Princes)

Bořivoj I	c.873
Spitihněv I	c.916
Vratislav I	c.920
St Wenceslas (Václav)	921–935
Boleslav I the Cruel	935–967
Boleslav II the Pious	967–999
. . . .	
Soběslav I	1125–40
Vladislav II	1140–73
. . . .	

(Kings)

Přemysl Ottokar (Otakar) I	1197–1230
Wenceslas (Václav) I	1230–53
Přemysl Ottokar (Otakar) II	1253–78
Wenceslas (Václav) II	1278–1305
Wenceslas (Václav) III	1305–6
. . . .	

After extinction of Přemyslids

John (Jan) of Luxemburg	1310–46
Charles (Karel) IV	1346–78
Wenceslas (Václav) IV	1378–1419
Sigismund	1419–37
Interregnum	1437–58/1471
George (Jiří) of Poděbrady	1458–71
Vladislav II Jagellon	1471–1516
Louis (Ludvík) Jagellon	1516–26

Habsburgs

Ferdinand I	1526–64
Maximilian II	1564–78
Rudolf II	1578–1611
Matthias	1611–19
Frederick of Palatinate (counter-king)	1619–20
Ferdinand II	1619–37
Ferdinand III	1637–57
Leopold I	1657–1705
Joseph I	1705–11
Charles (Karl) VI	1711–40
Maria Theresa	1745–80
Joseph II	1780–90
Leopold II	1790–92
Francis (Franz) I	1792–1835
Ferdinand I	1835–48
Franz Joseph	1848–1916
Charles (Karl) I	1916–18

Presidents of Czechoslovakia

Tomáš Masaryk	1918–35
Edvard Beneš	1935–38
Emil Hácha	1938–39
German occupation	1939–45
Edvard Beneš	1945–48
Klement Gottwald	1948–53
Antonín Zápotocký	1953–57
Antonín Novotný	1957–68
Ludvík Svoboda	1968–75
Gustáv Husák	1975–89
Václav Havel	1989–92

Václav Havel and Vladimir Mečiar were elected presidents of the Czech Republic and Slovakia, respectively, in 1992–93.

Art and architecture

Few European cities can match Prague in the scope and quality of their artistic heritage. In architecture, the city is virtually a museum of major European styles from the Middle Ages to the early 20thC. The result is often eclectic (a single house can bring together architectural details from each century between the 13th and 20th), but always full of beauty, charm, humor and technical virtuosity. In painting and sculpture, Prague produced some outstanding work in the Gothic, Late Renaissance and early modern eras, although it preserves only a modest fragment of the famous Rudolfine collections that once made it one of Europe's artistic capitals.

ROMANESQUE *(before 13th century)*
Stone and mortar came to the woods of Bohemia in the 10thC, and by the time Ibrahim ibn Jacob wrote his travelogue in 965, Prague had its fair share of solid architecture. Some were solid indeed: the Czech

St Vitus's Cathedral

word for church, *kostel*, goes back to a time when places of worship had to be strong enough to withstand a tribal raid. Three small fortress-churches of the 11thC survive in Prague in the rotundas of St Martin (Vyšehrad), St Longinus (Štěpánská ul.) and the Holy Cross (Konviktská ul.).

Buildings of a more civilized sort emerged toward the middle of the next century (Soběslav's palace, c.1140; St George's Basilica, 1142; Strahov abbey church, 1148; private houses in the Old Town), though many of these have now disappeared from view, having been buried under ten feet of earth when the burghers of Prague decided to raise the level of the city sometime around 1230.

More than a hundred Romanesque buildings continue to slumber under the surface of the Old Town, continuing to serve as tourist attractions (notably, the palace of the Lords of Kunštát and Poděbrady on Řetězova ul.) or restaurants and wine cellars (U zlaté konvice on Melantrichova ul.). One is put to good use as a discotheque (U bílého koníčka, off Old Town Square).

GOTHIC *(13th-16th century)*
The secret of using ribbed vaults to support roofs of previously unimaginable height was discovered in France around 1150. It made a tentative entry into Prague during the building boom of the 1230s (St Gallus, 1232; St James, 1232; the convents of St Agnes, 1234; houses in central Old Town), sputtered on for a hundred years (Old New Synagogue, c.1270; Stone Bell House, c.1330), then returned with a vengeance under Charles IV, to carry Bohemia into the artistic forefront of Late Gothic Europe.

The inspiration came mostly from France, although the outstanding name of this period was a German from Swabia, **Peter Parler** (1330–99). His buildings in Prague include some of the top landmarks of the city: St Vitus's Cathedral (see opposite), the Týn Church (illustrated on page 103), the Charles Bridge and right-bank tower, and the All Saints Chapel in the Castle.

The Caroline summer was equally rich in the other arts: Parler himself broke new ground in medieval sculpture with the realism of his statues in the Cathedral. **Master Theodoric** produced some of the most outstanding work of any 14thC European artist with his series of saints' portraits for Charles' castle at Karlštejn.

The boom continued under Wenceslas IV, though a more frivolous spirit is noticeable in the age of this playboy-king (sculptures of the Charles Bridge right-bank tower; oriel bays of the Carolinum and Old Town Hall; the church of St Barbara in Kutná Hora). It then collapsed in the fire and brimstone of the Hussite revolution: painting was declared idolatry, churches were confiscated and looted, and great projects — such as the Cathedral and Týn Church — remained incomplete.

When peace returned a half-century later under Vladislav II, it was a time of nostalgia for *le temps perdu:* medieval fashions came back into vogue, and Gothic acquired a new lease on life in Bohemia just as the rest of Europe was setting sail for new horizons. In the rebuilt royal palace of Hradčany, **Benedict Ried** (1454–1534) created a swansong of Gothic wizardry. The Charles Bridge left-bank tower (1464; illustrated on page 77) and the Powder Tower (1475) imitated Parler's style of the previous century. The turrets of the Old Town Hall and the completed Týn Church gave the city a deliberate tone of story-book unreality.

Nor was this the end of Prague's fascination with the Gothic. Until the close of the 16thC, the exuberant imagination of the Middle Ages held its ground in Bohemia against the purer disciplines of the Renaissance. Ferdinand I's architect **Boniface Wohlmut**, a man firmly schooled in the Italian style, reverted to Gothic forms to build the added chambers of the royal palace (c.1560) and the spectacular vaulting of the Karlov (1575). The chapel of St Roch in the Strahov Abbey (1599) carried Gothic design into Late Renaissance architecture. A slew of minor Gothic delights that contribute to the "medieval" charm of Prague today (e.g., the roofs of U malířů and U svatého Tomáše) were also products of this period.

Wood-carved sculpture, an art rooted in the Bohemian tradition, reached its pinnacle in the late 15th to mid-16thC with masterpieces like the anonymous *Žebrák Lamentation*, now in St George's Abbey, and the works of the 16thC master who signed his name **I.P.** (in St George's Abbey and Týn Church).

RENAISSANCE *(16th century)*
Echoes of Italy's infatuation with Antiquity reached Prague in Vladislav II's reign (windows of the Vladislav Hall, c.1500), and yielded some impressive fruit under Ferdinand I, a lover of all things Italian (Belvedere, 1538–63; Hvezda, 1555; Royal Ball Court, 1567). A fire that gutted the left bank in 1541 gave occasion for the wholesale rebuilding of aristocratic estates in the modern style (Schwarzenberg Palace, 1543; Martinitz Palace, 1570; many houses in the Lesser Side). But the pull of the Gothic on the one hand, and the puritanical streak of the Protestant Reformation on the other, meant that Bohemia was never entirely at home with the mainstream of the European Renaissance.

Sgraffito on the façade of the **Schwarzenberg Palace**.

One happy legacy of the Italian masters who came to Prague in droves under Ferdinand was the durable fashion for *sgraffito*, the art of decorating house exteriors with pictures made by chipping out colored layers of plaster. A majority of houses in the city were once covered with *sgraffiti,* a fact that is still visible under peeling layers of later (mostly Baroque) plaster.

RUDOLFINE MANNERISM *(late 16th to early 17th century)*

Having spent the 16thC on the margins of Europe, Prague returned to the limelight at the tail-end of the Renaissance, in the restless parenthesis between the revival of Catholicism and the onset of the Thirty Years' War, when all Europe seemed obsessed with the obscurer truths of mind and matter.

The eccentric court of Rudolf II (1576–1611) set the trend. Rudolf purchased art on a monumental scale (his Tintorettos, Dürers, Cranachs, Brueghels and El Grecos fill the world's great museums), and employed a stable of his own artists who deserve to be better known than they are.

Among them was **Giuseppe Arcimboldo,** a painter of psychedelic fantasies: his portrait of the emperor shows Rudolf as a creature made of fruits and cereals. The work of **Hans von Aachen, Aegidius Saddeler, Roelandt Savery, Bartholomaeus Spranger** and **Adriaen de Vries** was characterized by a fascination with the bizarre and unnatural, a brooding and violent eroticism, arcane symbols, and the distortion of natural forms.

In architecture, it was a barren time. The Jesuit church of St Salvator (sv. Salvátora, 1578) was more a cross between Renaissance and Baroque than a work of distinctive style. So too the Wallenstein Palace (1623), built a decade after Rudolf's fall, for the imperial warlord who inherited many of his artists and his obsessions. Its architecture is eclectic; its garden, with sculptures by de Vries and a magnificent painted terrace, is an apotheosis of Mannerist art.

BAROQUE *(17th-18th century)*

Baroque, the artistic language of the Counter-Reformation, came to Prague in the wake of the Catholic victory at the White Mountain (1620) and kept the city spellbound over the next 120 years. Its exuberance was a challenge to Slavic gloom. Its churches offered charm, pomp and illusion against the dour god of the Reformation, seducing where He moralized. Its saints appealed to the eros as well as the most astonishing recesses of the psyche to offer salvation.

Nearly all churches in Prague were either remodeled or rebuilt from scratch to cover the traces of their two centuries of errancy. A new nobility with vast reserves of booty from the Thirty Years' and Turkish wars vied to build monuments to its own triumph, often by pasting a curlicued face on the sober and solid houses of the old middle class. The trend ran amok in the decade of 1715–25, when the whole city must have looked like a vast construction site. It faded toward 1740, as the Habsburg treasury began to crumble under the weight of their excesses.

The first two generations of Baroque architects were almost all Italian expatriates who introduced the Roman models of Bernini and Guarini to Prague (**Silvestre Carlone** – Casa Santa in Loreto, 1626; **Carlo Lurago** – St Ignatius, 1665; **Domenico Orsi de Orsini** – the Strahov Abbey Theological Library, 1671; **Domenico Canevale** – the church of St

Francis Seraphicus, 1679; **Giovanni Alliprandi** – the Sternberg Palace in Hradčany, 1698, Hrzán Palace, 1702, and Lobkowicz Palace, 1703).

Germans, less imperious and more *gemütlich*, took over at the turn of the century. The Viennese **Johann Bernhard Fischer von Erlach** (1656–1723) gave Prague a number of monuments (Clam-Gallas Palace, 1707; designs for the mausolea of St John Nepomuk and Count Mitrowicz), and many pupils.

Baroque Prague came of age with the **Dienzenhofers**, the Bavarian **Christoph** (1655–1722) and his native-born son **Kilian Ignaz** (1689–1751). Their joint work combined the elegant, more conventional design of *père* with the soaring imagination of *fils* to produce such masterpieces as St Margaret's Abbey in Břevnov (1708–40), the Nativity church of Loreto (1717–34), St Thomas (1723–31), St John of Nepomuk on the Rock (1730–39) and St Nicholas in the Old Town (1732–37). St Nicholas in the Lesser Side (1704–53) was their crowning achievement.

Interior of **St Nicholas** in the Lesser Side, the masterpiece of the Dienzenhofers, father and son.

In sculpture, Baroque Prague reached a level of prolixity (and excellence) scarcely matched by any other city in Europe. An army of limestone saints, angels, gods and heraldic beasts invaded every church and palace, niche and pediment, courtyard and garden in town within the first four decades of the 18thC. The epitome was the Charles Bridge, which was furnished with a monumental row of gesticulating saints between 1683 and 1714. The best of them came from the hands of **Ferdinand Maximilian Brokoff** (1688–1731), a master of eloquent composition, or his rival **Matthias Bernhard Braun** (1684–1738), the less formal and more sensuous. In the following generation, **Ignaz Platzer** (1717–87) stood out as the sculptor of frightfully muscular giants.

Baroque painting made an autonomous start with the Italian-educated **Karel Škréta** (1610–74; *St Charles Borromaeus* in the National Gallery; altarpieces in Týn Church, Maltese Church and St Stephen). As the period wore on, however, painting became almost wholly subordinated to architecture. The best artists found their outlet in the acres of fresco that turned Baroque churches and palaces into theaters of illusion (**Wenzel Lorenz Reiner**, 1689–1743, ceilings of St Thomas and St Aegidius; **Cosmas Damian Asam**, 1686–1739, Břevnov Abbey prelates' hall). It is difficult to tell where painting starts or architecture ends in **Abraham Godyn**'s *trompe-l'oeil* ceiling for the great hall of Troja Château (1691), the most astonishing two-dimensional artwork of the era.

ROCOCO AND JOSEPHINE CLASSICISM *(late 18th century)*
The magnificent posturing of the high Baroque gave way after 1740 to the more coy manner of Maria Theresa's reign. Financial austerity put a lid on 1720s-style extravagance, and Enlightenment gnawed at its ideological roots. A new generation of "Rococo" architects (**Anselmo Lurago**: Sylva-Taroucca Palace, 1747, Kinsky Palace, 1755; **Nicolaus Pacassi**: new wing of the Castle, 1756–74) kept up Baroque appearances without the underlying spiritual intensity, stressing surface at the expense of volume, ornament at the expense of movement. Under Joseph II (1780–90), appearances too were discarded in favor of the cool rationalism of the Enlightenment (**Ignác Palliardi**: Strahov Library, 1782; the Kolovrat, Ledebur and Liechtenstein Palaces).

The church no longer provided a credible model, so artists turned to Graeco-Roman Antiquity for inspiration. At their best, the Estates Theater (1781) of Prague combined Classical simplicity of form with an inventive brilliance of detail. The star performer of its early years was, aptly, none other than Mozart.

In Rococo painting, Watteau and Tiepolo found their Austrian counterpart in **Franz Anton Maulpertsch** (1724–96), a virtuoso colorist who worked mainly in Vienna. The ceiling fresco of Prague's Strahov philosophical library (1795), his last work, forms a perfect résumé of the ideological obsessions of the Josephine era.

19TH CENTURY
The Habsburg imperial spirit declined with the French Revolution and the Napoleonic upheavals; Baroque was its moment of glory, and the Enlightenment proved a chimera.

In Bohemia, except for some rather quaint early efforts at a Czech national style, the first half of the 19thC was artistically dead. In the first few rooms of the convent of St Agnes, which holds the National Gallery's chronologically arranged collection of modern Czech art, one looks in vain for evidence of a country with a glorious artistic tradition of six centuries behind it.

Things improved in the second half of the century. A booming growth in industrial wealth brought with it correspondingly self-confident expressions of national identity. **Neo-Gothic** was the idiom of political conservatism. Its heyday was the 1850s (new statues on Charles Bridge, 1854–59), though it became fashionable again at the end of the century (extension of St Vitus from 1872; redecoration of the Powder Tower, 1875; the pseudo-cathedral of Sts Peter and Paul in Vyšehrad, 1885–1902).

Nationalists preferred **Neo-Renaissance** pomposity (National Theater, 1868–81; Rudolfinum, 1876; National Museum, 1885) to express the rebirth of the Czech nation. The middle class happily settled for an eclectic mishmash of styles with a good dose of **Neo-Baroque** pageantry. Good examples of historicist civil architecture abound in Prague's New Town (Na příkopě; Wenceslas Square), but its most extraordinary product is no doubt the *fin-de-siècle* resort towns of Karlsbad (Karlovy Vary) and Marienbad (Mariánské Lázně) in western Bohemia.

Josef Mánes (1820–71) counted as the founding father of the new Czech painting, perhaps more for his role in the patriotic rising of 1848 than his actual art. The better efforts of the next generation were still marred by an excess of national self-absorption. The painter **Mikoláš Aleš** (1852–1913) and sculptor **Josef Myslbek** (1848–1922) were the most popular of those affected, and their work greets the visitor on every other street corner and public hall in Prague.

ART NOUVEAU

The sassy, elegant, anti-historicist trend variously known as Art Nouveau, Jugendstil, Secession or Liberty style took Europe by storm in the mid-1890s; by 1910 it had exhausted its spark. Prague imported its particular version from Vienna, producing some fabulously playful architecture (Pařížská ul. has possibly Europe's most brilliant collection of Jugendstil apartment houses), an extraordinary outpouring of funereal elegance (the Vyšehrad national cemetery) and a successful popularizer in the person of the graphicist **Alfons Mucha** (1860–1939).

Mucha was born in Prague, made his fame in Paris as a poster designer for (and maybe lover of) Sarah Bernhardt, then returned to his native soil to sink gradually into the populistic kitsch of the 1930s (thus the stained-glass window in the new wing of St Vitus). **Ladislav Šaloun** (1870–1946) applied Art Nouveau forms to sculpture (the Jan Hus Monument in Old Town Square, 1915), while **František Bílek** (1872–1941) took them as a starting point to develop his highly idiosyncratic, religiously inspired art.

20TH CENTURY

Prague enjoyed a special place in Europe's artistic–intellectual vanguard, from the eve of World War I through the early decades of the republic. Cubism made an almost simultaneous appearance in the Czech capital as in Paris, producing world-class painters in **Antonín Procházka** (1882–1945) and **Josef Čapek** (1897–1945), and a brilliant sculptor in **Otto Gutfreund** (1889–1927). There were even architects (**Pavel**

Janák, 1882–1956, and **Josef Gočár**, 1880–1945) who tried to apply Cubist ideas to architecture. The unclassifiable **František Kupka** (1871–1957) claimed the distinction of painting the first nonfigurative work of modern art a year ahead of Kandinsky.

Devětsil, a group of Surrealist-influenced young artists led by **Karel Teige** (1900–51), dominated the interwar years. Its members included illustrious figures like the poet and Nobel laureate **Jaroslav Seifert** (1901–86), the linguist **Roman Jakobson** (1896–1982) and the painter **Josef Šíma** (1891–1971).

Munich smothered Czechoslovak culture, and the postwar years were no kinder to the Czechs. The Nazis had little time to build or create, but managed to send into exile, jail or gas chamber many of those who could. The communists set them to socially useful work as taxi-drivers and toilet-wipers. In 1968, Luis Aragon would call Czechoslovakia a "Biafra of the spirit."

The Stalin–Gottwald era could still aspire to greatness: witness the palatial International Hotel in Dejvice. The post-Stalin age only produced mediocrities, culminating with the Palace of Culture (1981) in Nusle. Mercifully, the damage to Prague's historic center was minimal, and the city was spared the worst excesses of our century.

Voluptuous **Art Nouveau** figures above a doorway in Široká, in the Jewish Quarter.

Prague portraits

A baker's dozen, in approximately chronological order, of the men and women who helped make Prague what it is. Look elsewhere in the book (via the INDEX) for other colorful personalities — **St Wilgefortis the Bearded**, **St John of Nepomuk**, **Master Hanuš**, **Dr Jessenius**, **Mydlář the Executioner** and **Jan Palach**, to name a few.

LIBUŠE *(9thC?)*
The tribe of Czech lived in peace and harmony under the daughters of Krok: Kázi, who was a medicinewoman, Teta, a priestess, and Libuše, who was the youngest of the three but took first rank because of her soothsaying and political skills. One day there was a dispute (some think it was over the birth of private property in a society that until then held land in common), and the men of the tribe asked Libuše to take up a husband to rule them. She sent out her horse on the search; it came back with a sturdy peasant by the name of Přemysl, and so started a dynasty that would rule Bohemia for 500 years.

Next, as she stood on the rock of VYŠEHRAD (see page 111), she had a vision of a great and famous city growing in the hills beyond the Vltava. A voice told her that the first stone should be laid on the spot where a man was building the threshold (*práh* in Czech) of his house. The man was duly found on the hill of Hradčany, and the 'CASTLE of Prague was established there at the dawn of Bohemia's history.

Her story bewitched the Romantics of the 19thC, German as well as Czech. Mendelssohn composed *Libussa's Vision;* Grillparzer wrote a drama on the same subject. Bedřich Smetana (1824–84) made her the heroine of an opera that counts as the pinnacle of Czech patriotic music.

ST WENCESLAS (VÁCLAV, WENZEL) *(c.903-935)*
Good "King" Wenceslas of Christmas carol was in fact a mere prince (a tribal chief, in other words), who made it to sainthood by being a Christian when the rest of his people preferred to continue worshiping ancestral gods and forest spirits. In practical terms this meant taking a German line in politics. The German king reciprocated by sending priests, monks, missionaries, church constructors and — the supreme gift of all — the pickled right arm of an obscure Roman saint called Vitus, who hereby became the patron and protector of the Czechs.

Half of his family opposed Wenceslas. His mother Drahomíra championed the anti-Christian cause and lobbied openly for her other son, Boleslav "the Cruel." Grandmother Ludmila had been Wenceslas' mentor since childhood; she was strangled on her daughter-in-law's orders. Wenceslas himself was murdered a few years later by his brother. But the old gods were by then beyond repair: Boleslav turned pro-Christian under German pressure; Drahomíra, according to medieval chroniclers, was swallowed up by Hell; and within a few years the body of the Good Prince came to rest in the shrine of St Vitus, securing a place for posterity as the national martyr and saint of Bohemia.

His legend was worked up into a national cult by Charles IV some 400 years later. It spread to Britain when Charles' daughter Anne married Richard II of England, and it worked its way into Christmas folklore about that time.

ST AGNES (ANEŽKA) *(1205-82)*

Agnes' father, Ottokar I of Bohemia, betrothed her firstly to a son of Germany's Frederick II, then to the king of England, and lastly to Frederick himself. She was not impressed, and set her sights on the King of Heaven instead. It was reported that she wore a hair shirt under her jeweled robes and a girdle studded with iron nails, and that she walked barefoot at dawn to share in the miseries of the poor people of Prague.

Convent was the logical next step and the obvious course of action in an age that had seen no less than Hedwig of Silesia, Elisabeth of Hungary, Yolanda the daughter of Béla IV and Isabella the sister of France's Louis IX — all relatives of Agnes by blood or betrothal — take up the nun's habit. Not content with one, Agnes asked dad to set up two convents for her, became abbess at the age of 28, and spent the rest of her life in exemplary saintliness.

In 1990, Pope John Paul II declared her a saint on the occasion of his first visit to post-communist Prague. In the national rejoicing that ensued, many people missed the papal point: that Agnes was honored because she chose a life of spiritual values over a politically and financially advantageous alliance with Germany.

CHARLES (KAREL, KARL) IV *(1316-78)*

Bohemia had been a German vassal state since at least the 11thC and a very powerful one since the 13th. With Charles it captured the German crown, and Prague was made the capital of Germany.

Times were ripe for such cross-national enterprise. Charles' grandfather had started out as duke of Luxemburg and ended as Holy Roman (i.e., German) Emperor. His father John the Adventurer lost the Empire but picked up Bohemia, fought hard to have the Italian crown as well, won Lithuania, and died fighting in the French ranks against the Black Prince's English army at Crécy. Charles himself grew up in the court of Paris. All his life, he would look back for his cultural model to the city of the Sorbonne and Notre-Dame.

Elected Holy Roman Emperor, Charles raised the Empire to the fullest extent of its medieval power, regaining control over Italy and persuading the pope to return to Rome from his "exile" in Avignon. At home, he tried to build Bohemia into what he hoped would be a position of permanent dominance in the Empire. His mother was a Přemyslid, which allowed him to wrap himself in Bohemian national legend. He spoke Czech and promoted the vernacular culture. He gave Prague its Cathedral, its university — the first in Central Europe — and a New Town as big and rich as the Old. His name is perpetuated in the town by a bridge (Karlův), a square (Karlovo), a street (Karlova) and a nearby castle (Karlštejn).

Wenceslas IV failed to live up to his father's ambitions; Sigismund, the younger and better son of Charles, took the Hungarian crown, and fought in vain for 60 years to gain his father's Bohemian inheritance. Meanwhile, Bohemia self-destructed in a fit of ideological madness.

JAN HUS *(1369-1415)*

A century before the Protestant Reformation, Hus preached against papal authority, church possessions, sinning priests and the Latin Bible. Intellectuals loved him, and made him rector of the university. The Pope invited him to explain his views at the Council of Constance, then had him promptly caught and roasted at the stake.

His followers retaliated by invading the town hall of the New Town and defenestrating — dumping out of the window — anyone rash enough to oppose them. Their demands were fourfold: abolish church property, allow free preaching of the gospel, suppress sin, and above all, administer the sacrament in Both Kinds — wine *and* bread — to laymen as well as priests.

A ragtag army took to the countryside under the one-eyed giant Jan Žižka, and started massacring Catholics, Sinners, Priests, One-kinders, and especially Germans. Soon all Europe was up in arms against the Czechs: the Pope issued an anathema, setting up a prize for anyone who killed a Czech and sending to Hell those who traded with or married one; Sigismund (Charles IV's son) chipped in with hopes of capturing his father's crown; and the Habsburg saw his chance to eliminate the house of Luxemburg once and for all from the competition for the Empire.

In a few years the rebels were split into at least three factions, which set upon each other with the predatory zeal of all moral purifiers. The Taborites, the purest bunch, lost out in 1434. The Bohemian and Moravian Brethren withdrew to the sidelines, to evolve in time into a Lutheran sect. The Prague-based Utraquists (Latin for "Both Kinds") made their peace with Sigismund, and remained the dominant sect in Bohemia until the '70s of the 16thC. The country itself never quite recovered from its holocaust.

Hus was a black name during the centuries of Austrian supremacy. The 19thC nationalists rediscovered in him a precursor of Czech patriotism and an embodiment of all the highest ideals of humanism, morality and righteousness that they expected a reborn Czechstan to represent. Masaryk's Czechoslovakia tried to model itself on a "Hussite" ideology; the Hussite church was revived after 300 years in abeyance and found some support among the patriotic elite. The communists, too, reserved a good seat for Hus in the national pantheon, partly because his populism and anti-clericalism appealed to their bolshie instincts, more because they found in him a useful hero of anti-Germanism. Other counsels have begun to prevail since 1989.

RUDOLF II *(1552-1611)*

Rudolf withdrew from the bitter world of religious wars to the seclusion of Prague's castle, gathering around him the greatest geniuses and cranks of Europe to brood over the arcane sciences of astronomy and alchemy. He was an obsessive collector of the rare, the curious and the extraordinary; his interests ranged from Dürers to unicorn's horns and from Hebrew manuscripts to dodo birds. His men sought the elixir of life and the philosopher's stone, attempting to resurrect mummies and to create men in the laboratory. Their presence meant a cultural revival for the city, which returned to the European center-stage after an absence of 200 years.

The emperor himself sank slowly from benign melancholia into serious madness. Childhood in the Most Catholic court of Spain had left its scars; the prophecy of his court astronomer that a mad monk would murder him threw him overboard. Obsessed with women (he spawned a menage of bastards), he would shrink with horror whenever the question of marriage came up. The issue of succession proved his undoing; quarreling with the Lobkowiczes and Rožmbergs, the most powerful families of the realm, supplied the cause. His brother showed up at the gates of Prague with an army, Rudolf abdicated, and the Thirty Years' War began to loom.

TYCHO BRAHE *(1546-1601)* **and JOHANNES KEPLER** *(1571-1630)*
The star-gazer that forecast Rudolf's mad monk was Tycho Brahe, a Danish astronomer who is credited with the most complete observation of the planets before the coming of the telescope. His hatred of monks was said to derive from a feud with the occupants of the Capuchin monastery neighboring his house in Hradčany. Another quarrel left him without a nose for most of his life, so he carried various prostheses including one made of gold that he only wore on Sundays and gala occasions; his tombstone in the Týn Church shows him with the artificial organ. The manner of his death was equally absurd: his bladder exploded at a feast where too much beer was consumed. The highest mountain on the moon carries his name.

Kepler, his successor at the court of Rudolf, has a more orthodox reputation as one of the founders of modern science. His work on celestial motion was the first to describe the orbits of planets as elliptical rather than circular, and formed the immediate basis of Newton's laws. But he was no less prone to the occult side of the stars than any of his contemporaries. His duties as court astronomer included drawing up a horoscope for the emperor (and, later, for Wallenstein); his book on the planets featured a treatise on the music of celestial spheres and a section on the spiritual powers of the stars. Worse: his mother was a witch.

A modern statue of the two astronomers stands at the intersection of Pohořelec and Keplerova, in Hradčany.

RABBI LOEW *(1512-1609)* **and JOSEF GOLEM**
Rabbi Loew ben Bezalel was a fitting Chief Rabbi for the Prague of Rudolf II: his tales have become Yiddish folk classics. In one famous episode, the clever rabbi builds a magic device — a *laterna magica* — to bring back the biblical patriarchs for the emperor's benefit: Rudolf breaks up into hysterical laughter, almost bringing down the universe on his head. In another, Rabbi Loew sets to work with his son-in-law Yitzak and an apprentice to create a man of clay — a *golem* — from the mud of the Vltava.

The creature comes to life when a slip carrying the unutterable name of God — a *shem* — is inserted under his tongue. He is introduced to the world as Josef Golem, the rabbi's helper, and performs many good deeds, helping maidens and saving the ghetto from the evil machinations of Brother Thaddaeus, so long as his master remembers to unplug the *shem* before each Sabbath. But finally he forgets, and the creature runs amok — as man-made monsters invariably do. Loew is called to undo his work, manages to pull out the *shem*, and Golem is laid to rest with a big funeral on the roof of Prague's Old New Synagogue. The rabbi's own tomb in the Old Jewish Cemetery is a major tourist attraction.

Frankenstein is the parallel that comes to mind, but the more direct descendant of Golem was the Robot, which first appeared in a play by the Czech writer Karel Čapek (1890–1938) and became one of the few words of Czech to join the international vocabulary. Golem also inspired a novel by Gustav Meyrink (1888–1932) and a silent movie classic directed by Paul Wegener.

ALBRECHT VON WALLENSTEIN (WALDSTEIN, VALDŠTEJN) *(1583-1634)*

The Thirty Years' War made Wallenstein into one of the most formidable warlords of European history. He led the imperial army to victory with ruthless cynicism, with no belief in their cause and no other goal than his own self-aggrandizement. At his peak, he was more powerful than anyone in the empire, and wealthier than the emperor he served. Yet he was suspected of dealing with the enemy, and in the end did so to escape those who suspected him of double-dealing.

Albrecht Eusebius Wenzel von Waldstein (better known in English as Wallenstein), a member of the minor Bohemian nobility, was an Utraquist until a timely conversion to Catholicism landed him on the winning side in 1620. Contracted as a mercenary commander by Ferdinand II, he conquered almost all of Germany for the emperor, coming within an inch of stamping out Protestantism in the continent. In 1630 he was dismissed on suspicion of disloyalty; next year the Saxons sacked Prague and he had to be recalled with greater powers and higher titles than before. In 1632 he defeated the Swedish king Gustavus Adolphus at Lützen; two years later he turned against his employer in collusion with the Swedes. His supporters wanted to make him king of Bohemia, but before he could act, the emperor's agents assassinated Wallenstein in the town of Cheb (Eger).

His moral ambiguity has fascinated dramatists: Schiller made him the hero of one of the greatest works of German theater in his *Wallenstein;* Sartre used him as the subject of his Existentialist play *Les Mains Sales.* His palace and garden remain one of the most impressive monuments to aristocratic vainglory in Prague.

JOSEPH II *(1741-90; ruled 1780-90)*

The most radical reformer to ascend a European throne in modern times, Joseph tried to accomplish by *fiat* what the French Revolution would tackle by blood and fire. Already as co-regent in 1776 he had helped expel the Jesuits from the empire whose cornerstone they had been for two centuries; as enlightened despot, he followed up by banning most religious orders and shutting up some 700 monasteries whose inmates could not prove to be engaged in "productive" work. His Patent of Tolerance gave civil rights to Protestants and Jews, dissolving the ghetto and permitting the return of Lutheran exiles to Bohemia.

To break the power of the nobility, he abolished serfdom; to quash the privileges of burghers, he reorganized ancient townships into uniformly administered cities. To promote Enlightenment — and, incidentally, to make life easier for a centralized bureaucracy — German was made the official language of the empire to the exclusion of both Latin and rustic dialects of the provinces.

Even the dead were not immune to reform: an ordinance in 1784 banned them from churchyards and crypts to modern cemeteries outside the town limits, set standards for coffins and tombstones, recommended reusable coffins, and prohibited all "excessive" forms of funeral rite. The ultimate memorial of Josephinism driven to its logical extreme can be seen in Theresienstadt/Terezín, a model town built on Joseph's orders in northern Bohemia, which the Nazis used as a concentration camp.

Without a base of support, Joseph's reforms crashed. His language policy proved his undoing in Bohemia, as in Hungary. ("In Bohemia the imperial nobility, which had been imported by the Habsburgs, cloaked their hostility to social reform in a display of Bohemian patriotism, and in the ante-rooms of [the Viennese palace] the descendants of German, Scottish, or Spanish adventurers ostentatiously exchanged a few words of Czech which they had laboriously learnt from their stable-boys" — A.J.P.Taylor, *The Habsburg Monarchy*). Czech was a dying language when Joseph came to power; yet within a generation, it would be the banner of a reborn and rebellious nation.

WOLFGANG AMADEUS MOZART *(1756-91)*

Mozart hated his native Salzburg, was often snubbed in his adopted Vienna, but adored ("My Praguers understand me") Prague, and that allowed the Czech capital to claim its fair share of the bicentenary hullabaloo. The composer first came to Prague in January 1787 to conduct *The Marriage of Figaro,* whose performance at the ESTATES THEATER was a runaway success, possibly because the rebellious traditions of the Bohemian capital were more receptive to the subversive message of the opera than unctuous Vienna. He had the time of his life, made good friends and composed a new symphony (*The Prague,* K504) while in town.

He returned in August that year for a three-month stay that saw the world premiere of *Don Giovanni.* Twice more he returned in 1789, and finally three months before his death to conduct the first performance of *La Clemenza di Tito* as part of the coronation rites of Leopold II as king of Bohemia.

The most famous memorial of his visits is the BERTRAMKA, the country house of his friends the Duscheks, which was the setting for a couple of the best-selling myths about his life. The Mozart Tavern on Templová, however, no longer carries the inscription, "Here Mozart ate, drank and composed, respectively, schnitzels, wine and *Don Juan.*"

FRANZ KAFKA *(1883-1924)*

Kafka died a respected name in the Czechoslovak insurance world, but few could guess at the time that modern literature had lost one of its trailblazers, and not even they could dream of his future metamorphosis into a tourist attraction for his native Prague.

The author of *The Castle, The Trial* and *Metamorphosis* was born into a modest Jewish family, which was, like most Prague–Jewish households of the time, bilingual in Czech and German. He spent all but his last two years in the city, nearly all of it in the shadow of the fantastic spires of the Týn Church. His deep sense of insecurity contrasts with the rich and confident age he was born into, and his bleak vision of society sits awkwardly with the backdrop of warm and quaint humor that Prague supplied.

His unproletarian pessimism was enough to put him into the communists' bad books. It only made matters worse that he wrote, unpatriotically, in German, and Kafka remained a nonentity in his native land for some 60 years after his death. The wind has turned since 1989: his name now feeds an entire industry of souvenir books, T-shirts, tours, plays, "Kafka pissed here" shops, and much fashionable angst.

VÁCLAV HAVEL *(born 1936)*

It was perhaps natural that a playwright should be the leader of a nation whose protector, St Vitus, is the patron saint of actors and dancers. At a time when Czechoslovakia was called the "Biafra of the spirit," Havel insisted on the moral responsibility of the writer to "live in truth" and to rise above the sordid reality of a police state. While his colleague Milan Kundera *(The Unbearable Lightness of Being)* emigrated to the West, he chose to stay behind to fight, with the quiet stoicism of a sage rather than the bitterness of a militant.

Charter 77, the human rights organization he helped to found, was a ray of hope in the suffocating atmosphere of Husák's regime. It led to his first arrest in 1977, which was followed by a $4\frac{1}{2}$-year prison term in 1979 for supporting the Committee for the Unjustly Prosecuted, and four months' imprisonment in 1989 for taking part in a demonstration in memory of Jan Palach, a student who burned himself to death in protest after the 1968 invasion.

In October that year, he was detained again on the eve of anticipated protests. Two months later he was President of the Republic.

The Prague coat-of-arms

The emblem showing three towers and the city wall with open gate was the Old Town coat-of-arms, adopted around the time of the town's incorporation c.1230. The walls were originally silver but became gilded in 1471 as part of the price that Vladislav II had to pay to the city in order to gain its support for his election as king. The arm with sword was granted in 1649 by Ferdinand III as a token of the gallantry of the Old Towners who had fought off Swedish invaders on the Charles Bridge during the final days of the Thirty Years' War.

The two lions rampant symbolize the Bohemian kingdom. The third one on top replaces the imperial Austrian two-headed eagle, which disappeared after Czechoslovakia's independence in 1918. A socialist red star crowned him until 1990. The flags represent the 24 communities that came together at different times to form the city of Prague. The third from the right, showing a star of David and a Swedish cap on red ground, is that of the Jewish town.

The motto on linden branches, *Praga caput rei publicae* ("Prague, capital of the republic"), is an adaptation of the original *Praga caput regni* ("Prague, capital of the kingdom"), the device granted by King John of Luxemburg in 1338.

Practical information

Before you go

DOCUMENTS

The Czech Republic requires no **visa** from citizens of the USA, Canada or any European countries except Albania. Nationals of other countries are asked to apply for a visa at a Czech consulate abroad, although visas are also issued on the spot at major (but not all) entry points, including Prague's Ruzyně airport. At the time of writing, a Czech visa is valid for entry into Slovakia and vice versa.

HEALTH CARE

Avoid Prague in winter (October to March) if you have respiratory problems or any other reason to worry about the quality of the air you breathe: decades of ecological neglect have left the Czech capital with one of the worst cases of air pollution of any major European city. No other specific health hazard calls for a warning. Inoculations are not needed for the Czech Republic. Medical services are adequate within the limits imposed by a bureaucratic system in transition.

For minor ailments, a **pharmacy** *(lékárna)* can provide hassle-free advice and recommend medication. Many pharmacies (most centrally, the one at Na příkopě 7, map **5**C6) are open 24 hours, though you may sometimes need to bang doors for a while to wake up the person on duty.

English-speaking doctors are employed by the foreigners' department of the **Fakultní Poliklinika** *(2nd floor, Karlovo nám. 28, map 4E5, open Mon 7.15am–5pm, Tues–Thurs 7.15am–3.45pm, Fri 7.15am–2.30pm).* Treatment here costs very little by Western standards. Not so at the **Diplomatic Health Center for Foreigners** *(Na Homolce 724, Smíchov* ☎ *529 21 11, map 1 C2, near main western highway),* open at all times (including dental care). Take your passport and at least kč1,000 as down-payment.

The Czech national health service has a reciprocal arrangement with the British health service, which entitles British citizens to full insurance cover while in the country: keep your receipts for medical fees and drugs to claim a refund back at home. No comparable arrangement exists for US nationals, though some private insurance packages cover medical expenses while abroad. Temporary insurance coverage is not available to foreign visitors in the Czech Republic.

The **IAMAT** (International Association for Medical Assistance to Travelers) is a nonprofit organization that has a list of English-speaking doctors who will call, for a fixed fee. There are member hospitals and clinics throughout Europe, including Prague. Membership is free, and other benefits include information on health risks worldwide. For further information, and a directory of doctors and hospitals, write to IAMAT headquarters in the US or Europe *(at 417 Center St., Lewiston, NY 14092, USA, or 57 Voirets, 1212 Grand-Lancy, Genève, Switzerland)*.

CUSTOMS

Customs control is relaxed and friendly, a striking change from the ordeal it used to be before the revolution. Items intended for personal use can be brought in free of customs duty, and that includes 250 cigarettes, 1 liter of spirits, 2 liters of wine and 500 centileters of perfume. There is a kč500 limit on gifts that can be brought out of the country, but inflation has rendered it meaningless. Regulations on the export of art and glass are more serious, and you should be advised about them before you make any significant purchases. See under ANTIQUES, pages 157–8.

MONEY

The Czechoslovak crown *(koruna,* pl. *koruny)* gave way in 1993 to separate Czech and Slovak currencies, abbreviated *kč* and *kš* respectively. The two units were initially set at par, but they have already begun to go their separate ways. The *haléř,* 100 of which make up a crown, has become irrelevant.

After a sharp fall, the value of the crown seemed to stabilize somewhat in 1992 at about kč26 to US$1. A prodigious number of **exchange bureaux** *(směnárna)* operate in all places likely to be touched by a tourist's itinerary, including, obviously, the airport and train stations. Rates are posted, but be aware that many private bureaux will charge hidden fees to the tune of 10 percent or more. Banks, in general, pay better rates. Shops and individuals will be glad to take payment in Deutschmarks, Austrian Schillings or — less often — US dollars. Changing unused crowns back into harder currency is a very major hassle, so it makes sense to buy only as needed.

The **black market** is technically illegal, though rates are now regularly published in the press, including the *Prague Post*. These often hover within 10 percent of the bank rate. Money-changers are thick on the ground around Wenceslas Square and Na příkopě. **Be very alert,** for they are known to perform all sorts of nasty tricks, and the chances of ending up with a wad of worthless old bills or Polish zlotys is higher than you might wish to believe.

Travelers checks issued by American Express, Thomas Cook, Barclays and Citibank are widely recognized. Make sure to read the instructions included with travelers checks. **It is important also to note separately the serial numbers and the telephone number to call in case of loss.** Specialist travelers check companies such as **American Express** provide extensive local refund facilities through their own offices or agents.

Charge and credit card usage is growing fast and seems set to catch up with Western levels soon. Nearly all hotels, better restaurants (but few pubs and beer houses) and the more ambitious private shops now accept plastic. Readily accepted cards are American Express, Diners Club, MasterCard/Eurocard and Visa.

A personal check supported by a **Eurocheque Encashment Card** can be cashed at major banks. Cash advances are available as follows:

- **American Express**   Václavské nám. 56, Prague 1. Map **5**D6 ☎26 17 47 ☒26 15 04. American Express cash advances and travelers check cashing.
- **Čekobanka**   Branches throughout Prague, open Monday to Sunday until 7pm, 9pm or 11pm. 24-hour branches at Staroměstské nám. #21, map **4**C5, and at 28. října #13, map **5**D6. Diners Club, MasterCard/Eurocard, Visa, JCB advances, Eurocheque cashing.
- **Komerční banka**   Branches at Na příkopě 3 and 28 (map **5**D6) have ATM machines that provide MasterCard/Eurocard cash advances.
- **Obchodní banka**   The central branch at Na příkope 14 (map **5**D6) cashes international bankers' checks and handles money wires via the SWIFT network.
- **Thomas Cook**   Václavské nám. 47, Prague 1. Map **5**D6 ☎26 31 06 ☒26 56 95. Cashes Thomas Cook travelers checks.
- **Živnostenská banka**   Na příkopě 20 (map **5**D6), open Monday to Friday 8am-5pm. Cash advances on Visa and MasterCard/Eurocard, no limit and no local fee.

American Express has a **MoneyGram®** money transfer service that makes it possible to wire money worldwide in just minutes, from any American Express Travel Service Office. This service is available to all customers and is not limited to American Express Card members.

COSTS

Prices have risen wildly since liberalization but still remain low by Western standards. Most nonimported items now hover between 30 and 50 percent below Western European (read: German) equivalents. Conversely, the official muggery of state-run tourist monopolies and state-set prices is largely gone, so a visit to Prague today may actually cost less than the times when a full restaurant meal could be had for $1 but you had to pay $80 for a dingy Interhotel room. Some examples are: • Dinner for one in a good restaurant: kč400. • Take-out sandwich: kč15. • Liter of high-grade gasoline: kč18. • Pint of beer: kč12-25. • Average monthly salary: kč4,000.

CLIMATE AND CLOTHING

Summer day temperatures in Prague vary between 15˚C (59˚F) and 30˚C (86˚F). Chilly days are common, so a light or not-so-light sweater is essential even in high summer. Likewise an umbrella and/or light rainwear. Midwinter temperatures range from 0˚C (32˚F) down to -15˚C (5˚F).

Gambling casinos are just about the only place where formal attire (tie, jacket, no jeans) is obligatory, but as a rule the Central European dress code is rather more conservative than that of either New York or London: a certain amount of dressing up will be expected at concerts, restaurants and posher hotels. Remember, on the other hand, that a couple of years ago Havel and half his cabinet roamed the halls of Hradčany in ski jackets and roller-skates.

Pack a comfortable pair of walking shoes: armed with this book, you are presumably expecting to do a lot of walking.

ELECTRICITY

Local current is **220 volts.** Sockets are either of the unearthed, two-hole, round-pronged variety (the European norm) or the hermaphrodite sort with a stick-out earth pin in addition to two holes. Plugs fitting the latter type are hard to find outside the Czech Republic and Slovakia, but you can buy an adaptor at any appliance shop in Prague or borrow one from the receptionist of your hotel.

TIME ZONE

The Czech Republic observes **Central European Time**, which is six hours ahead of Eastern Standard Time and one hour ahead of Greenwich Mean Time. Summer time starts at the end of March and finishes at the end of September, along with the rest of continental Europe — which is almost a month after Britain, the US and Canada, so the time difference with these countries is one hour greater for a few weeks in April and October.

TOURIST INFORMATION OVERSEAS

Čedok, the state-run travel agency, doubled until recently as the national tourist office of Czechoslovakia. This is no longer the case, but as of this writing the Czech Republic had yet to organize its new tourist office. Čedok has branch offices in the US and UK. Contact them for ideas, but think twice about their vacation packages, which as of mid-1993 remained unimpressed by market forces.

- 10 East 40th St., New York, NY 10016 ☎(212) 689 9720 ☒(212) 481 0597
- 49 Southwark St., London SE1 1RU ☎(071) 378 6009 ☒(071) 403 2321

A range of agencies have begun to offer specialist packages to the former Czechoslovakia, ranging from ballooning tours to art-and-opera vacations. Inquire about them through your travel agent.

Getting there

BY AIR

Prague has good airline connections with most European cities and many North American ones. In addition to the usual companies, several recently established private carriers have begun to offer flights (scheduled service, charter or air taxi) to and from some Central European locations, notably Vienna and Munich.

The winds of economic reform and the break-up of the country make the future of **Czechoslovak Airlines** (ČSA), the state company, somewhat cloudy. As it is, ČSA offers twice-daily flights from London, 5-times-weekly flights from New York, and assorted other routes. Its domestic destinations, beside Prague, are Bratislava, Košice, Ostrava, Piešťany, Sliač/Banská Bystrica and Tatry/Poprad (all in Slovakia). ČSA offices in Prague:

- **Travel office**   Revoluční 1, Prague 1. Map **5**C6. Metro: Nám. Republiky ☎2146. Reservations ☎235 27 85.
- **Vltava Terminal**   Revoluční 25, Prague 1 (near Švermův most). Map **5**B6 ☎2146. Information ☎231 73 95.
- **Airport**   ☎334 11 11.

The **Ruzyně Airport** is 15km (9 miles) w of the city center. The ČSA shuttle bus runs at 45-minute intervals between the airport, the Dejvická metro station, the Vltava Terminal and the Central Train Station (Hlavní nádraží). Municipal buses 119 and 254 also serve the airport from the Dejvická metro. A taxi to the city center costs about kč150 (S6).

- For airport information call   ☎38 78 14.

BY TRAIN

Prague has the benefit of frequent, punctual and comfortable railway connections with all points in Central Europe. Most international trains arrive at the Central Train Station (Hlavní nádraží), which is indeed centrally located. Others stop at the Masaryk Station (Masarykovo nádraží), a few blocks away, or the Holešovice Station (Nádraží Praha-Holešovice) in Prague 7. Addresses of train stations:

- **Hlavní nádraží**   Wilsonova, Prague 2. Map **5**D7. Metro: Hlavní nádr. (Also known as Wilsonovo nádraží.)
- **Masarykovo nádraží**   Hybernská, Prague 1. Map **5**C7. Metro: nám. Republiky.
- **Nádraží Praha-Smíchov**   Nádražní, Smíchov (Prague 5). Map **1**D3. Metro: Smíchovské nádr. Suburban and national lines only.
- **Nádraží Praha-Holešovice**   Prague 7. Map **2**C4. Metro: nádr. Holešovice.

Train arrival *(příjezd)* and departure *(odjezd)* information is prominently and intelligibly displayed in all stations. In addition to the basic fare, you can reserve a seat by paying a small surcharge (obligatory on night trains and some express trains). Tickets for international lines are sold in a separate section in the upper floor of the Central Station. Avoid buying sleeper and/or first-class tickets here, as the same services can be obtained much more inexpensively and with much greater goodwill by paying a friendly supplement to the conductor on board.

BY CAR

Prague is situated 1,200km (750 miles) by road from London, 500km (310 miles) from Frankfurt and 310km (195 miles) from Vienna.

A **national driver's license**, **car registration papers** and proof of **valid insurance** are required from drivers coming to the Czech Republic. If you don't have an international insurance certificate ("green card"), you may be asked to buy local insurance at the border crossing. The state-owned distribution company dominates the gas station *(Benzína)* network with (mildly) subsidized prices and the occasional (mild) shortage, but this is expected to change quickly as subsidies are abolished and foreign companies enter the market in greater numbers.

Roads are generally up to the best European standards, often very scenic and rarely crowded, so driving is a real pleasure. Speed limits are 110kph (69mph) on motorways, 90kph (56mph) on other main roads and 60kph (37mph) in towns unless otherwise posted. Road police, however, are a mere shadow of their mighty totalitarian past and you can, if you are so minded, get away almost with murder so long as you keep enough 10DM bills in readiness.

Report all **accidents** to the police, and to the Czech Insurance Company at Spálená 14-16, Prague 1 *(map 4 D5)*, if you mean to collect insurance.

In case of **breakdown**, contact the Yellow Angel tow-away service at ☎154 in the country or at ☎22 49 06 in Prague. Alternatively, hitch a ride to the nearest village, where people are likely to be friendlier, more competent, considerably less greedy and will probably offer you a beer as well. Schooled in the vagaries of Eastern-bloc cars, nearly all Czech drivers carry a towing rope, extra fuel, a sucking pipe and enough other tools and tricks to put the deadest car back on the road. Flag anyone down, and be ready to promise a guaranteed job in America.

Getting around in Prague

PUBLIC TRANSPORT
The all-purpose **transport ticket** *(jízdenka* or *lístek)* costs kč4 and is valid on the metro, buses, trams and trolleybuses as well as the Petřín funicular. It is sold in all newspaper kiosks and most food stores, restaurants and hotel reception desks. In metro stations you can *only* obtain it from vending machines, which may or may not return change. There is also an "ecological ticket" *(ekologická jízdenka)*, slightly cheaper than the standard ticket, which is valid on the metro, trams and trolleybuses, but not on buses.

Passengers are supposed to validate their ticket at the metro station entrance or on boarding a bus/tram/trolleybus by sticking it into the stamping automat: there is no one to check this on the spot, but occasionally a plainclothes inspector will turn up to nab unsuspecting dodgers. A ticket is valid for only one ride, with no transfers allowed, although you are of course allowed to change lines on the metro.

There exist unlimited-use tickets and passes for practically every interval of time between 24 hours and one year. They provide substantial savings if you plan to use the system frequently.

METRO
The metro has three lines labeled A, B and C. *Vstup* means "way in," *výstup* is "way out," and *přestup* indicates "transfer" or "passage," e.g., to another line. *Smĕr* means "direction" and is usually followed by the name of the last metro stop on a given line. At each stop a mellifluous

voice announces the name of both the current stop *and* the next stop, so listen carefully before rushing out. The system shuts from midnight to 5am.

The entire fleet of sturdy, clean and perfectly functional Soviet-made subway cars will be replaced by German ones by 1994 for no more obvious reason than ideological correctness or financial arm-twisting. The change will cost the city DM 20 million. A simultaneous extension of the B line from Nové Butovice to Zlíčín is planned.

BUSES, TRAMS AND TROLLEYBUSES

Trams run on precise and highly reliable timetables, which are displayed at each stop. A system of **night trams** takes over after midnight (in summer) or 10pm (in winter). There are only nine lines of these, numbered 51–59, and all pass through Lazarská in the New Town *(map 4E5)*. A white-on-blue sign at your local tram stop indicates the number of the nearest night tram line, along with a simple route map.

Buses function more or less like trams, except that they have 3-digit route numbers and generally keep out of the city center. The old Škoda and Ikarus smoke-belchers, famous contributors to Prague's pollution problem, are in the process of being replaced on many lines by electric-powered **trolleybuses**.

TAXIS

It is essential to remind the driver to turn on the meter *("Taximetr, prosím")*, and to make sure that it starts and ticks up at the usual rate (currently kč6 start-up, then kč5 per kilometer). When in doubt, demand a receipt before paying *("Potvrzení, prosím")*. A 5-to-10-percent tip is justified only in the case of exceptionally good conduct.

The **central exchange** for all Prague taxis is ☎20 29 51, 20 39 41 (24-hour service). For **advance booking** call ☎236 58 75, 235 26 11. Many of the smarter hotels have their own (rather expensive) taxi service.

Renting a taxi for a full day is usually an inexpensive alternative to renting a car. One of the cheapest companies is **Interkontact** (sic) ☎22 12 55.

CAR

Driving in central Prague is madness: there are no straight streets, and getting from point A to point B is often an altogether baffling exercise in deviations, one-way drives, and streets that suddenly terminate in a dead-end valley. Many streets in the historic part are legally closed to traffic, although you would not know it by seeing all the cars that are, or act as if they are, exempt.

The red circle sign means "restricted access," usually followed by *mimo* ("except") and, if you are lucky, some intelligible words like "auto" or hours of access. Exercise caution with direction signs as they are often deceptive, or else deliberately falsified to keep innocent drivers out of certain parts of the city.

There is a strong chance that your car will be towed away if you park illegally. In the event of this cataclysm, call ☎158 or proceed to the *parkoviště odtažených vozidel* at Kutnohorská ul. in Prague 10, 9km (5½ miles) E of the center

CAR RENTAL

Renting a Škoda, the perfectly nice, solid, reliable domestic make, is usually about half the cost of the least expensive imported model. Typical daily rates in summer for a 7-day rental with unlimited mileage, inclusive of 12-percent tax and insurance, hover just below $50 for a Škoda Favorit and $100 for an Opel Kadett. As always in the case of international rental companies, it is often considerably cheaper to reserve in advance before you leave home. The following are the major car rental firms (for hotel addresses see listings in WHERE TO STAY):

- **Avis (Pragocar)** Head office: Opletalova 33, Nové město, map **5D7** ☎22 23 24 ⓕₓ22 30 94. Branches at: airport ☎334 10 97; Hotel Atrium ☎284 20 43; Hotel Forum ☎419 02 13.
- **Budget** Head office: Strešovická 49, Nové město, map **3B1** ☎333 07 77. Branches at: airport ☎334 32 53; Hotel Inter-Continental ☎280 09 95; Čedok, Na příkopě 18, map **5C6** ☎236 33 80.
- **Europcar** Pařížská 26, Staré město, map **4C5** ☎231 02 78.
- **Hertz** Branches at: airport ☎312 07 17; Hotel Atrium ☎232 25 51; Hotel Diplomat ☎331 41 74; Hotel Palace ☎236 16 37.
- A local agency with lower prices is **Esucar**, Husitská 58, Žižkov (Prague 3), off map **5C7** ☎691 22 44. Reserve in advance, as usually there is a waiting list.

Listings of other local renters can be found under *půjčovny aut* in the classified section of various periodicals (the weekly *Pro* is a good source). Prices here can be as low as $10 a day, but nearly all advertisers are fly-by-night operators with one car to rent ("It is free next week, maybe") or none ("I suppose I must borrow father-in-law's"). Count on spending a frustrating day or two on the telephone.

BOAT

Sightseeing boats depart from the right bank of the river (New Town) near the Palacký Bridge *(Palackého most, map 4F4)*. In the same area is the landing for regular excursion boats (summer only) to Lake Slapy in the s or Troja, Stromovka and Roztoky in the N (see BOAT EXCURSIONS, page 166). For information ☎29 38 03, 28 83 09.

BICYCLE

Cyklo Centrum rents regular and mountain bikes at about $10 a day *(Karlovo nám. 29, Nové město, map 4E5 ☎29 94 44 ⓕₓ29 80 49)*.

On-the-spot information

TOURIST SERVICES

It seems to be very fashionable these days in Prague to open a tourist agency. About 3,500 of them are already in business, including five in the Central Train Station, one occupying the guard's tower of a historic bridge, and others that are run from back desks of government offices.

Their services include tours and excursions, private guides (usually a friend who speaks English), accommodation (usually a friend's apartment), money exchange, car rental (a friend's jalopy), transport and theater tickets, and in general any sort of help that a tourist may reasonably need or demand. Some are more professional than others, and some will no doubt grow to be tomorrow's travel giants.

Čedok

The former state tourist monopoly of Czechoslovakia, Čedok, was semi-privatized in 1992, but it is still by far the largest tourist concern, with 150 branches in the Czech Republic and an incoming capacity of 400,000 visitors a year. It owns three of Prague's top hotels (PALACE, ATRIUM and the new CLUB HOTEL PRUHONICE sport hotel), organizes a wide agenda of tours, and offers blocks of tickets for cultural events, including the Prague June festival and the new Laterna Animata multimedia show, for which Čedok is the sole sales agent.

In their main office at Na příkopě 18 *(map5C6* ☎*212 71 11* Fx*232 16 56)*, you may be told, with a straight face, that there is absolutely no accommodation left in Prague that day or the next day or the next ten days. Try elsewhere.

Information bureaux

Two tourist information bureaux have semiofficial status:

- **Prague Information Service (Pražská informační služba: PIS)** Offices at: Staroměstské nám. 1, map 4C5 ☎22 44 52; Na příkopě 20, map 5C6 ☎26 40 20; Hradčanská metro station, map 3A3 ☎32 29 17.
- **Pragotur** Municipal Building, U obecního domu 2 (metro: nám. Republiky), map 5C6 ☎231 72 81. The information service of the city government.

Private bureaux

Among private outfits, **Pragolem** *(Matějská 3, Prague 6* ☎*311 60 68)* and **City Point** *(Novotného lávka 1, Staré město, map 4C4* ☎*22 82 34)* are useful.

International travel companies

American Express, Thomas Cook, Wagons-Lits and other international travel companies have opened branch offices in Prague:

- **American Express Travel Service** Václavské nám. 56, map 5D6 ☎26 17 47 Fx26 15 07
- **Thomas Cook** Václavské nám. 47, map 5D6 ☎26 31 06 Fx26 56 95.

American Hospitality Center

The American Hospitality Center *(Malé náměstí 14, off Old Town Square* ☎*236 74 86* Fx*26 61 79, open daily 10am-10pm)* is information bureau, accommodation broker, exchange office, café, pizza parlor and souvenir store rolled into one. Jointly sponsored by the city of Prague and American business interests, it opened within days of the revolution and has been a popular meeting place ever since with Americans and non-Americans alike.

Other tour operators

Central European Adventures organize bicycle tours in and around

Prague and canoe tours on the Berounka river. Contact them through Pragotur (see above).

Evangtour is a Christian (Protestant) travel and contact service, at Korunní 60, Vinohrady (Prague 2), off map **5E7** ☎25 41 54 ⓔˣ25 45 16.

Wittmann Tours specialize in Jewish-interest tours throughout the Czech Republic and Slovakia. Their address is Uruguayská 7, Vinohrady (Prague 2), map **5F7** ☎823 87 95 ⓔˣ25 12 35.

LANGUAGE

A large majority of Czechs speak or understand some German. English is less widely spoken but quite common among tourist-service personnel and younger people. Don't hesitate to address your hotel receptionist or waiter in English: it is part of their job to speak the Bard's tongue. Czech itself is hopelessly opaque to anyone not versed in Slavic languages.

Public signs, displays, information etc. are usually in Czech alone, or at best bilingual in Czech and German. Many museums, however, observe the very civilized habit of keeping plastic-coated explanatory sheets for visitors in just about every known language: ask for them at the desk and return them before you leave.

ENGLISH-LANGUAGE PUBLICATIONS

Two excellent **English-language periodicals** have been in publication since 1991. The weekly *Prague Post* is stronger on news, the bi-weekly *Prognosis* on art and entertainment listings.

Melantrich, with six branches in central Prague, offers a decent selection of English-language books. Their best-stocked shop is at Na příkopě 27, map **5C6** ☎26 28 37, open Monday to Friday 8.30am-8pm, Saturday, Sunday 8.30am-6pm.

RADIO AND TV

The **OK3** television channel broadcasts the BBC Breakfast News on weekdays from 8.30am to 9am, and **CNN** programs on weekdays from midnight to 7am, 9 to 10am, and noon to 1.30pm. On weekends it transmits CNN from 6 to 7.55am and from noon to 1.30 or 1.55pm.

The **BBC World Service** can be received daily on 101.1 FM. **VOA Europe** broadcasts news and pop music on 98.1 FM.

SHOPPING AND BUSINESS HOURS

The basic opening hours are 10am-6pm on weekdays and 10am-2pm on Saturdays, but privatization has brought a wonderful elasticity to the working day. Many **shops** in central Prague start early (6am in the case of food stores, 8.30 or 9am for others) and stay open until 8pm or later; quite a few work full hours on Saturdays and Sundays. Some take a short lunch break, usually 12.30 to 1pm. The ubiquitous "non-stop" sign means that the business is open round the clock, or at least until late at night, or at the very least that it plans to work on weekends.

The same applies to **banks**, which open and close at eccentric hours. One recently established private bank lists seven separate sets of opening hours for its different branches in the city.

Museums generally stick to the regular 10am-6pm schedule Tuesday to Sunday. Virtually all of them are closed on Mondays, except the State Jewish Museum, which keeps the Sabbath.

PUBLIC HOLIDAYS
January 1, **Easter Monday**, **May 1**, **May 8** (Liberation from Nazi occupation, 1945), **July 5** (Sts Cyril and Methodius), **July 6** (Martyrdom of Jan Hus, 1415), **October 28** (Independence Day, 1918), **December 24-26** (Christmas).

Offices, banks, museums and some shops are closed on these days, but enough places stay open to change money or to buy necessaries. **November 17**, the anniversary of the 1989 revolution, is likely to be commemorated with a variety of public events.

POSTAL SERVICES
The **main post office** *(Hlavní pošta)* is located at Jindřišská 14, Nové město *(off Wenceslas Square, map 5D6)*, and stays open 24 hours a day, seven days a week. If you become confused, go to window 30 for information. There is a fax/telegram room to the right of the main entrance. Poste restante is received at window 28 *(address letters c/o Poste restante, Jindřišská 14, 110 00 Praha 1)*. You can try to send out parcels from windows 10-12, but the chances are that you will be told to go to the **customs office** at Plzeňská 59 or the **parcel post** at Plzeňská 139 (both in Prague 5) to have a taste of red tape.

There are **post offices** at Kaprova 12 in the Old Town *(map 4C5)*, Josefská 4 in the Lesser Side *(map 4C4)*, and one opposite St Vitus's Cathedral in the Castle *(map 3B3)*. Faxes can also be sent from the business centers of all major hotels or from the **American Hospitality Center** on Malé náměstí (see page 42).

TELEPHONE SERVICES
Public telephones come in four varieties: orange, black, old gray and digital gray. The first two take kč1 coins only: you place them in the slot before you dial and they drop when someone picks up at the other end. The older type of gray telephones also take higher-value coins, which you insert after you are connected. Gray phones with a digital display accept all coins and return the unused amount at the end of your call. Cards can be purchased at post offices for the increasing number of card telephones in use. The gurgling sound you hear after dialing is normal and means your call is going through.

Telephone numbers in Prague have six or seven digits. The **country code** for both the Czech Republic and Slovakia is **42**. Prague's **city code** is **2**. For unknown numbers in Prague ☎**120**; for unknown numbers in the rest of the two countries ☎**121**.

International calls can be made from all public phones provided you have enough coins. The international operator is reached at ☎**0135**; collect calls are placed through ☎**0132**. You can also call from a post office, where you first pay a deposit, then dial the number yourself from a booth, and at the end reclaim anything left of your deposit.

PUBLIC LAVATORIES (*ZÁCHOD* OR *WC*)

Public lavatories are scarce, although you will now find some automatic WCs in central Prague. There is usually an attendant, whom you pay as you enter, the amount depending on the facilities you wish to use. The attendant will also sell you toilet paper, by the sheet. It is generally acceptable to use the bathrooms in restaurants and pubs, and there are often WCs at metro stations. Standards of hygiene tend to be low.

LAUNDRY

Laundry Kings, Prague's only real laundromat, is located at Dejvická 16, near metro Hradčanská *(map 3 A3, open all week 8am-10pm)*.

TIPPING

With prices of consumer goods running way ahead of formal wages, a tip (gratuity, commission, bribe, etc.) is often a welcome supplement to the average Czech household's income. Waiters and taxi drivers have learned to expect the usual Western tipping levels (10 percent or so).

CONSULATES AND CULTURAL CENTERS

Australia   Čínská 4, Bubeneč (Prague 6). Map **1C3** ☎311 06 41. Tram 20, 25 from metro Dejvická. Monday to Thursday 9am-4pm, Friday 9am-1.30pm.

Canada   Mickiewiczova 6, Hradčany. Map **4B4** ☎312 02 51. Metro: Hradčanská. Monday to Friday 9am-11am.

UK   Thunovská 14, Malá strana. Map **3C3** ☎53 33 47. Monday to Friday 9am-noon. The **British Council** is located at Národní 10, Nové město. Map **4D5** ☎20 37 51.

USA   Tržiště 15, Malá strana. Map **3C3** ☎53 66 41. Monday to Friday 8am-4pm. The **American Library** is a few doors up at Vlašská 11.

Citizens of other Commonwealth countries are advised to contact the British Consulate if difficulties arise.

RELIGIOUS SERVICES

Active **Roman Catholic** churches in central Prague include St Vitus's Cathedral and the churches of Holy Cross, St Apollinaris, St Henry (Jindřišská), St Mary of Victory, St Mary of the Snows, St Nicholas in the Lesser Side, and St Stephen. More churches have returned to active use since the revolution. Services of the **Czechoslovak (Hussite) Church** are held in St Nicholas on the Old Town Square. The **Bohemian (Evangelical) Brethren** hold services in the churches of St Clement and St Martin.

English-language services are held at the following:

Anglican   St Clement's Church (sv. Kliment), Klimentská, Nové město. Map **5B6**. Metro: nám. Republiky. Services on Sunday at 11am.

Ecumenical   International Church (Církev bratrská), Vrázova 4, Smíchov (Prague 5). Map **1D3**. Metro: Anděl. Service daily at 11.15am ☎311 53 91.

Reformed   Church of Scotland (Husova kaple), U pošty 6, Karlín (Prague 8). Map **2C4**. Metro: Palmovka. Service daily at 11am, Sunday at 9am and 11am.

Roman Catholic (English)   St Joseph's Church (sv. Josef), Josefská,
Malá strana. Map 4C4. Metro: Malostranská. Mass daily at 10.30am
☎311 54 74.
Seventh Day Adventist   Peroutkova 54, Smíchov (Prague 5). Map
1D3. Metro: Anděl, then bus 137. Service on Saturday at 9am, 2pm.

Jewish services are held in the Staronová synagoga *(Old New Synagogue, Maislova, Staré město, map 4 C5)* and Jubilejní synagoga *(Jubilee
Synagogue, Jeruzalémská 7, near Central Train Station, map 5 D7)*. For
information, call the Jewish Society at ☎231 86 64.

Emergency information

POLICE
In emergencies ☎158. The central police station is located, aptly, at
Konviktská 14, Staré město, map 4D5; metro: Národní třída. Do not
expect anyone to speak English, but German may help.

MEDICAL AND DENTAL
- **Ambulance**   ☎155 or ☎333.
- **Dentist referral** (24-hour)   ☎26 13 74.
- **First aid**   Palackého 5, Nové město. Map 5D6. Metro: Národní
  třída ☎236 14 08, 236 14 09. 24-hour service.
- **General Hospital**   Karlovo nám. 32, Nové město. Map 4F5.
  Metro: Karlovo nám ☎29 93 81. 24-hour service at the
  department for foreigners (doctors speak English and German).
- **Pharmacy** *(lékárna)*   One or more pharmacies in each of
  Prague's ten districts stay open round the clock. The only one to
  do so in the central district (Prague 1) is the pharmacy at Na
  příkopě 7, map 5C6 ☎22 00 81; metro: Můstek.
- **Diplomatic Health Center for Foreigners**   A private clinic:
  see HEALTH CARE, page 34.

LOST AND FOUND
The lost-and-found bureau *(Ztráty a nálezy; Fundbüro* in German) is
located at Bolzanova, Nové město (near the Central Train Station). Map
5C7. Metro: Hlavní nádraží ☎236 88 86.

In case of lost passports, car papers or other documents, go to
Olšanská 2, Žižkov (Prague 3). Map 2C4 ☎24 51 84. Tram 5, 9.

CAR PROBLEMS
- **Accidents**   ☎158 or 236 64 64 to report to the police.
  ☎158 for medical aid.
- **Breakdown**   Call Yellow Angel at ☎154. 24-hour repair
  garages exist at Limuzská 12, Prague 10 *(map 2 C5)* ☎77 34 55,
  and Macurova 1640, Prague 4 *(map 1 D3)* ☎855 83 81.

Note on street names

Under the old regime, many of the streets, squares and bridges of Prague celebrated the great and good of the world's proletariat (Karel Marx, Bedřich Engels, Lenin, Gottwald, The Soviet Tankist) or the edifying moments of its history (May Day, the October Revolution). These names were changed in 1990-91, in most cases back to what they were before 1948 or even 1939. Hardly anyone remembers the old ones now, but there is potential for confusion still if you are using an outdated street map.

The easiest way to check is to find the next bridge south of Charles Bridge, which now bears the name of **Most legií**: if you see Most 1. Máje then the map is no good.

STREET NUMBERS

Most buildings in Prague carry two number-shields, a **blue one** showing the street number in the usual way, and a **red one** indicating the "registry number" within a city district. The latter system was established during the reorganization of the city in the days of Joseph II, and follows the order by which buildings were noted in the land registry — the lower the number, in other words, the older the building.

MAP LEXICON

most   bridge
nábřeží (nábř.)   embankment, quay
náměstí (nám.)   square
trh   market
třída (tř.)   avenue
ulice (ul.)   street

- Note that many streets are designated by prepositional expressions with *u, v, na, k* or *pod* (at, in, by, up, under) — thus *U radnice*, "By-the-City-Hall," *Na příkopě*, "In-the-moat." The word *ulice* (street) is not used in these cases.

Planning
your visit

An overview of the city

Prague straddles the **Vltava**, a subsidiary of the Elbe which is also known by its German name Moldau. **Staré město** (the **Old Town**) occupies the right (east) bank, surrounded on the east and south by **Nové město** (the **New Town**). The latter was already called "new" at its birth 650 years ago, though it took its present form mostly in the late 19thC, when it grew into the core of modern Prague. The streets Národní třída, Na příkopě and Revoluční separate the Old and New Towns along the course of the old (no longer extant) city walls.

The left (west) bank of the river is dominated by the hill of **Hradčany**, or Castle Hill, the seat of Bohemian kings from the Middle Ages onward and of Czechoslovakia's presidents since 1918. Nestled below the hill is **Malá strana** (the **Lesser Side**), a charming old town settled as early as Staré město but governed as a separate entity until modern times. A green belt separates the historic center from the newer districts surrounding it.

The population of Prague had its fastest growth from the early 19thC to 1939, increasing from 48,000 around 1820 to 676,000 in 1922 and 962,000 in 1938. Since the end of World War II it has been nearly stable just above the one-million mark.

Administratively, the city is divided into ten districts *(obvod)*. The historic center forms District 1, which includes Staré město, Lesser Side, Hradčany, and a part of Nové město. The remainder of Nové město and the castle of Vyšehrad constitute District 2. Districts 3 to 10 surround the center in clockwise succession. They are, with few exceptions, of little interest to the general tourist.

• **Throughout this book, we usually give the district number for addresses in Prague 2 to 10, but omit it in Prague 1.**

When to go

Avoid August unless you have *very* firm hotel reservations, carry your own food, and delight in the company of Europe's vacationing masses. The tourist season runs from **Easter to October**, and the streets of Prague are a semipermanent festival for much of this time. Off-season, some hotels, out-of-town castles, river cruises and the like will be shut for business.

The celebrated **Prague Spring** music festival starts rolling on the anniversary of Smetana's death on May 12, with musicians of the Czech Philharmonic walking from the composer's tomb in Vyšehrad to Obecní dům and there playing his cycle of symphonic poems, *Má vlast*. Since 1992, an extra four weeks of music and arts have stretched the festival into a so-called **Prague June**. Tickets for this are sold exclusively through Čedok, the semi-state travel agency.

The **Prague/Europe Music Festival** was inaugurated in September 1992 with a big display of fireworks and a program that brought a brilliantly fresh approach to the classical repertoire. Sponsored by various European governments and a battery of big-time celebrities, it promises to be the more successful of the two festivals.

December is another good time to be in the land of Good King Wenceslas. On St Nicholas' day (December 6), Santa and attendant angels parade the streets of Prague, collecting candies. On December 8, a march and outdoor concert is held in Malá strana to commemorate John Lennon's death. Carp, the Czech equivalent of the Anglo-Saxon turkey, makes its appearance in shops, menus and street stands. On Christmas Eve, Baby Jesus (and not Santa Claus) delivers presents.

What to see

The best way to enjoy Prague is to walk, more or less randomly.

One reason is practicality. The old part of the city is a maze of ancient alleys and passageways, which twist and curve in so many unexpected ways that it is hard for wondering strangers to follow any pre-set route without spending half their time checking a map.

Second, almost every alley hides a few items — a back-street church, a row of ancient houses, an eccentric house sign, a sooty statue — of singular charm and historic value. So there is usually little reason to choose one over another.

Third, none of the individual points of interest (museums, palaces and the like, with a few obvious exceptions) is of overwhelming importance on its own. As with Venice or Amsterdam, Prague's great attraction is the city itself, rather than any particular set of monuments.

Fourth, the historic center is compact enough to permit exploring on foot, if also large enough not to exhaust itself in a day, or two, or three.

Finally, there are few compelling sights in the outer part of the city that really and absolutely call for a planned sally out of the walkable core.

So set aside a few days and plunge into the labyrinth of Old Prague with only your instincts (and, of course, your *American Express Prague*) to direct your steps.

PRAGUE IN A NUTSHELL
Several key sights form the obvious building blocks of any tour: it is hard to imagine a first-time itinerary without the **Castle** of Hradčany, the **Charles Bridge**, the **Old Town Square** or **Wenceslas Square**.

Some three dozen splendid old churches lie along the way. Two — **St Vitus's Cathedral** in Hradčany and **St Nicholas** in Malá strana — are the splendidest, and any one of several others (the **Týn Church** on the Old Town Square, **St James** in Staré město, **St Thomas** in Malá strana, the **Loreto** shrine) would be enough by itself to put any city on the tourist's map. Other architectural high points include the **Royal Palace** in Hradčany, the **Town Hall** on the Old Town Square, and the fabulous libraries of the **Strahov Abbey**.

None of Prague's museums is quite a Louvre or Hermitage, but a couple of them — the **National Gallery**'s collections of Old Bohemian Art and European Art, located in two separate buildings in Hradčany — are full of brilliant work within their relatively modest scale. Just as exciting are the various **art galleries**, which bubble and sparkle with the tide of creativity that has gripped the nation since the Velvet Revolution.

The streets that carry the most tourist traffic, and so possess the most and the best shops, cafés, jugglers, street musicians and bauble sellers, are **Nerudova** and **Mostecká** in Malá strana, **Karlova** and **Celetná** in Staré město, and **Na příkopě** on the border between Staré and Nové město. These also feature some of the nicest and best-restored rows of pretty old houses.

Join these points, and you get a standard itinerary prescribed by every tour operator in town:

- Start at **Hradčany**, visit the **Royal Palace**, the **Cathedral**, the Old Bohemian collection in **St George's Abbey** and the European collection in the **Sternberg Palace**.
- Go down **Nerudova** to see **St Nicholas's Church**.
- Follow **Mostecká** to the **Charles Bridge**.
- Take **Karlova** to the **Old Town Square**, visiting the **Town Hall and Týn Church**.
- Amble along **Celetná ul.** and **Na příkopě**.
- End at **Wenceslas Square**.

Follow this route by all means if you don't particularly mind having to push and elbow your way through prodigious loads of weekending Germans. Or turn off into any side street, where the crowds suddenly vanish and the unrestored face of Old Prague shows through, crumbling with age yet quite as magical as the better-packaged part.

The three walks we propose in the following chapter combine the two approaches, covering nearly all of the city's main attractions while periodically abandoning the beaten track to discover a private nook or an uncrowded cranny.

Walking tours

Hidden Prague

Here, then, are three suggested walking itineraries. They should be read against the background of what has been said in the preceding pages — that just about any street in Old Prague is as lovely as the next, and that you will get happily lost anyway as soon as you take your eyes off the map.

Nearly all of the individual sights mentioned here are discussed in greater length in SIGHTS AND PLACES OF INTEREST. Any item written in **BOLD SMALL CAPITALS** has a full entry of its own in that chapter. Other places of interest get fuller treatment under some appropriate broader entry. Look for them under a relevant, more general place-name (thus St Vitus's Cathedral under CASTLE; the Týn Church, Old Town Hall and Malé náměstí under OLD TOWN SQUARE), or check the INDEX at the end of the book.

Each of the following itineraries should keep you walking for the better part of a day (4–6 hours), depending on how deeply you immerse yourself in details.

WALK 1: OLD TOWN AND NEW TOWN
See Walk 1 map overleaf. There are detailed plans of Old Town Square on page 101 and the Jewish Quarter on page 88.

Wenceslas Square (Václavské náměstí) is the center of modern Prague, and the Old Town Square (Staroměstské náměstí) that of the historic town. Devote your first walk to familiarizing yourself with the living core of the city.

Start at the **Můstek** ("Small Bridge"), where Wenceslas Square touches on the perimeter of Staré město and forms one of the busiest intersections in Prague. Elude the army of money-changers who blitz you in a dozen languages, and turn right into **Na příkopě**, Prague's shiniest window on the Consumer Society. The name of the street ("In the Moat") comes from the moat that once used to run here along the Old Town walls. The palace at #10, now a gambling casino, is the **Sylva-Taroucca Palace** (Sylva-Ta-rouccovský palác). Excellent bookstores at **#3** and **#27** help you arm yourself with enough maps, postcards, guidebooks and sightseeing ideas to last you through your stay in Prague.

The far end of Na příkopě, where it joins Náměstí Republiky, is punctuated by the **Powder Tower** (Prašná brána), the Gothic tower house of what used to be the main city gate. The adjoining **Municipal**

WALK 1

Starý Židovský Hřbitov (Jewish Cemetery)

Staronová Synagóga

MALÁ ŠTUPARTSKÁ

Palác Kinských

U kamenneho zvonu

sv. Jakuba

Paříž Hotel

ŠIROKÁ

PAŘÍŽSKÁ

MASELOTA

Týnsky dvůr

ŠTUPARTSKÁ

Obecní dům

Kafka's Birthplace

STAROMĚSTSKÉ NÁM. (OLD TOWN SQUARE)

CELETNÁ

NÁM. REPUBLIKY

sv. Mikuláše

U RADNICE

Staroměstské radnice (Town Hall)

U minuty

P. M. před Týnem

Karolinum

ŽELEZNÁ

Cubist House

OVOCNÝ TRH

Prašná brána

MALÉ NÁM.

U dvou medvědů

MELANTRICHOVA

HAVELSKÁ

sv. Havla

Stavovské divadlo

NA PŘÍKOPĚ

RYTÍŘSKÁ

MŮSTEK ◀— **START HERE**

N

JUNGMANNOVO NÁM.

VÁCLAVSKÉ NÁM. (WENCESLAS SQUARE)

Adria Building

P. Marie sněžné

Grand Hotel Evropa

To Národní muzeum

0 — 100 — 200 — 300m
0 — 100 — 200 — 300yds

House (Obecní dům), considered to be Prague's finest specimen of Art Nouveau, houses a popular café. Go all the way around it to admire the extravagantly eclectic **Paříž Hotel** on **U obecního domu**, then return to the Tower and turn right on CELETNÁ ULICE for one of the city's most famous line-ups of quaint old houses. Observe the hard-pressed Baroque caryatids of the old **Mint** at #36 and the **Cubist house** (U cěrné Matky boží) at #34, enter the attractive courtyard of **#17**, and note Franz Kafka's childhood homes at **#2** and **#3**.

The Old Town Square is directly ahead of you, but hold off for a while to wander first into the strangely run-down alleys of the oldest part of Staré město, which lie on your right. Turn into **Štupartská** and left on **Malá Štupartská**: you will be facing the church of ST JAMES (sv. Jakuba), whose sculpted portals, ceiling and altar are among the most extravagant products of the Baroque in Prague.

Almost directly across the road from sv. Jakuba, an entranceway leads left into the **Týn Court** (Týnsky dvůr), a medieval shopping complex

52

which has been shut for repairs for some years and seems likely to remain that way for a while more. Go through, if you can, or around if the gate is blocked up, to emerge at last into the hubbub of the **OLD TOWN SQUARE** (Staroměstské náměstí). Enjoy the scene from any one of the sidewalk cafés; alternatively, choose a higher lookout on the second floor of **Café Amadeus** at #14.

The fantastic towers of the **Týn Church** (Panny Marie před Týnem) form the square's visual signature. Enter the church (if it is open, which is not often the case) through the plain little gateway under the arcade of the **White Unicorn House** (U bílého jednorožce), and note **Tycho Brahe's tombstone**, with the 16thC astronomer's artificial nose. Check the current expositions at the **Stone Bell House** (I kamenného zvonu) next to the church and the **Kinsky Palace** (Palác Kinských) adjoining it.

Pařížská, the Art Nouveau showcase of Prague if not of all Europe, leads straight NW off the Old Town Square toward the former **JEWISH QUARTER** (Josefov), where a cluster of memorials constitute the **State Jewish Museum** (Statní Židovské muzeum). The **Old New Synagogue** and **Jewish Cemetery** (Staronová synagóga and Starý židovský hřbitov) merit the greatest attention among a half-dozen synagogues and other buildings scattered over several city blocks.

Return toward the square via **Maislova**, which eventually lands you beside the church of **St Nicholas** (kostel sv. Mikulaše), a little Baroque gem not to be confused with the more famous St Nicholas in Malá strana. In the house beside the church, now featuring a blatantly commercial "museum," Franz Kafka was born in 1883.

Continue through the arcades of **U radnice**, which soon bring you to **Malé náměstí**, the lesser sidekick of the Old Town Square. Observe the 16thC *sgraffiti* covering the house **U minuty** and the much newer color frescoes of the **Rott House** (U Rottů) at #3. If you have timed your arrival to the hour, you can watch the parade of saints and ghouls at the venerable cuckoo clock of the **Town Hall** (Staroměstská radnice). Otherwise, while the hour away at the top of the Town Hall's tower, surveying the square and the city from the vantage of birds.

Leave the square again heading s by **Melantrichova**, the old, curving alley that starts opposite the Town Hall. Past the arches, note the 16thC portal of **The Two Golden Bears** (U dvou zlatých medvědů) in the dead-end alley on the left, and the ruined church of **St Michael** (sv. Michala) hidden in a courtyard on the right. The first real cross-street is **Havelská**, which features a permanent **street market** and the strangely eloquent Baroque facade of **St Gallus** (sv. Havla).

Go left, past the church, and turn right on **Železná**, where you will be facing the main hall of the **CAROLINUM**, one of Europe's oldest universities. Enter the alley separating this from the **ESTATES THEATER** (Stavovské divadlo) to see the fanciful **oriel bay**, a surviving part of the original 14thC building of the university.

Now go around the theater, which was the stage for the premieres of two of Mozart's operas as well as a set for Miloš Forman's *Amadeus*, and linger for a while in **Ovocní trh**, a ring of candy-colored historic houses perfectly suited to the stage-set of an 18thC play.

Next, follow **Rytířská** and turn left toward **Můstek**. You have made a full circle back to the starting point of this walk, and WENCESLAS SQUARE (Václavské náměstí) beckons ahead, with its neon lights and evening crowds. If you are hunting for photos you may just catch the **National Museum** (Národní muzeum) blazing in the late sun and looking magnificent at the head of its ramp.

Make a final detour, if you wish to go on, on to **28. října ul.** and **Jungmannovo nám.** The latter features the curious black facade of the **Adria Building** (Palác Adrie), a specimen of the 1920s architectural movement known as Rondocubism. Off to one side, a courtyard conceals behind an unpromising huddle of modern buildings the gigantic rump of the never-finished Gothic church of **Our Lady of the Snows** (Panny Marie Sněžné).

Return to Wenceslas Square and stroll as far as the **statue of St Wenceslas**, noting the monuments of turn-of-the-century *folie de grandeur* that line the boulevard. The grandest of them is arguably **Grand Hotel Evropa**, and its café could be the right place to sit down to write all those postcards that have piled up through the day.

Old Town Square houses combine medieval foundations with Baroque gables and 19thC details.

WALK 2: OLD TOWN AND LESSER SIDE

See Walk 2 map overleaf. There are detailed plans of Old Town Square on page 101, Lesser Side Square on page 93, and Hradčany Square on page 85.

Prague actually has two Old Towns, and the one not called by that particular name is in many ways the quainter and more hoarily historic. Nearly every street and alley in the Lesser Side (Malá strana) deserves to be strolled through, so there is little point in feeling bound to any particular itinerary. Here is one path you might want to follow.

Start at the OLD TOWN SQUARE (Staroměstské náměstí), which hardly loses any of its charm on a second (or third, or fourth) visit. Proceed to **Malé náměstí** (Lesser Square), where the **American Hospitality Center** offers the triple amenities of tourist bureau, pizza parlor and souvenir store, then follow the twists and bends of KARLOVA ULICE toward the Charles Bridge.

Note the mighty caryatids of the **Clam-Gallas Palace** (Clam-Gallasův palác) on the first corner on the right, and the house at **#4** where the astronomer Johannes Kepler lived during his tenure at the court of Rudolf II. One of Prague's finest antiquarian bookstores is located at **#2**, almost beside the bridge. The huge complex of the KLEMENTINUM, the former Jesuit school that now houses the National Library, juts over into the street on the right with the eloquent rotunda of the **Italian Chapel** (Vlašska kaple).

Next comes the church of **St Salvator** (kostel sv. Salvátora), facing the Charles Bridge with one of the finest exteriors in Prague. Opposite it on the right side of **Křížovnické náměstí** is yet another Baroque church, that of **St Francis** (kostel sv. Františka serafinského), with its immense bronze cupola. The **statue of Charles IV** guards the entrance of the bridge that carries his name. It looks, as Neo-Gothic statues usually do, like a minor film star dressed up for a historical epic. Under his feet, some wild-looking Goths usually mint coins with great bangs and clinks for the amusement of passers-by.

The CHARLES BRIDGE (Karlův most) is thoroughfare, art gallery, bazaar and theater stage rolled into one. It has 30 groups of statues, some of them genuine masterpieces, and at different points along the way as many as a dozen street musicians will be performing at any given moment. There are two fabulous medieval towers on each end, which you can climb for a better view. The more famous of the two is the **Old Town Tower** (Staroměstská mostecká věž) on the E bank: an important battle was fought under it during the Thirty Years' War, and the chopped heads of the Bohemian nobility were dangled from its walls for public instruction in another phase of the same conflict.

Having crossed to the W bank, you encounter a quietly attractive corner of Old Prague under the bridge this side of the **Lesser Side Towers** (Malostranské mostecké věže). Take the first street to the right as you leave the bridge, passing in front of **The Three Ostriches** (U tří pštrosů), one of Prague's best-known hotel/restaurants. The street is called **Mišeňská** at first but soon curves into **U lužického semináře** and provides some of the nicest snapshots of picture-book Prague.

Turn right toward the canal separating the island of KAMPA from the

WALK 2

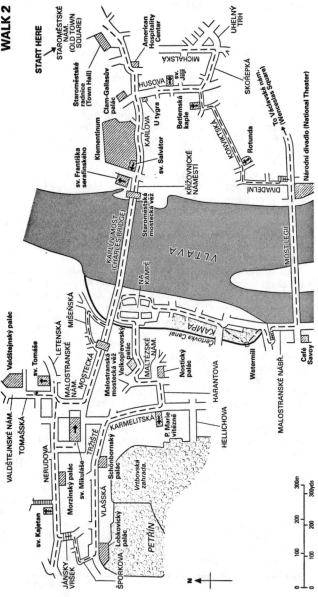

START HERE

STAROMĚSTSKÉ NÁM. (OLD TOWN SQUARE)

American Hospitality Center

Staroměstské radnice (Town Hall)

Clam-Gallasův palác

HUSOVA

sv. Jiljí

MICHALSKÁ

UHELNÝ TRH

SKOŘEPKA

Klementinum

KARLOVA

U tygra

Betlémská kaple

sv. František serafínského

sv. Salvator

KŘÍŽOVNICKÉ NÁMĚSTÍ

KONVIKTSKÁ

Rotunda

To Václavské nám. (Wenceslas Square)

KARLŮV MOST (CHARLES BRIDGE)

Staroměstská mostecká věž

DIVADELNÍ

Národní divadlo (National Theater)

VLTAVA

NA KAMPĚ

Čertovka Canal

KAMPA

MOST LEGIÍ

Valdštejnský palác

sv. Tomáše

LETENSKÁ

MÍŠEŇSKÁ

Malostranská mostecká věž

MOSTECKÁ

Velkopřevorský palác

MALOSTRANSKÉ NÁM.

MALTÉZSKÉ NÁM.

Nostický palác

HARANTOVA

Watermill

Café Savoy

MALOSTRANSKÉ NÁBŘ.

VALDŠTEJNSKÉ NÁM.

TOMÁŠSKÁ

sv. Kajetán

NERUDOVA

Morzinský palác

sv. Mikuláše

TRŽIŠTĚ

Schönbornský palác

VLAŠSKÁ

KARMELITSKÁ

P. Marie vítězné

HELLICHOVA

JÁNSKÝ VRŠEK

ŠPORKOVA

Lobkovický palác

Vrtbovská zahrada

PETŘÍN

N

0   100   200   300m
0   100   200   300yds

56

mainland, and right again until you re-emerge on the side of the bridge beside the Ostriches.

Now head W, following **Mostecká**, the lively main street of Malá strana, to the LESSER SIDE SQUARE (Malostranské nám.). This actually consists of two separate spaces divided by the bold mass of **St Nicholas** (kostel sv. Mikuláše) and the barracks-like compound of the former **Jesuit College** (Jezuitská kolej) beside it.

Proceed first up the eastern side of the square to admire the astonishing exterior of **St Thomas** (kostel sv. Tomáše), in a tiny alley off Letenská and to take a look, if the church is open, at its majestic frescoes. Detour up **Tomašská** to see the amazing statue on the front of #4, where an exasperated deer stares down a bewildered **St Hubert**, and continue to **Valdštejnské nám.** to admire the exterior of the Wallenstein Palace (Valdštejnský palác, whose extraordinary garden, entered by the back street, is part of WALK 3).

Now retrace your steps to the N side of the square, to climb upward along the stately but crumbling facades of the **Sternberg** and **Smiřický Palaces** (Šternberský palác and Palác Smiřických) and the **Jesuit Gymnasium** (Jesuitska gymnazium). Now enter St Nicholas (its entrance is from the upper square) and permit yourself to be overwhelmed by its gesticulating saints and frenzied curves.

NERUDOVA ULICE climbs gently westward toward Hradčany through one of Prague's most attractive districts. Note the arrogant moors of the former **Morzin Palace** (Morzinský palác) on the left at #5 (the Romanian Embassy), and the contortionist eagles of the **Thun-Hohenstein Palace** (Thun-Hohenštejnský palác) across the road at #20 (the Italian Embassy). Visit the church of **St Cajetan** (kostel sv. Kajetana), discovering the hidden stairway between this and the Italian Embassy that leads up to the castle. Browse through the toy stores at **#21, #31** and **#45**, and view the ancient house signs that decorate almost every doorway on Nerudova.

The *sgraffiti*-covered rear of the **Schwarzenberg Palace** (Schwarzenbersský palác) rises over the upper end of the street where a short ramp would bring you up to Hradčany Square (HRADČANSKÉ NAMĚSTÍ). Leave this until WALK 3. Instead, turn left and come back down to the stairway, called **Janský vršek**, which leads into a confusion of alleys down the side of the Castle Hill.

Turn right on **Šporkova**, a peaceful alley that winds past two cul-de-sacs full of unexpected details, to emerge in front of the **Lobkowicz Palace** (Lobkovický palác), now the German Embassy. Behind the palace rises the wooded hill of PETŘÍN with a park incorporating the gardens of several former aristocratic estates and church properties. Walk along the base of the hill, following **Vlašská** and then **Tržiště**. Note the **Schönborn Palace** (Schönbornský palác: the US Embassy), and peek into the forecourt of the **Vrtba Gardens** (Vrtbovská zahrada), one of Prague's finest parks, which for some years has been closed for repairs (entrance at Karmelitská #25, around the corner from Tržiště).

Reaching **Karmelitská**, you return momentarily to the world of cars and crowds. A short distance ahead, a raised platform on the right carries the church of OUR LADY OF VICTORY (kostel Panny Marie vítězné), remarkable mainly for the doll of Child Jesus, the "Bambino di Praga," which attracts pilgrims from around the Catholic world. Follow **Harantova**, the alley facing the church, eastward into the peaceful seclusion of MALTÉZSKÉ NÁMĚSTÍ.

Note the majestic **Nostitz Palace** (Nostický palác: the Dutch Embassy) on your right, then turn left to walk past the pastry-puff **Turba Palace** (Turbů palác: the Japanese Embassy) toward Brokoff's statue of **John the Baptist**, which stands in the middle of the square. Study the menu of **U malířů** ("At the painter's", at #11), the most expensive eating place in Prague, and the fortress-like exterior of the church of **Our Lady Under the Chain** (Panny Marie pod řetězem). The Maltese Knights who gave the square its name have returned to the adjoining **Grand Prior's Palace** (Velkopřevorský palác), which they have restored in lovely detail.

The garden wall of the Prior's Palace, facing the French Embassy (the former **Palais Buquoy**/Buquoyský palác) across chestnut-lined **Velkopřevorské nám.**, carries the youngest of Prague's art treasures, the **John Lennon Wall**. Follow the trail of graffiti over the little bridge that crosses into the island of KAMPA, then take the alley on the left, which unexpectedly emerges at the foot of the **Charles Bridge**.

The delightful square here, **Na kampě**, usually remains untouched by the hustle and bustle reigning on the bridge. Note the **Blue Fox** (U modré lišky) at #1, walk to the riverbank for an unusual view of the Charles Bridge, then cross the park heading s to the edge of the **Čertovka Canal** to see the venerable old watermill hidden in the foliage. Climb the stairs to the **Malostranské nábř.**, where there is a splendid old apartment building with an enviable river view. Check out the elegant **Café Savoy** as a potential venue for a lazy afternoon another day. Cross back to the E bank by the **Legions' Bridge** (Most legií), noticing how its four towerlets echo the Neo-Renaissance roof of the NATIONAL THEATER (Národní divadlo) across the river.

From the theater it is a quick walk E past the pathetic department-store windows of **Národní třída** to WENCESLAS SQUARE (Václavské náměstí). If you still have any energy, you may take another plunge (heading N) into the narrow streets of Staré město. The part below Betlémské nám. is at first disappointing: you go down the stairs opposite the National Theater, a favorite hangout of Prague's street-pissers, follow **Divadelní** and turn right along the gray 1920s apartment blocks of **Konviktská**. The stumpy **Rotunda of the Holy Cross** (Rotunda sv. Kříže) at the corner of ul. Karolíny Světlé is the oldest building in Staré město, with about 900 years to its credit. The **Bethlehem Chapel** (Betlémská kaple, on Betlémské nám.), a modern fake like most other monuments of Czech nationalism, is a reconstruction of the chapel that saw the birth of the Hussite revolution a little less than 500 years ago.

Some of the finest pubs in Prague now lie between you and the triangle defined by Karlova and Můstek. Try **The Golden Tiger** (U zlatého tygra), a legendary meeting-place of Prague's literati: to reach it, go left on Husova, past the Dominican church of **St Giles** (sv. Jiljí) until you get almost to the corner of Karlova. If the Tiger is too full or too smoky or too talky for you, then head along Skořepká toward **Uhelný trh**, where you will find **The Two Cats** (U dvou koček). Or check the string of wine houses along **Michalská**, which are a favorite hangout of younger people on summer evenings.

WALK 3: HRADČANY

See Walk 3 map overleaf. There are detailed plans of Hradčany Square on page 85, Prague Castle on page 66, and the Jewish Quarter on page 88.

The centerpiece of this route is the Prague Castle, which is less a castle than a fortified acropolis storing the accrued baggage of 1,000 years of Czech history. Touring it means browsing through several churches, four or five museum collections, assorted palace halls and long rows of trinket-sellers' stands, which together demand the better part of your day. Nearly everything worth seeing in the castle is closed on Monday, so choose another day for this walk.

Start at the STRAHOV ABBEY, which stands where the SW tip of Hradčany joins the hill of PETŘÍN. You can get there by following **Úvoz** ("The Dip") past the upper (W) end of **Nerudova**, or by following **Vlašská** to its western end and going through the park (see WALK 2). But undoubtedly the most exciting way is to take the **Petřín funicular**, then walk NW through the park, whose eastern part is a big orchard full of all sorts of unattended fruit trees. The abbey itself possesses a library that is one of Prague's wonders.

The gently sloping cobblestones of **Pohořelec** ("Firegrounds") lead, by way of many little antique stores and small cafés, to **Loretánské náměstí**, whose principal features are the imposing **Czernin Palace** (Černínský palác), now the Foreign Ministry, on the left, and the cherub-filled frontage of the LORETO on the right. Visit the Loreto for one of the most unrestrained outpourings of Baroque fancy to be found anywhere, and do wait to hear the hourly carillon whenever it is not canceled/being repaired/out of order.

Walk down **Černinská**, the steep alley leading off to the right of the Czernin Palace as you face it from the Loreto, and soon you are in the enchanted world of **Nový Svět** ("New World"). This was once a poor man's neighborhood that somehow survived as a genuine village street at the edge of the city. Follow it along the park wall into **Kanovnická**, which in turn will let you emerge into Hradčany Square (**HRADČANSKÉ NAMĚSTÍ**) beside the sgraffiti-covered facade of the **Martinitz Palace** (Martinický palác).

The square is one of Prague's most monumental spaces, dominated at one end by the main entrance of the castle and surrounded on three sides by the palaces of leading members of the Habsburg aristocracy. Note the **Toscana Palace** (Toskánský palác) on your right as you come into the square; the black-and-white checkered **Schwarzenberg Palace** (Schwarzenberský palác: now the Military History Museum) on the far right of the square, and the adjoining **Salm Palace** (Salmovský palác); and the pink-and-cream **Archbishop's Palace** (Arcibiskupský palác) on the left. A gate beside the latter leads to the **Sternberg Palace** (Šternberský palác), which houses the National Gallery's small but excellent

WALK 3

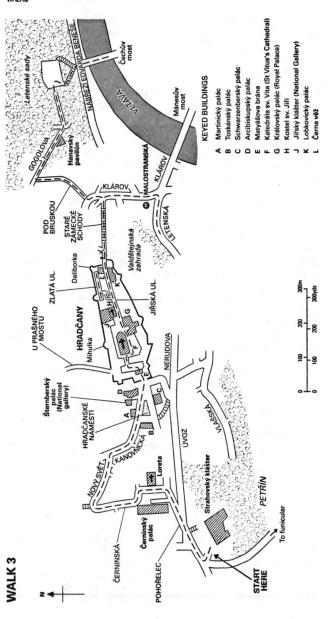

KEYED BUILDINGS

A   Martinický palác
B   Toskánský palác
C   Schwarzenberský palác
D   Arcibiskupský palác
E   Matyášova brána
F   Katedrála sv. Víta (St Vitus's Cathedral)
G   Královský palác (Royal Palace)
H   Kostel sv. Jiří
J   Jiřský klášter (National Gallery)
K   Lobkovický palác
L   Černá věž

collection of European (i.e., non-Czech) masters. At the far end of the square, the observation terraces on the left of the castle entrance command a classic panorama of Prague.

Enter the CASTLE (Hrad, Hradčany) between the extravagant giants that protect the outer gateway. Go through the **Matthias Gate** (Matyášova brána), an early 17thC portal incorporated into Maria Theresa's barracks-like 18thC palace. This complex, which encloses a huge courtyard and continues with a wing on the right side of the Cathedral Square, houses the offices and residence of the President: the President of just *what* is an open question at the time of this writing.

Two sections of the palace that are accessible to the public are both entered through the second courtyard: on the right, the **Holy Cross Chapel** (Kaple sv. Kříže), which hosts an exhibit of the cathedral treasury, and on the left, the **Castle Gallery** (Hradní galerie), which holds works of art from the former royal collection (currently closed for restoration).

Cross the second gateway and you will be facing the gigantic pile of **St Vitus's Cathedral** (Katedrála sv. Víta). The part you see on this side is actually a 20thC extension built in imitation of the original 14thC style. Go around to the right to enter through the splendid portal — the "**Golden Gate**" (Zlatá brána) — of the original church, and do not let the permanent jam at the ticket-desk discourage you from entering the **Wenceslas Chapel** (Kaple sv. Václava) to the right of this entrance. Cross the nave to see Alfons Mucha's stained-glass composition of the lives of Sts Cyril and Methodius.

Directly across the courtyard from the Golden Gate is the entrance to the **Royal Palace** (Královský palác), one of Europe's finest monuments of Gothic civil architecture. The centerpiece of the palace is the Vladislav Hall. A jutting wing to the right was the setting for the famous defenestration that launched the Thirty Years' War. Go upstairs to view the impressive halls of the Land Registry and the Bohemian Chamber, and downstairs into the basement for the extensive remains of the older, Romanesque, palace of King Soběslav.

Leave the palace by the back exit, which faces the red Early Baroque facade of **St George's Basilica** (kostel sv. Jiří). This hides a severely empty interior, while the adjoining **St George's Convent** (Jiřský klášter) is the setting for possibly the most memorable of Prague's art treasures: the National Gallery's collections of Medieval and Baroque Bohemian art.

As you leave St George's Square, a passageway on the left leads to the **Golden Lane** (Zlatá ulička), the most hyped-up alley in Central Europe. On the right is the **Lobkowicz Palace** (Lobkovický palác), the most dispensable of Hradčany's museums. Come out of the castle precincts by the **Black Tower** (Černa věž), stopping outside to take in the incomparable cityscape. Descend by the **Old Castle Stairs** (Staré zámecké schody), pushing on as well as you can through the tide of tour groups, peddlers and street artists.

The **Malostranská** metro station, a short distance from the bottom end of the stairs, is a possible point to end the walk.

However, for a more fantastic place to rest your feet, walk a further block down and turn right into **Letenská** toward the rear entrance of the

WALLENSTEIN GARDENS (Valdštejnská zahrada). Designed in the waning days of the Renaissance for the man who was at that time Europe's most powerful warlord, the garden features a sumptuous portico and pathways lined with de Vries' bronze statues.

It is a two-minute walk from the Wallenstein Gardens to either the **Lesser Side Square** or the **Charles Bridge** (see WALK 2). But if you still wish to go on, an alternative could be to retrace your steps back to the Malostranská metro and the base of the castle stairs. A tiresome but short climb here up the pedestrian path of **Pod bruskou** takes you to an entrance of the LETNÁ GARDENS (Letenské sady).

Enter the park and enjoy a fabulous view of Prague while sipping your beer on the terrace of the **Hanau Pavilion** (Hanavský pavilón). Walk next to the vast and empty platform from which a colossal statue of Stalin once used to look down on the city. Climb down and cross the Art Nouveau **Bridge of Svatopluk Čech** (Čechův most) to the JEWISH QUARTER in Staré město (see WALK 1).

Sights and places of interest

Exploring Prague

The principal sights of Prague are listed in this chapter in alphabetical order. Some entries deal with an individual building or monument. Other entries cover an area or a cluster of sights — examples include CASTLE, LESSER SIDE SQUARE and OLD TOWN SQUARE — which in our opinion are more easily toured, understood and described as an ensemble.

Inevitably this is not a perfect solution. For example, you have to look for the Týn Church and St Nicholas under OLD TOWN SQUARE, while some less top-ranking churches, because they stand on their own, have their own entry. But we feel that the alternative of unbundling every large entry into its constituent pieces would be less readable and less useful as an on-the-spot guide.

If you don't immediately find something that you look for, try the INDEX at the end of the book.

To avoid cluttering the main A to Z, three much shorter alphabetical lists follow it. They include Prague's lesser CHURCHES (page 115) and MUSEUMS (page 119), and a miscellany of OTHER SIGHTS (page 122).

OPENING TIMES
Nearly all **museums** work standard hours, 10am–6pm from Tuesday to Sunday. Virtually all of them close on Mondays (except, notably, the State Jewish Museum, which keeps the Sabbath). No such generalization can be made about **churches**, whose opening hours are unpredictable.

EXPLAINING OUR TYPE STYLES
- **Bold type** generally indicates points of outstanding interest.
- Places named without addresses and opening times are often described more fully elsewhere: look out for **cross-references**, which are printed in SMALL CAPITALS.
- In this chapter, look for the ★ symbol against the outstanding, not-to-be-missed sights.
- If you have more time, look for the ☆ symbol, indicating places that we think you should make an effort to see.
- Places of special interest for children (⚲) are also indicated.
- For guided tours, look for the 𝒦 symbol: details follow this symbol where appropriate.
- **For a full explanation of all the symbols used in this book, see page 7.**

Sights A to Z

BERTRAMKA (Mozart Museum)
Mozartova 2, Smíchov (Prague 5). Off map 3F2 ☎ 54 38 93 ☒ Open daily 9.30am–6pm ✗ with mini-concert July–Sept daily at 11am and 5pm. Indoor concerts Thurs, Fri, Sat at 5pm. Garden concerts July–Sept every Fri at 7pm. Metro: Anděl.

The charming country house now engulfed by a semi-industrial suburb owes its fame to Wolfgang Amadeus Mozart, who stayed here as a guest of Franz and Josephine Duschek, a pianist and a singer. It is now a Mozart museum and a venue for chamber music concerts. Exhibits include some period furniture and a harpsichord said to have been played by Mozart, as well as 13 hairs belonging to the composer.

The name refers to one Franz Bertram von Bertram, a previous owner who gave the house its present appearance in the early 18thC.

Mozart's longest stay at Bertramka was in September–October 1787, during his presence in Prague for the first performance of Don Giovanni. *While there, he put the finishing touches to his opera, and composed the overture over a bowl of punch on the legendary night before the premiere.*

Several semi-believable anecdotes attach to this visit. According to one, Mozart promised to compose a piece for Mrs Duschek. As his departure neared and it was not yet ready, she locked him in a garden pavilion of the Bertramka and threatened to throw away the key unless he kept his promise; so was born the concert aria Bella mi fiamma addio. *Curiously, the same thing happened with Count Pachta, who owned a now-vanished palace at the corner of Národní and Mikulandská where Mozart attended several parties. Before one of these, the Count locked the composer up and swore he would not be released until he composed some dances for the evening. That was the origin of* Sei Tedeschi (Six German Dances), *K509.*

CAROLINUM (Karolinum; Charles University)
Železná 9, Staré město. Map 4C5. Metro: Můstek.

The first university of the German- (and Slavic-)speaking world was founded in Prague in 1348 by Charles IV, who dreamed of making his capital into the intellectual center of the Holy Roman Empire. During its first three centuries of independent existence, the Collegium Carolinum — Charles University — was ranked among the leading academic institutions of Central Europe, as it has been again since its revival in the 19thC.

Charles' university was organized into the four independent corporations, or "nations," of Bavarians, Saxons, Poles and Bohemians. German was the language of daily use for the first three, while the fourth became the birthplace of medieval Czech vernacular culture. Relations between the two linguistic camps turned sour during the church-reform movement of the 1390s, which the Czechs championed, and it came to blows and daggers over the election of the reformer Jan Hus to the rectorate in 1402. The Czechs won with royal support from Wenceslas IV, a son of Charles. The German dons left Prague in a huff and founded Leipzig University.

For the next 200 years the Carolinum was a hotbed of Hussite and Protestant radicalism. Its illustrious sons included Jan Amos Comenius, a founder of modern pedagogy, and the anatomist Jessenius, a pioneer in human dissection. The White Mountain dealt a devastating blow; placed under the care of Jesuits in 1627, the university sank into insignificance. Reform came in the 18thC under Joseph II. Separate Czech and German sections were once more established in 1882. The Germans were eventually expelled in 1945.

The aula *(main hall) of the university has occupied the same Gothic house on Železná ul. since 1383. Having been embroiled in every riot and uprising in Prague's fitful history (notably 1393, 1419, 1547, 1618, 1848, 1945, 1968 and 1989), and burned or demolished many times as a result, it retains little of its original structure apart from a cloistered inner courtyard. The lovely* **Oriel Bay** *(✫), which juts over the alley beside the ESTATES THEATER, was reconstructed in the 19thC in imitation of the 14thC original.*

CASTLE (Pražsky hrad; Hradčany) ★

Map 3B3. From Malá strana: metro to Malostranská. From N: metro to Hradčanská, then tram 22.

The Castle dominates the skyline of Prague, rising high above the Vltava in a cluster of spires, towers and Baroque masonry. It has been the residence of the kings of Bohemia, the site of its first Christian church and its only cathedral, the repository of all four of its patron saints, of its crown treasury and its once-fabulous art collections. Today it holds the offices of the Czech president, several museums, and a splendid range of architecture spanning eleven centuries.

History

A tribal settlement must have existed on the hill of Hradčany as early as the 6thC, and a stronghold of wood and adobe was reported in existence by the year 873. It served the early Přemyslids in their rise from tribal chiefdom to royal power. Here Prince Bořivoj and his wife Ludmila were baptized by St Methodius; they must have built the first church in Bohemia, a wooden structure whose remains were discovered in 1950 buried in the wall of the Castle Gallery. The basilica of St George (sv. Jiří) was erected under their son Vratislav (921), and soon thereafter received the body of St Ludmila, Bohemia's first Christian martyr.

In 926, St Wenceslas built the first chapel of St Vitus — a four-apsed rotunda in imitation of Charlemagne's imperial chapel in Aachen — to house the miraculous hand of Vitus, a gift of the German king; he was buried in the chapel himself after his own martyrdom. The bishopric of

PRAGUE CASTLE

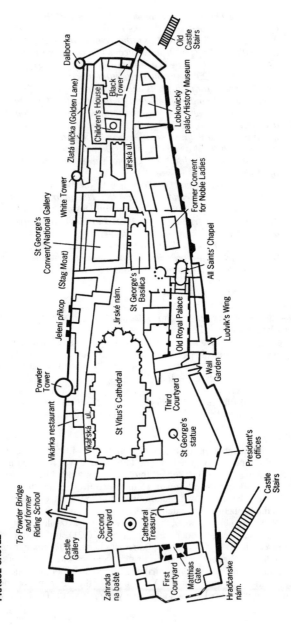

To Powder Bridge and former Riding School

Castle Gallery

Zahrada na baště

Second Courtyard

Cathedral Treasury

First Courtyard

Matthias Gate

Hradčanské nám.

Castle Stairs

President's offices

Vikárka restaurant

Powder Tower

Vikářská ul.

St Vitus's Cathedral

St George's statue

Third Courtyard

Jeleni příkop (Stag Moat)

St George's Convent/National Gallery

White Tower

Jiřské nám.

St George's Basilica

Old Royal Palace

Ludvik's Wing

Wall Garden

All Saints' Chapel

Zlatá ulička (Golden Lane)

Children's House

Jiřská ul.

Daliborka

Black Tower

Lobkovický palác/History Museum

Old Castle Stairs

Former Convent for Noble Ladies

66

Prague was established in Hradcany in 973. Benedictine nuns founded Bohemia's first monastery in the same year beside the church of St George.

A Romanesque palace with a stone base and wooden superstructure replaced the old tribal kraal during the reign of Soběslav I (1125–40). Its upper stories were to be rebuilt several times again, but the bottom part survives today in the shape of the musty cellars of the Royal Palace.

A fire in 1303 destroyed most of the previously existing buildings on the hill, clearing the site for Charles IV's builders to go to work. Having obtained the Pope's consent to elevate Prague into an archbishopric in 1344, Charles invited the French cathedral-master Matthew of Arras to build a Gothic cathedral in place of the old rotunda of St Vitus. After the premature death of the Frenchman, his work was carried on by Peter Parler up to 1399, and then by his sons, until the Hussite cataclysm forced a break in 1419. Construction was only resumed in 1873, and the western half of St Vitus is 500 years younger than its eastern half.

The royal palace remained unoccupied from the time Wenceslas IV was forced to take up residence in the Old Town in 1394 until Vladislav II moved back to the castle nearly a century later. Vladislav then commissioned Benedict Ried to rebuild the upper stories of his residence into a dazzling *tour de force* of late-Gothic architecture. A generation later, it was the turn of Ferdinand I and his architect Boniface Wohlmut to pursue the Gothic experimentation to new heights.

The first two Habsburg rulers of Bohemia, while in principle based in Vienna, spent much of their time in Hradčany; the third, Rudolf II, came to reside there full-time. From his reign date the Spanish Hall (1589–96), and possibly the gateway that has become known by the name of his successor, Matthias (1610s). However, the Baroque era barely touched the castle, which lacked a royal tenant after 1620. Additions during this period were the remodeled Lobkowicz residence, the Convent for Noble Ladies (1677) and the new facade of St George's Basilica (1680).

A major modernization got under way only around the middle of the next century, under the auspices of Maria Theresa. Using as excuse some destruction that took place during the French occupation of Prague in the Seven Years' War, the empress ordered a complete redesign that would integrate the architectural hodgepodge of the castle into a rational whole to serve the needs of her newly-created army of bureaucrats. The task was given to Nicolaus Pacassi, the architect of Vienna's Schönbrunn Palace, and over a period of three decades turned the s and sw wings of the castle into the dull Classical block that they are today.

The Neo-Gothic part of St Vitus, the only major new construction on the hill in the last 200 years, was completed in 1929.

Access to the Castle

The most popular approaches are from the Lesser Side, from the sw via the **Castle Stairs** (Zámecké schody) or from the se via the **Old Castle Stairs** (Staré zámecké schody). Since the revolution, both have been occupied by a colorful crowd of street artists, bead sellers and peddlers of Soviet army surplus. There is a third entrance on the nw by way of the **Powder Bridge** *(Prašný most)*.

The guards who delight snapshooters with their flamboyant red-white-and-blue uniforms are a recent addition to the castle's charms. In the days when the occupants of Hradčany felt a more serious urge for security, the guards wore khaki and carried a red star on their caps. The new outfit was created for President Havel by his friend Theodor Pištěk, a designer whose earlier credits included the costumes for Miloš Forman's *Amadeus*. More recently, Pištěk was commissioned to redesign uniforms for the new Czech army.

Office wings

Maria Theresa's 18thC compound, now housing the offices and residence of the President of the Czech Republic, encloses an outer and an inner court, and extends a wing on the s side of the central square of the Castle (Jirské nám.). The menacing **giants** over the entrance of the outer court (the First Courtyard on our plan) are modern copies of Ignaz Platzer's 18thC originals. A 17thC gateway, the so-called **Matthias Gate** (Matyášova brána), retained when the rest of the buildings received their post-Baroque face-lift, gives access to the central court (the Second Courtyard).

Parts of the official compound are open at least some of the time to the public — for example, the **Castle Gallery** (Hradní galerie ✮), a collection of art from the former royal possessions; it has been only spasmodically open since a visitor walked away in 1991 with a masterpiece by Lucas Cranach the Elder, which was never heard of again.

The collection holds a couple of dozen paintings from Rudolf II's legendary stock of 600, as well as reproductions of some that were looted, sold, lost or have otherwise disappeared from Prague. Rudolf's court painters, von Aachen, Spranger and de Vries, are represented with several works that do not rank among their best. Rudolf's acquisitions included Guido Reni's *Centaur Nessus Abducting Deianeira*, Gentileschi's *Amor Triumphant*, Tintoretto's *Flagellation of Christ* and several Veroneses. Rubens is present with an exuberant *Gathering of Olympian Gods*. A room is devoted to Habsburg family portraits, a fascinating series of character studies painted c.1570 for the instruction of some royal prince.

The gallery occupies the former royal stables, constructed under Rudolf over the remains of an archaic church from the tribal period. Upstairs is Rudolf's **Spanish Hall** (Španělský sál), a gala room of lavish decoration, which occasionally admits the public for concerts or receptions.

An 18thC chapel in the courtyard houses the **Cathedral Treasury** (✮), a collection of saintly relics (star turns include a thorn from the Crown of Thorns, a piece of the tablecloth from the Last Supper, fragments of the True Cross, and the veil of the Virgin Mary) and assorted jewel-encrusted devotional articles. Replicas of the royal jewels that used to be exhibited here have now been moved to the History Museum in the Lobkowicz Palace (see page 75).

St Vitus's Cathedral (Chrám / katedrála svatého Víta) ★

The eastern half of the cathedral, including the apsis, choir, transept and s portal, belongs to the original phase of building that was abandoned in 1419. It carries the stamp of Peter Parler, one of the great geniuses of the Middle European Gothic. The nave, twin spires and w '(main) portal were added early in this century in a meticulous but too-formal imitation of the original. The unfinished bell tower on the s was capped with a balustrade in the 16thC, then topped up with a totally incongruous Baroque bulb, which in time has grown into an inseparable part of Prague's skyline.

St Vitus was a Sicilian youth who was fed to the lions during one of ancient Rome's anti-Christian purges. His connection with Prague began many hundreds of years later when King Henry the Fowler of Germany sent a piece of the saint's arm to Wenceslas (later a saint himself) as a token of his goodwill. Vitus thus became the first saint to touch the soil of newly-converted Bohemia, albeit in an incomplete state. The rest of his body was acquired in 1355 by Charles IV and interred in the cathedral.

Charles IV was a devotee of St Wenceslas, the founder of Bohemian Christianity and a hero of the imperial *Ostpolitik* that reached its culmination with himself. The cathedral accordingly downplays Vitus, replacing the Roman with the Bohemian saint as its spiritual as well as architectural focus. The centerpiece of Parler's design was the tomb/chapel of Wenceslas, and a correspondingly lavish portal was erected on the s, immediately beside the chapel, in the first stages of the construction of the cathedral. For five centuries, the **Golden Gate** (Zlatá brána ✰) was the main entrance of St Vitus. The mosaic above it depicts *The Last Judgment* with the figures of Charles IV and Elizabeth of Pomerania, his fourth wife.

Parler himself is featured, along with Matthew of Arras and a battery of their employers (Charles IV, four wives, two sons and in-laws, three successive archbishops, and various directors of the cathedral chapter), in the series of 21 **sculpture portraits** lining the triforium, the half-height gallery along the inner arcade of the choir. Of a realism wholly unusual for medieval art, they count among the masterpieces of Gothic sculpture.

Parler's father, who may have been of French origin, built the church of the Holy Cross in Schwäbisch Gmünd, a turning point of the German Gothic. At the age of 23, Peter (1330-99) was invited by Charles IV to take on the job that the death of Matthew of Arras had left vacant. His other commissions included the All Saints Chapel in the palace, the Charles Bridge and the Týn Church. He lived at #10 HRADČANY SQUARE and was laid to rest in the Wallenstein Chapel in the cathedral (the fourth chapel left of Wenceslas).

His sons Václav and Jan continued the family tradition after his death. Other sons, brothers, nephews and cousins were active in the cathedral-building business in Cologne, Strasbourg, Freiburg, Nürnberg, Cracow, Vienna and Milan.

The **Chapel of St Wenceslas** (kaple sv. Václava ✰), a glittering treasure-trove of painted and gold-plated medieval art, was built by Parler (1362–67) in place of the original rotunda of St Vitus, where Wenceslas had been buried by a fratricidal but remorseful Boleslav four centuries

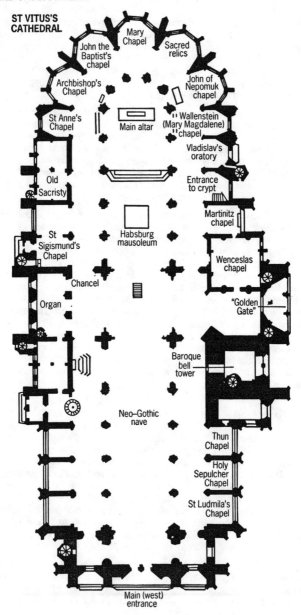

**ST VITUS'S
CATHEDRAL**

Mary Chapel

John the Baptist's chapel

Sacred relics

Archbishop's Chapel

John of Nepomuk chapel

St Anne's Chapel

Main altar

Wallenstein (Mary Magdalene) chapel

Vladislav's oratory

Old Sacristy

Entrance to crypt

Martinitz chapel

St Sigismund's Chapel

Habsburg mausoleum

Wenceslas chapel

Chancel

Organ

"Golden Gate"

Baroque bell tower

Neo–Gothic nave

Thun Chapel

Holy Sepulcher Chapel

St Ludmila's Chapel

Main (west) entrance

earlier. Its contents include a statue of Wenceslas by a nephew of Parler, a series of brilliant paintings of his life and dastardly death, and various pointers to the unpleasant results of perfidy (Peter wretched after denying Christ, Judas having his tongue extracted, Doomsday). The tomb of the saint, a dull 20thC work, replaces the original, which was looted by the Hussites 500 years earlier.

Boleslav invited his brother Wenceslas to his castle of Mladá Boleslav on the pretext of a feast to celebrate his son's baptism. Wenceslas smelled danger — Boleslav was not yet a Christian, so it was unusual for him to baptize a son — but submitted to Providence. At the table, he excused himself to go out to pray alone in a church. His brother followed, and the prince was stabbed to death just as he laid his hand on the doorknob to enter the church. The doorknob itself, brought to Prague, is among the prize exhibits of the chapel.

A chamber behind the Wenceslas Chapel holds the **Crown Jewels of Bohemia** (✫), kept under seven locks whose keys are in the custody of seven different institutions. They are not ordinarily shown to visitors, who must make do with the replicas in the Lobkowicz Palace (see page 75).

The **Martinitz Chapel** (kaple sv. Ondřeje či Martinická), next on the left, holds the body of Jaroslav of Martinitz, the royal legate who died a peaceful death many years after surviving defenestration in 1618, and was nearly made a saint by the Catholic party. The **Royal Crypt** (královské krypty) is the final resting place of several Bohemian kings and their families, Charles IV, Rudolf II, and one of Maria Theresa's 16 children. The **Chapel of St John Nepomuk** (kaple sv. Jana Nepomuckého ✫) rivals that of Wenceslas on account of the sarcophagus of the saint, a glorious example of Baroque fantasy run amok. The extravaganza of silver (3,700 pounds of it) and fake marble was built to a blueprint created by the leading architect–sculptor of the Viennese Baroque, Fischer von Erlach, in 1731.

Read more about John of Nepomuk under CHARLES BRIDGE (page 79). The tight-lipped confessor was made a saint in 1729 after the Jesuits exhumed his body and discovered that his tongue, so unyielding in life, had remained miraculously incorrupt in death. The saintly organ is now removed from public display. It is apparently the lumpy object pointed at by the cherub on top of the coffin.

The next three chapels hold the tombs of six Přemyslid kings. The first has a statue of Ottokar I by Parler; the third features a bronze chandelier that one of the 12thC Přemysls carried off from Milan on a booty raid. The last chapel on the left of the high altar contains two interesting wood-carved reliefs from 1631 depicting, respectively, the flight of Frederick the Winter King and a panorama of Prague as it then appeared.

The modern half of the cathedral suffers from the dull formalism of the 19thC Neo-Gothic. One celebrated sight is a **stained-glass window** by Alfons Mucha (first chapel left of the main entrance) illustrating the lives of Sts Cyril and Methodius: a late (1931) work of the artist, it departs from the kitschy elegance of his Art Nouveau posters for the wooden didacticism of 1930s "social" art. A far better artwork is the woodcut **Crucifixion** (1896–99) by the Symbolist sculptor František Bílek, which is placed in the adjoining chapel.

Prague's revered Cardinal Tomášek, who died in 1992, lies in the next chapel on the left.

Old Royal Palace (Starý Královský palác) ★

Open Apr–Sept Tues–Sun 9am–4.15pm; Oct–Mar Tues–Sun 9am–3.45pm.

One of Europe's most brilliant examples of Gothic civil architecture took shape under Vladislav II and Ferdinand I, in the 16thC, above the gloomy cellars of Soběslav's 12thC castle. The centerpiece of it is the **Vladislav Hall** (Vladislavský sál ★), an enormous room measuring 62 by 16 by 13 meters (203 by 52 by 43 feet), designed expressly to hold crowds of mounted knights with colors unfurled. It remains one of the largest interiors ever built of stone and mortar without the support of either dome or pillars. The wizardry lies in the rib-vaulting, the Gothic stock-in-trade, transformed by Benedict Ried into a fantastic exercise in ribbon curves and flourishes. At the time that it was done (1493–1500), Gothic was already passé in the rest of Europe, and the windows of the hall reflect the newer manner of the Italian Renaissance.

On December 29, 1989, Václav Havel was sworn in as President of Czechoslovakia in the Vladislav Hall with a ceremony that marked the formal end of 42 years of communist rule.

There is more vaulting to see in the adjoining halls. Oldest is that of the **All Saints Chapel** (kaple všech Svatých), where Parler experimented with the first example of a net-vault in Central Europe (1370–87). The arches of the **Knights' Staircase** (Jezdecké schody; 1500) were designed to achieve sufficient height on a slant to permit knights to ride up into Vladislav Hall without getting off their horses. The ceiling of the **Hall of the Diet** (Stará sněmovna) is an intricate web of broken ribs, a homage to Ried by his successor as royal architect, Boniface Wohlmut (1559–63). The Diet was where the lords of Bohemia met as a court of justice; the **New Land Registry** upstairs, decorated with a dazzling collection of family crests, cataloged their titles and land claims.

A passage leads from the Vladislav Hall to the chambers of the **Bohemian Chancellery** (Česká kancelář), the seat of Bohemia's government for most of the 16thC (also called Ludvík's Wing, after Louis/Ludvík of Jagellon, Vladislav's son and successor: note his initials on the portal of the first room). The chambers made history in much the same way as the infamous streetcorner in Sarajevo: from their windows (the second one on the left, to be precise) the more famous of Prague's two defenestrations took place on May 23, 1618, launching one of the worst wars in European history. Two obelisks mark the spot in the garden below where the three defenestrees came to rest, alive, after a 50-foot fall.

The victims were William of Slavata and Jaroslav of Martinitz, the hated vice-regents of the emperor. The secretary Fabricius, who protested too loudly, followed them. The bizarre act was planned a day earlier at a meeting of Protestant conspirators in the Smiřický Palace (see LESSER SIDE SQUARE). Their leader was Count Thurn, who paid for his crime three years later by getting drawn and quartered on the OLD TOWN SQUARE.

The regents' fall was eased, according to eyewitnesses, by the Virgin Mary in person; others say they fell in a dungheap. Thurn and his men followed with pistols, but the three men managed to run to safety in the Lobkowicz Palace, from which they were spirited away by Countess Polyxena von Lobkowicz. After the Catholic victory, she paid her debt to the Virgin by bringing the miraculous Bambino di Praga to town (see OUR LADY OF VICTORY).

St George's Basilica (Bazilika sv. Jiří) ★
Jiřské nám. ▣ *Open daily: Apr–Sept 9am–5pm; Oct–Mar 9am–4pm.*

The oldest stone church in the Czech lands (founded 921) became firmly associated with St Ludmila when it became her place of burial after her martyrdom. The current building, an austere basilica in the Romanesque manner, dates from 1142; the adjoining chapel of St Ludmila is of slightly later age. The imperious facade is in the style of the early Italian ("Jesuit") Baroque of the 1680s belies the stark interior, a favorite place for concerts because of its unearthly acoustics. A Baroque chapel of St John Nepomuk was grafted on in the 1720s.

The equestrian **statue of St George** that stands in the square outside the basilica dates from about 1370, and counts among the oldest public statues in medieval European art.

Ludmila was the wife of Prince Bořivoj, and grandmother of Wenceslas, the future Good "King". She remained committed to

*Christianity at a time when a pagan revival affected the Czech
nobility, including most of her own family. She took little Wenceslas
under her wing, which so exasperated the boy's mother Drahomíra
that she ordered the saintly woman's neck wrung in 925; Wenceslas himself was martyred ten years later. Ludmila was buried in
St George's Basilica, which her son had founded some years earlier.*

Dvořák composed a splendid oratorio in honor of Ludmila.

St George's Convent and National Gallery Old Bohemian Collection

(Klášter sv. Jiří / Národní galerie) ★

Jiřské nám. ☎ *53 52 46* 🚇 *Open Tues–Sun 10am–6pm.*

Next to Ludmila's church, the first convent in Bohemia was established
in the year 973 by her great-granddaughter Mlada, a daughter of Boleslav the Bad and sister of Boleslav the Good. She became the first
abbess; the next three, Bertha, Agnes and Kunhuta, were also members
of the ruling family. In 1782 Joseph II evicted the nuns and turned their
convent into a military barracks and a jail for recalcitrant priests.

Today the building accommodates a superb collection of pre-19thC
Bohemian art (officially, but misleadingly, labeled "Czech" art). The
collection is in three parts.

MEDIEVAL (c.1350–1520s): The greatest period of Bohemian art is
represented by church paintings and statues from the reigns, mainly, of
Charles IV and his son Wenceslas IV. A room is devoted to the enormously
expressive portraits of saints by Master Theodoric, the first Bohemian
painter to emerge from anonymity, who painted a cycle of 127 for
Charles's castle at KARLŠTEJN (see page 171; the Karlštejn collection is
closed pending restoration). Works by the Master of the Třeboň Altar
reflect the worldlier sophistication of Wenceslas' court. Two 16thC masterpieces — the anonymous *Žebrák Lamentation* and a carved wood altar
by the acronymous I.P. — demonstrate the seamless elision of Bohemian
art from medieval formalism to Mannerist contortion.

MANNERISM: Rudolf II's court is represented by a small number of
outstanding works soaked with sex and morbid imagery. Among them
are Bartholomaeus Spranger's *Epitaph of Müller the Goldsmith* (c.1590),
a bronze *Hercules* by Adriaen de Vries, and several landscapes by
Roelandt Savery.

BAROQUE: The high points of the collection are the powerful sculptures by Ferdinand Maximilian Brokoff *(Archangel Raphael)* and Matthias Braun *(St Jude Thaddaeus),* the two rival geniuses of the Prague
Baroque. Also notable are an anonymous *Annunciation* and the strangely
disturbing portraits of Jan Kupecký (1667–1740).

Powder Tower (Prašná věž; Mihulka)

🚇 *Open Apr–Sept Tues–Sun 9am–5pm; Oct–Mar Tues–Sun 9am–4pm.*

The tower was built in the 15thC as an armory; in Rudolf II's reign it
became a laboratory where alchemists from around Europe — among
them the English duo of John Dee and Edward Kelley, inventors of the
crystal ball and reputed recipients of world-shattering secrets com-
municated to them by the angel Uriah — gathered to try to transmute

base metals into gold. Today it houses a museum devoted to its own history. The more famous tower of the same name is in the Old Town.

Golden Lane (Zlatá ulička) ✰

This quaint alley of miniature cottages is subjected to torrents of tourists, who wash through it without respite, trampling on its fragile charm. The houses, scarcely more than huts, were built in the 1540s to accommodate the castle guards. Originally there were two rows of them with only a tiny passage in between; one row was later demolished to make way for tourists. Residents of the row at various dates included Franz Kafka, who lived briefly at the house #22 in 1917, and the Nobel laureate poet Jaroslav Seifert, who spent several years in the 1930s in a now-demolished house at the far end of the street. The last inhabitants were expelled in 1951 and replaced with a line of souvenir shops. The name of the street has no firm explanation, but the attempt to trace it to Rudolf's gold-making alchemists is tourist-guide humbug.

The tower at the end of the alley obtains its nickname, **Daliborka**, from the knight Dalibor who was jailed in it in 1498 for either robbery or inciting a serf revolt or both, depending on which sources you choose to believe. He is said to have played the violin while awaiting the axeman, and reportedly still does if someone is around to hear him at midnight. Smetana turned the story into an opera.

Lobkowicz Palace (Lobkovický palác; National History Museum)
Jiřská 3 📧 *Open Tues–Sun 9am–5pm.*

The palace of Rudolf II's chancellor, originally built in Renaissance style, received its Baroque accouterments in 1677. Restored recently, it now houses a concert and exhibition hall, and a museum devoted to "the Treasures of National History," an interesting attempt to come to terms with the country's (pre-communist) past free from pat formulas and ideological certitudes.

Another palace of the same name in the Lesser Side belongs to the German Embassy (see NERUDOVA ULICE).

Palace Gardens and Belvedere

Across the wooded **Stag Moat** (Jelení příkop) on the N side of the castle lies the **Royal Garden** (Královská zahrada), which was laid out by Ferdinand I for the pleasure of his wife Anna. The queen was also the recipient of the **Belvedere** (Belvedér, Královský letohrádek ✰), at the eastern end of the gardens, a Renaissance garden palace (1538–63) of great elegance whose colonnade has a relief showing Ferdinand presenting a flower to her. In another part of the garden, their son Maximilian II commissioned from Boniface Wohlmut the **Royal Ball Court** (Míčovna; 1567–69), decorated with a superb series of *sgraffiti.* Both buildings, reopened following restoration, host periodic exhibitions.

Two gardens on the s side of the palace, the **Paradise Garden** (Rajská zahrada) *(entrance from the Castle Ramp)* and **Wall Garden** (Zahrada na válech) *(entrance through a stairway beneath Royal Palace)* offer excellent views over the city.

CELETNÁ ULICE ★
Staré město. Map 5C6. Metro: nám. Republiky.

In the Middle Ages, Celetná (Zeltnerstrasse; Tentmaker Street) was part of the royal procession route that began at the **Powder Tower** (Prašná brána: see page 97) and wound up in the CASTLE. It is still part of the city's meticulously kept-up showfront. Most houses retain their dainty Baroque exteriors, although the underlying structures tend to be Gothic and date from the 14thC. Older yet are the underground cellars that were buried in the 1230s when the city floor was raised to the present level to prevent further flooding by the Vltava.

The former **Mint** at #36 served as such from 1420 until the abolition of local minting privileges under Joseph II. The burly miners flanking its gate are by Ignaz Platzer, the 18thC sculptor who specialized in Baroque equivalents of Arnold Schwarzenegger. The **Black Mother of God** (U černé Matky boží) at #34, designed by Josef Gočár in 1911, is a curious attempt to apply Cubist ideas to architecture. Its name refers to a black Madonna inherited from an earlier house on the site, now perched incongruously in a cage on the lintel. The house at #13, now part of Charles University, carries the Caretto-Millesimo family crest with the Habsburg double-eagle, an archiepiscopal hat and a lot of flourish. The **Hrzán House** at #12 was given the Baroque treatment in 1702 by Giovanni Alliprandi and decorated with sculptures from the Brokoff workshop.

The **Sixt House** at #2 obtains its name from Theodor Sixtus of Ottersdorf, one of the leaders of the 1618 revolt who escaped decapitation through the good offices of a Catholic relative, but who, in a supreme irony, lost his house to none other than the scribe Fabricius who had been thrown out of the window along with the two regents for protesting on their behalf (see page 73). Kafka lived in this house as a child in 1888–89. Later he moved with his parents to the **Three Kings House** (U tří králů) across the street, where for 11 formative years he could look out of his bedroom window over the towers of the Týn Church.

Celetná ul. leads into OLD TOWN SQUARE. (See page 100.)

CHARLES BRIDGE (Karlův most) ★
Map 4C4. Metro: Staroměstská.

A wonderful old bridge, possibly the most beautiful in Europe, this has been a landmark of Prague since 1357. Charles IV commissioned it from Peter Parler at a time when he (Charles) had grandiose plans to develop Prague into the permanent capital of the Holy Roman Empire. For nearly 500 years afterward, it was the only bridge on the Vltava and thus a critical point on Central European trade and invasion routes. Decorated with 30 groups of statues after 1683, it became, additionally, one of the greatest showcases of Baroque sculpture on the continent.

The bridge, traffic-free since 1950, carries a perpetual crowd of musicians, street artists, jugglers, and people selling this and that.

The Judith Bridge, the first stone bridge in Prague and the second in medieval Europe after that of Regensburg, was built in 1158 slightly downstream and at an angle to the present span. Its collapse in 1342 was the immediate occasion for Charles' great opportunity.

Old Town Bridge Tower (Staroměstská mostecká věž)

Parler was the architect of this splendid defense tower with its pointed cap and rich Gothic decoration. It was completed under Wenceslas IV, Charles' son, who appears over the E (city) gateway along with his father and St Vitus, presiding over the coats of arms of the lands he ruled. Above them are Sts Adalbert and Wenceslas, patrons of Bohemia. An anonymous figure is seen on the left running his hand under a nun's skirt.

For several years after 1621 the tower served the grisly purpose of displaying the chopped heads of some of the 27 Bohemian nobles who had led the revolt against the Habsburgs (see OLD TOWN SQUARE). In 1648 it was the site of the heroic stand of a band of university students and Old Town Jews, which saved the Old Town from the marauding Swedes who had occupied — and thoroughly looted — the left bank.

The W (bridge) side of the tower was blown up during that fight, and instead of Gothic finery it carries a florid 18thC tablet commemorating the battle.

After years of restoration, it is now possible to go inside the tower and climb the **observation terrace** (✪) on top. The palindromic Latin words on the ceiling of the second floor (*signatesignatemeremetangisetangis* and *romatibisubitomotibusibitamor*, which seem to mean respectively "Beware, beware, you touch and torture me" and "Rome, love comes to you with sudden force") are medieval devices meant to trap evil spirits by locking them into a vicious circle from which — being purely mental creatures — they could never escape.

Outside the tower on Křížovnické nam. is a bronze **statue of Charles IV** erected in 1848 in Wagnerian Neo-Gothic. The four female figures on the pedestal are said to be allegories for the four "nations" of the university (see page 64), but more probably represent the four wives of Charles.

> *The most famous of the four was the last, Elizabeth of Pomerania, who was reputedly strong enough to bend a horseshoe with her bare hands.*

Lesser Side Bridge Towers

(Malostranské mostecké věže)
The asymmetrical twin towers of the Left Bank (pictured) offer a medley of architectural styles. The shorter of the two was built in the mid-12thC as part of the

defensive apparatus of the old stone bridge that Charles replaced; its wholly incongruous but amiable Renaissance-style cap was added in 1591. The taller tower, built in 1464 under George of Podebrady, is modeled closely on Parler's Old Town Tower. Its **terrace** (✭) is worth climbing.

Beside the tower before you leave the bridge is the **Three Ostriches** (U tří pštrosů), a Renaissance house with an added Baroque gable. The birds painted on the facade are a reminder of the time in the 16thC when the house belonged to one Jan Fux who bred ostriches here to sell for their plumage. The house is now a hotel with an expensive restaurant (see pages 128 and 137).

The statues

Charles' original bridge was adorned with a simple crucifix. After the Thirty Years' War, which unleashed a manic drive to fill up the city with glories of the reconstituted Catholic Church, it turned into a theme park of hagiography. Noblemen and civic bodies subscribed to individual monuments, and top sculptors of the time were set to work; Ferdinand Maximilian Brokoff, the greatest of them, contributed eight. When the program reached completion in 1714, the bridge was a gallery of 30 ecstatic, gesticulating, wriggling, exhorting saints. In due course, some of these were washed away into the Vltava, and in the mid-19thC, they were replaced with rather more demure Neo-Gothic figures. A final group of statues was added in 1938.

The Brokoff dynasty began with Johann, who died in 1718, and continued with his sons Michael Josef (died 1721) and Ferdinand Maximilian (died 1731). Works by all three carry the signature of Joh. Brokoff as a family trademark.

A characteristic feature of the Baroque statues (as of Baroque monuments elsewhere) is the manner of dating, where the letters I, V, X, L, C, D and M occurring in the inscription add up to give the year of construction.

A list of the statues follows, starting from the Old Town side, with the name of the sculptor, the date, and often some comment. (Commenting fully on each and every one of them would be beyond the scope of this book.) We cover first the right (statues 1–15) and then the left (16–30) side of the bridge.

Right side

1. **Madonna with St Bernard**, Matthias Wenzel Jaeckel, 1709.
2. **Madonna with Sts Dominic and Thomas Aquinas**, Jaeckel, 1708.
3. **Crucifix**, Christ's body in bronze from 1667.
- The oldest statue on the bridge. An earlier, wooden Christ, which had shocked the English-born queen of Frederick, the Winter King, by its explicit manliness, perished during the fight with the Swedes. The huge inscription in Hebrew reads, "Holy, holy, holy is the Lord of hosts." It is said to have been donated under duress by a Jew who had been caught muttering a blasphemy as he passed by the cross in 1696.

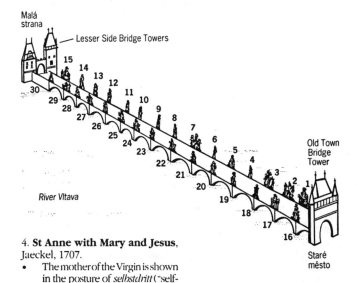

Malá
strana

Lesser Side Bridge Towers

15
14
13
12
11
10
9
8
7
6
5
4
3
2
1
16
17
18
19
20
21
22
23
24
25
26
27
28
29
30

River Vltava

Old Town
Bridge
Tower

Staré
město

4. **St Anne with Mary and Jesus**,
Jaeckel, 1707.

• The mother of the Virgin is shown
in the posture of *selbstdritt* ("self-
in-three"), accompanied by child
Mary and child Jesus. The strange iconography was first seen at the
time of the wedding of Charles IV's daughter Anne to the king of
England, and became immensely popular afterwards.

5. **Sts Cyril and Methodius**, Karel Dvořák, 1938.

• The only modern statue on the bridge replaced Brokoff's St Ignatius
Loyola, who fell into the river during a flood. Ignatius was a Jesuit
and therefore distasteful to Czechoslovak national sentiment. Cyril
and Methodius were brothers from Constantinople who founded the
Slav national church in the 9thC. During the interwar years, a time
of pro-Russian public sympathy, they became politically correct.

6. **John the Baptist**, Josef Max, 1857.

7. **Sts Wenceslas, Norbert and Sigismund**, Josef Max, 1857.

8. **St John Nepomuk**, Joh. Brokoff and Matthias Rauchmüller, 1683 (✮).

• John of Nepomuk was martyred in 1393 by being lobbed into the
Vltava by the king's men, allegedly at this precise spot on the Charles
Bridge. Legend tells that he incurred the royal wrath by refusing to
disclose intimate details of the confession of 21-year-old Queen
Sophie; more prosaic accounts say that John, who was an archbishop's
deputy under Wenceslas IV, antagonized the king by appointing an
abbot against his wish.

The manner of his death made him, according to the logic of
antidotes, the protector of bridges and all who cross them, so his
statue naturally became one of the most popular on this particular
crossing: note the patina left by millions of devout fingers on the

saint's face in the pedestal relief. Five stars appeared above his head as he floated in the river, and that is how he is shown in all representations.

9. **St Antonius of Padua**, Johann Mayer, 1707.

10. **St Judas Thaddaeus**, Johann Mayer, 1708.

11. **St Augustine**, Johann Friedrich Kohl, 1708.

12. **St Cajetan**, F.M. Brokoff, 1709 (✮).

• The 16thC Italian nobleman-turned-monk was an important promoter of reform within the Catholic Church. The burning heart is a symbol of the Theatine order, which he founded.

13. **St Philip Benitius**, Michael Bernhard Mandl, 1714.

14. **St Vitus**, F.M. Brokoff, 1714.

• For Vitus, see under his cathedral (page 69). This saint is a protector of epileptics as well as of those suffering from the nervous disorder called St Vitus's Dance — and, by extension, of dancers and actors. He is invoked against the bites of mad dogs and venomous snakes, and against over-sleeping.

15. **Christ with Sts Cosmas and Damian**, Johann Mayer, 1709.

Left side

16. **St Ivo**, Matthias Bernhard Braun, 1711 (copy 1908).

• The statue of the patron saint of lawyers was donated by the Law Faculty of Prague University.

17. **Sts Barbara, Margaret and Elizabeth**, F.M. Brokoff, 1707.

18. **Pietà**, Emanuel Max, 1859.

19. **St Joseph**, Josef Max, 1854.

20. **St Francis Xavier**, F.M. Brokoff, 1711 (copy 1913) (✮).

• The co-founder of the Jesuit order is shown supported by Asiatic coolies, a reference to his missionary activities in India, Japan and China.

21. **St Christopher**, Emanuel Max, 1857.

22. **St Francis Borgia**, F.M. Brokoff, 1710 (✮).

23. **St Ludmila with child Wenceslas**, workshop of Matthias Braun, after 1720.

• For St Ludmila, grandmother of Good "King" Wenceslas, see page 73.

24. **St Francis Seraphicus**, Emanuel Max, 1855.

25. **Sts Vincent Ferrer and Prokop**, F.M. Brokoff, 1712 (✮).

• According to the inscription, the two saints between them converted 100,000 sinners, saved the souls of 8,000 Saracens and 2,500 Jews, suppressed 70 demons and raised 40 from the dead. Vincent, the Spanish ex-philosopher, is shown clad in a Dominican cloak, attending to a remorseful sinner and a man possessed by the devil; Prokop, the Moravian abbot, coolly drives a crozier into Satan's throat.

On a supporting pier below this statue stands young knight **Bruncvík**, or Brunswick. Legend identifies him with either Roland or Přemysl Ottokar II, who is supposed to have dropped his sword into the river at this spot on his way back from a lucky battle with King Béla of Hungary, and will return again to lead the Czech nation to glory in their hour of darkest need.

26. **St Nicholas of Tolentino**, J.F. Kohl, 1708.
27. **St Luitgard**, Matthias Braun, 1710 (★).
- Luitgard, a Cistercian nun, is shown in ecstasy as Christ bears down from the Crucifix to embrace her and she reaches over to kiss His wound. She had this vision late one night and was made a saint as a result. Braun's statue surpasses all others on the bridge in its sensuous intensity.
28. **St Adalbert**, M.J. Brokoff, 1709.
- Adalbert, or Vojtěch as he was known in his native Czech, was the second bishop of Prague, who died a martyr's death in 997 while on a campaign to convert the pagan Lithuanians. He is one of Bohemia's four patron saints along with Vitus, Sigismund and Wenceslas.
29. **Sts John of Matha and Felix of Valois with Blessed Ivan and a Turk**, F.M. Brokoff, 1714 (★).
- The largest and most popular group of statues shows a Turk and a mad dog keeping some hapless Christians in jail while two gentle friars, an unkempt monk and a stag look on. The friars are the founders of the Trinitarian Order, which specialized in ransoming Christian captives from Muslim hands. The monk with long hair and grizzled beard is Blessed Ivan, a 10thC hermit who spent his life in a cave and was brought to the attention of Prince Oldrich of Bohemia by a doe who befriended him. The stag commonly represents Christ. The mind reels at the possible range of symbolic references (stag–doe, cave–jail, good works versus solitude), but generations of Prague schoolchildren have been more interested in the potbellied Turk — how many buttons on his vest? why is his hand behind his back? what is on his mind?
30. **St Wenceslas**, Josef Böhm, 1858.

CHARLES SQUARE (Karlovo náměstí)

Nové město. Map 4E5. Metro: Karlovo nám.

The central square of Charles IV's New Town is more like a park than a square. Until 1848 it carried the name of "Cattle Market."

The Gothic **Town Hall** (Novoměstské radnice ★) is nearly as attractive a building as its Old Town counterpart, though not remotely as touristy (main building 1411–18, tower 1451–56, exterior with gables 1520–26). Prague's trend-setting First Defenestration took place here in 1421, when a mob led by the Hussite firebrand Father Želivský stormed the hall and threw out Catholic members of the council to their death. The building was laid waste a few years later by the Old Towners, who carried off Želivský as their prize and decapitated him in the OLD TOWN SQUARE, setting another famous precedent.

Halfway down the square is the attractive Early Baroque church of **St Ignatius** (Carlo Lurago, 1665–78). The hospital complex to which it is attached was formerly a Jesuit college.

Vicinity

Three churches in the immediate neighborhood of the square are of considerable interest.

The church of **Sts Cyril and Methodius** (kostel sv. Cyrila a Metoděje) on Resslova ul. was born in 1733–40 under the name of St Charles Borromeo, one of the pet saints of the Catholic Counter-Reformation. The rebaptism under its current name took place in 1935 (see the note on the saints' statue on CHARLES BRIDGE on page 79), when the church was given over to the Russian Orthodox rite. The bullet holes riddling its walls are a reminder of the 120 members of the Czech resistance (including, coincidentally, the team that had carried out the assassination of Reinhard Heydrich) who were found holed up in the crypt in June 1942 and killed after an all-night gun battle with the Gestapo.

St John of Nepomuk on the Rock (kostel sv. Jana Nepomuckého na skálce ✪) on Vyšehradská ul. is a masterpiece of Kilian Ignaz Dienzenhofer, the architect of St Thomas and St Nicholas in the Lesser Side. A *trompe-l'oeuil* ceiling fresco depicts the heavenly adventures of the saint (see pages 71 and 79).

The futuristic roof of the former **Emmaus Abbey** (Emauzy; Klášter na slovanech) was built in 1967 to replace one blown away by a freak Allied air raid during World War II. The monastery, established in 1347, belongs to a peculiar sub-sect of the Benedictines who conduct liturgy in Old Church Slavonic and have followed the Hussite track at various points in their history (they returned in 1991 after a 40-year exile). Their cloister features a series of 14thC **frescoes** (✪) commissioned by Charles IV.

CLEMENTINUM (Klementinum; Národní knihovna)
Křižovnické nám., Staré město. Map 4C5 ☎26 65 41 (for concerts and programs). Observatory open Mon, Thurs 2–7pm; Tues, Fri 9am–7pm; closed Wed, Sat, Sun. Metro: Staroměstská.

The former headquarters of Prague's Jesuits, on the Old Town approach to the CHARLES BRIDGE, is the largest Baroque complex in the city. In the past the Clementinum comprised a college, an observatory, and the living quarters of the padres. Today it houses the **National Library**, as well as several publicly accessible Baroque halls and some of the loveliest enclosed courtyards of Prague.

The Society of Jesus, founded in 1540 and supported chiefly by the two Habsburg capitals of Vienna and Madrid, played a key role in re-Catholicizing the lapsed parts of Europe after the Protestant Reformation. Its main weapon was education, to which the "subtle Jesuits" brought psychological insight and a certain doctrinal flexibility. The Jesuits came to heretic-infested Prague in 1556, consolidated their position in the first part of Rudolf II's reign, and established a virtual monopoly of power after the White Mountain. In 1776 their order was driven from the Habsburg lands, a victim of the Enlightenment.

The ornate **main entrance** is located on Křižovnické nám. opposite the bridge. Within lies a vast compound of five courtyards, a splendid Baroque **library hall** (✪), a **chapel** sometimes used for concerts, and the former Jesuit **observatory** (✪). The observatory contains fascinating old models of the universe, astronomical charts, allegories and statues, and owns the oldest continuous weather records in Europe. The library displays among other treasures the so-called *Coronation Evangeliary of Vyšehrad* (✯), the oldest illuminated manuscript in Bohemia (1086).

The second courtyard on the right holds the **statue of a goateed student**, a tribute to the scholars who held off the Swedish army on the Charles Bridge in 1648 long enough for news of the conclusion of the Thirty Years' War to seep into town. Two very long corridors illustrate in serial fashion the lives, respectively, of Sts Ignatius Loyola and Francis Xavier, the twin founders of the Jesuit order.

Forming part of the Clementinum are three churches. **St Salvator** (kostel sv. Salvátora), the oldest Jesuit church in Bohemia, was founded in 1578. Its **facade** (✯), dating from 1600 (outer portico 1653; statues 1673) and based on Il Gesù, the Jesuits' mother church in Rome, is one of the most elegant in Prague, combining quasi-Renaissance formalism with an exuberant parade of Baroque saints. The **Italian Chapel** (Vlašská kaple; properly Chapel of the Assumption, or Nanebevzetí P. Marie) is located immediately outside St Clement. The chapel (1590–1600) has served the Italian community since the reign of Rudolf II. **St Clement** (kostel sv. Klimenta) dates from 1711–15, and is decorated with statues by Matthias Braun.

Vicinity

Křižovnické nám. is dominated by the bold dome of **St Francis Seraphicus** (kostel sv. Františka Serafinského), the church of the Knights of the Cross. Based on a design by Jean-Baptiste Mathey (realized by Canevale, 1679–89), this is the only Baroque church in Prague to follow a French rather than Italian model. The interior, rich and dark, possesses a splendid altar flanked by the extraordinary **statues** (✯) of Sts Joachim, Anne, George and Martin by Jeremiah Süssner of Dresden.

ESTATES THEATER (Stavovské divadlo) ✯
Železná 11, Staré město. Map 4C6. Metro: Můstek.

The only surviving theater in which Mozart himself actually worked was built in 1781–83 at the initiative of Count Nostitz: it counts as the finest work of Josephine Classicism in Prague. Mozart's *Marriage of Figaro* was staged in the Estates Theater in December 1786 to wild acclaim (Mozart reported seeing baker's boys who whistled tunes from his opera), so he returned twice to conduct on the same stage the world premieres of two new operas, *Don Giovanni* in 1787 and *La Clemenza di Tito* in 1791.

More recently, Miloš Forman used the theater for the interior scenes of his film *Amadeus*, much of which was shot in and around Prague. The communist authorities used the income from the film to launch an ambitious renovation program that returned the building to its precise 18thC shape. Six years later, and two years after the fall of the communists, the curtains reopened on December 5, 1991, the bicentenary of Mozart's death.

The old name of the theater was restored as well on that occasion, superseding the less class-conscious "Tyl Theater," which it had been renamed in the years following World War II.

An argument has since raged between Western investors aiming to turn the theater into a glitzy new stop on the international opera circuit and Czech cultural groups who demand that it should serve mainly as a platform for native talent.

Ovocní trh ("Fruit Market" ☆), the small square behind the theater, is surrounded by townhouses of predominantly 17th and 18thC origin.

GOLDEN LANE
A 16thC alley of tiny cottages. See CASTLE.

HRADČANY
Castle Hill, the seat of Bohemian kings and, in the 20thC, of Czech presidents, dominates the w bank of the Vltava. See CASTLE.

HRADČANY SQUARE (Hradčanské náměstí) ☆
Map 3C2. Closed to vehicle traffic.
The monumental space outside the main gate of the CASTLE is dominated by the residences of the cream of the Habsburg aristocracy. Nearly every stone around the square has some legend going back to the time of tribes and forest spirits, but the architecture dates largely from the aftermath of the great Hradčany fire of 1541.

Outstanding buildings include the **Archbishop's Palace** (Arcibiskupský palác), whose freshly restored Rococo facade (1765) incorporates a gateway from an earlier phase of building. The current appearance of the as-yet-unrestored **Salm Palace** (Salmovský palác), across the square (note the huge "S" of the Counts Salm), dates from 1800–10.

The next-door **Schwarzenberg Palace** (Schwarzenberský palác ☆), dating from 1543–63, provides one of Prague's visual signatures with the abstract black–white *sgraffiti* covering its whole surface (illustrated on page 20). The original owner was George of Lobkowicz, a powerful nobleman and early protector of the Jesuits who forfeited his estates to the crown under Rudolf II; the Schwarzenbergs inherited the house from the Eggenbergs.

Today the palace houses a **Military History Museum** (Vojenské historické muzeum) with displays of old armor, swords, blunderbusses, some war booty and a World War II tank.

Georg Ludwig, founder of the Schwarzenberg fortunes, was a German upstart who paid loyal service to the Austrian cause in the Thirty Years' War and was rewarded with vast Bohemian estates confiscated from Protestants. Prince Karl Philip, a descendant, led the Austrian armies to victory against Napoleon in 1812 and 1813. His son Felix helped quell the revolution of 1848 in Vienna and became a byword for reactionary politics as Franz Joseph's chancellor. Karl, the current prince, was the influential chief-of-staff of President Václav Havel.

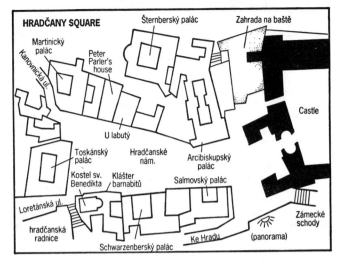

Next is the former **Barnabite Abbey** (Klášter barnabitů: c.1655), now a guest-house for visiting heads of state, and the church of **St Benedict** (kostel sv. Benedikta), which it encloses (c.1350, rebuilt 1720). The former **Town Hall of Hradčany** (Hradčanská radnice: 1589) is a reminder of times when the tiny area outside the castle constituted a separate and independent town.

The **Toscana Palace** (Toskánský palác: 1689–91), which rears its imposing Baroque facade on the w, was built for the Thun-Hohensteins but passed on shortly afterwards to the Dukes of Toscana. To its right is one of the most charming of Prague's noble houses, the **Martinitz Palace** (Martinický palác: c.1570). The colored *sgraffiti* covering its exterior (1634) depict Joseph running away from Potiphar's wife, and other merry scenes. The interior, used for concerts or exhibitions, has a main hall with a remarkable painted-wood ceiling, a chapel displaying paintings by Dürer's students, and a courtyard with more *sgraffiti.*

Sternberg Palace and National Gallery European Collection (Šternberský palác / Národní galerie) ★
Hradčanské nám. 15 ☎ *35 24 41* 📧 *Open Tues–Sun 10am–6pm.*

A passage beside the Archbishop's Palace leads to the residence of the Sternbergs (1698–1720; architects Martinelli and Alliprandi), now the repository of Prague's most famous art museum. The collection is small in size, but it runs the gamut of the great names of Western painting and includes several top-drawer masterpieces.

The core of the collection comes down from the acquisitions of Rudolf II. Rudolf was a compulsive purchaser of works of the Late Italian and Northern Renaissance. Of his collection of 600 pieces, two-thirds were looted in 1648 by mercenaries on contract to Queen Christina of Sweden;

85

Joseph II sold off or disposed of much of the rest in his Enlightened drive to clean up the empire's cluttered attics. Horror stories about Dürers and Cranachs that periodically turn up as rainguards in Hradčany's leaking roofs or as fodder for its mice form part of Prague's folklore.

The gallery does not have numbered rooms. The **first floor**, devoted to medieval and Early Renaissance art, has been closed for some years and may in the future move to another site. The **second floor** contains Old Masters grouped according to national schools. Outstanding among the Italians are Sebastiano del Piombo's statuesque *Madonna with Veil*, Lorenzo Lotto's melancholy *Musician*, Tintoretto's *St Jerome*, Bassano's *Flogging of Christ*, and Bronzino's masterful portraits of *Cosimo de' Medici* and *Eleonore of Toledo*. The German section holds some superb work by the two Holbeins, Albrecht Altdorfer and Lucas Cranach the Elder *(Adam and Eve, Christ Emmanuel, Madonna with Sts Catherine and Barbara)*.

The pride of the collection is Dürer's *Feast of the Rosary* (✰), one of the acknowledged pinnacles of the northern Renaissance. It shows the Virgin and Child with Maximilian I, Pope Julian II, St Dominic and assorted other guests (Dürer himself is on the far right) at a vast outdoor party. Dürer painted it in Venice in 1505 for the local German merchants' collective; 90 years later Rudolf engaged "four stout men" to carry it on foot over the Alps.

Among the Dutch and Flemish works are Jan Gossaert's *St Luke Painting the Virgin*, Pieter Brueghel's joyful *Haymaking*, Leonaert Bramer's powerful *Raising of Lazarus*, and several by Rubens, including a dramatic *Martyrdom of St Thomas* that once belonged to the altar of St Thomas in the Lesser Side. The French and Spanish are poorly represented except for a *Head of Christ* by El Greco, a recent acquisition.

Two floors of the **northwest wing** are devoted to European art of the 19th and 20thC. Artists include Delacroix, Courbet, Corot, Monet *(Ladies in Flowers)*, Pissarro, Renoir *(Lovers)*, Cézanne, Gauguin, van Gogh *(Green Rye)*, Henri Rousseau, Toulouse-Lautrec, Seurat, Signac, Vlaminck, Matisse, Braque, Derain, Chagall, Klimt, Kokoschka and Munch. Picasso is present with more than a dozen paintings spanning his entire career; Rodin with several original sculptures *(Age of Bronze, Martyr)* and a copy of his *Balzac*. The **upper floor** holds a beautiful collection of works by the Russian Ilya Repin.

The museum was hit by one of the most spectacular art heists of recent times in May 1991, when burglars got away with four Picassos worth $30 million. The paintings turned up months later in Germany, on their way to Japan. They are now back on display.

JEWISH QUARTER (Josefov) ✰

Map 4C5. Jewish Museum (Státní židovské muzeum): at Jáchymova 3 ☎231 07 85 ▨ open Sun–Fri 9am–5pm (last entry 4.30pm); closed Sat. Metro: Staroměstská.
What remains of the old Jewish ghetto has become one of Prague's most popular tourist attractions. Its monuments are among the oldest survivors of Jewish culture in Europe, and some of the works of art on display are of great interest to Jew and Gentile alike, but the spirit of

quiet retrospection one might wish to find in such places has fallen victim to the souvenir stands and busloads of loud people.

History

Paradoxically, it was the Nazis who turned the ghetto into a cultural monument. The Jews of Prague were transferred to the concentration camp of Theresienstadt/Terezín (see EXCURSIONS), but the German occupation authorities decided to preserve their neighborhood as the scientific museum of a race they expected to vanish soon; they stuffed its synagogues and communal buildings with items they salvaged from destroyed Jewish communities throughout Bohemia and Moravia. The Czechoslovak state took the museum over after the war, and used it intensively in the framework of its anti-German propaganda.

The walled, self-governing ghetto of Prague was formed after the Lateran Council of 1173 ordered all European Jews to live in segregated neighborhoods. For the next 700 years it fascinated visitors to Prague with its narrow lanes and exotic squalor. Its closed intellectual world (Europe's first Hebrew printing press was set up in Prague in 1512) was glimpsed by outsiders through a veil of superstition, and contributed to the widespread perception of Prague as a city of mysteries and ghouls-at-large.

Joseph II abolished the Jewish laws in 1780. The ghetto thereby lost its walls and renamed itself Josefstadt/Josefov in gratitude, but otherwise retained its physical appearance. A more radical turn came when gentrifiers set to work in 1893, demolishing the old ghetto with the exception of a handful of historic buildings, and replacing it with apartment houses whose end-of-century elegance characterizes the district today.

More than a hundred of these buildings were confiscated by the Nazis and later inherited by the Czechoslovak government. Of Prague's pre-war Jewish population of 30,000, less than 1,000 remain.

The question of Jewish properties in the former ghetto remains embroiled in controversy. The Restitution Law of 1990, which returns all assets nationalized by the communist regime to their former owners, seems to have overlooked the victims of earlier injustices, including those of the Nazi regime.

A new chief rabbi for Prague's Jewish community was elected in 1992 after a long vacancy in the office. The incumbent Karol Sidon was a screenwriter, novelist, civil rights activist and founder of the Charter 77 dissident movement before he was forced to leave Czechoslovakia in the early 1980s. He returned to Prague after the revolution. He is a colleague of Ivan Klíma, who survived Terezín to become one of Czechoslovakia's foremost novelists.

What to see

The ghetto lies immediately off the OLD TOWN SQUARE on Pařížská ul. The **State Jewish Museum** comprises six synagogues, two civic buildings and a cemetery distributed in a compact area, and forms a tragic testimony to the history of what was once one of the largest and most active Jewish communities in Europe.

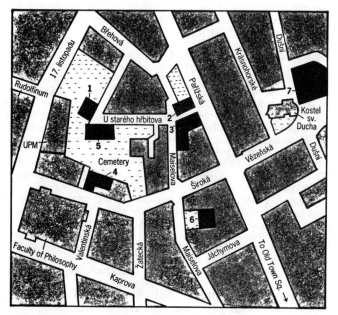

Old Jewish Cemetery (Starý židovský hřbitov) ★

Brochures call it "one of the world's ten most interesting sights." That may be a slight exaggeration, but the ancient cemetery can be a singularly evocative place with its tens of thousands of tombstones standing pell-mell in a quiet garden full of elder trees. For 600 years (until 1784), nearly all of the ghetto's dead were buried in this minuscule space: hence the extraordinary density of tombs and the lumpy ground where each man-made mound holds as many as nine layers of bodies resting on top of one another.

The tombstones carry emblems that denote profession, name or ancestry: scissors for a tailor, hands for a Cohen, a jug for a Levi, a woman for a virgin, a woman with raised left hand for a virgin bride. The inscriptions form an invaluable source for historians. The oldest belongs to the poet **Avigdor Caro**, who died in 1439; older stones were evidently destroyed during a pogrom in 1389. Another marks the grave of **Rabbi David Oppenheim** (1664–1736) whose 5,000-book library forms the Oppenheimer collection of Oxford's Bodleian Library. The most famous of all is that of **Rabbi Loew**, the creator of the *golem* (see page 29), which you will find along the w wall of the cemetery, roughly opposite the entrance gate.

The **Ceremonial Hall (1)** of the cemetery, a pseudo-medieval building from the 1890s, holds a permanent exhibition of pictures made by Jewish children at Terezín. (Bold numbers refer to the map above.)

Synagogues

Architecturally the most significant of the six is the **Old New Synagogue** (Staronová synagóga ✪ **2**), a Gothic building from c.1270, which has been the oldest synagogue in Europe since the destruction of the one in Worms during World War II. The name was originally New Synagogue, but time took its toll. Its builders may have been Cistercian monks, who specialized in this type of building; they evidently chose the unique five-ribbed vaulting over the usual four-ribbed sort so as to avoid the symbol of the cross. The brick stepped roof, one of the characteristic sights of Prague since the Middle Ages, has been the object of many unsuccessful attempts (most famously by the essayist Egon Erwin Kisch in the 1920s) to spot the *golem* in his final resting place.

The **Town Hall** of Josefov (Židovská radnice **3**), which stands opposite the Old New Synagogue on a narrow alley, was built in 1568 but took on its present appearance in the 1890s. Its most curious feature is an 18thC clock which has figures in Hebrew and Arabic and runs backward. On the upper floor (with a separate entrance next door) is the **High Synagogue** (Vysoká synagóga **3**), holding a collection of Jewish ceremonial textiles and embroideries.

The **Pinkas Synagogue** (Pinkasova synagóga **4**) was built in stages between 1479 and 1625 over the 11thC foundations of what is believed to have been the oldest Jewish place of worship in Prague. After the war it was converted into a memorial for the victims of National Socialism, and the names of all 77,297 Czech Jews killed by the Nazis were inscribed on its walls. It reopened in 1992 after many years in restoration.

The **Klausen Synagogue** (Klausova synagóga **5**), a 17thC building remodeled in 1884, houses a museum devoted to the history of literature, printing and the art of book-making in the ghetto. The **Maisel Synagogue** (Maislova synagóga **6**) carries the name of Mordecai Maisel (1528–1601), mayor of the ghetto under Rudolf II and one of the wealthiest men of his time in Europe thanks to a trading monopoly granted by the emperor. The family synagogue that he founded was rebuilt in the Neo-Gothic of the 1890s and now contains a collection of Jewish silver objects. The Neo-Moorish **Spanish Synagogue** (Španělská synagóga **7**) served the Sephardic community, whose ancestors came from Spain in 1492. It remains closed to the public pending restoration.

KAMPA ✪
Malá strana. Map 4D4. Closed to vehicle traffic.

A quietly romantic islet on the Vltava, separated from the Lesser Side by a little canal, the Čertovka, and dubbed, inescapably, Venice-in-Prague. Its proper name goes back to a gentleman by the extraordinary name of Rudolf Tycho Gansnebo Tengnagl vom Campo, who owned a farm here during the reign of Ferdinand III.

Na kampě, the main square beneath the foot of the CHARLES BRIDGE, retains the character of a village marketplace with houses of predominantly 17thC vintage. The stairway to the bridge was added after many inhabitants of the island perished during one of the Vltava's habitual floodings.

A much-repeated legend says that the icon of the Virgin on the balcony of #9, off the bridge, was carried away by high water during one of these floods. The owner jumped in after the miraculous relic, whereupon it reversed course and towed the man back to safety. Later it also healed his daughter whose hands had been caught in the rollers of the house laundry — hence the pair of carved rollers beside the picture.

The southern half of the island is a **park** covering ground once owned by the Counts Nostitz. The Nazis planned to drive a multilane highway through here, but the timely outbreak of World War II postponed the project indefinitely. The park was turned instead into exercise grounds for the Hitler Youth by demolishing the walls of the Nostitz estate. A fine 18thC **portal**, left intact, stands incongruously at the edge of the grass.

Off the southern tip of Kampa is the small Gothic church of **St John at the Laundry** (kostel sv. Jana Křtitela na prádle), the name of which arises from its lengthy stint (1787–1935) as a public washing facility.

KARLOV (Karlshof)
*Ke Karlovu, Nové město (Prague 2). Map **5F6**. Church open only Sun 2–5.15pm. Bus 272 from metro I.P. Pavlova.*

The octagonal **Church of the Assumption and Charles the Great** (kostel Nanebevzetí Panny Marie a Karla Velkého ☆) and the adjoining abbey building form part of a monumental but unfinished ensemble initiated by Charles IV in 1350 as a memorial to Charlemagne, the founder of the Holy Roman Empire.

The Roman crown that Charlemagne (742-814) revived was later assumed by the German emperors, who on that basis claimed universal authority over all of Christian Europe. Charles IV rebuilt the Empire after a time of crisis. His Golden Bull regularized the imperial succession, till then at the mercy of warring lords, by setting up a college of seven Electors, with the King of Bohemia as senior member. He adopted the name of Charles at his coronation (his original name had been Wenceslas) to signalize his empire-building intentions.

The church is distinguished by its painted and gilded **star-vault** (☆), a work by Boniface Wohlmut (c.1575), which constitutes one of the latest and grandest flourishes of Gothic art in Prague. The **Scala Santa**, added in 1708, represents the stairway of the palace of Pontius Pilate on which Christ faced interrogation on Maundy Thursday. The **abbey** formerly housed a Museum of the Interior Ministry documenting the heroic achievements of the Czechoslovak Security Police against assorted classes of criminals, subversives and foreign spies.

KARLOVA ULICE (Charles Street) ☆
*Staré město. Map **4C5**. Closed to vehicle traffic.*

An attractive old lane that connects the OLD TOWN SQUARE with the

CHARLES BRIDGE, and once formed part of the royal procession route. Several beautiful old buildings jostle for attention with the cafés and antique stores along the way.

The **Clam-Gallas Palace** (Clam-Gallasův palác), around the corner of Husova ul., was designed by the Viennese master J.B. Fischer von Erlach (1713) for Count Gallas, Marshall of Bohemia and Viceroy of Naples and, incidentally, a grandson of the above-mentioned vom Campo (see KAMPA). It now holds the city archives, and some tact is needed to gain access to the stupendous **stairway** (★) of the lobby. The **giants** (★) supporting the gate are the work of Matthias Braun.

The recently restored **Golden Well House** (U zlaté studně) at #3 decorates its 16thC facade with an elaborate Baroque relief featuring Sts Rochus and Sebastian, joint guardians against the plague. The **Golden Serpent** (U zlatého hada) at #18, now a fashionable wine bar (see page 142), was where an Armenian from Damascus by the unlikely name of Deodatus ("God's Gift") opened Prague's first coffee house in 1708. A few doors down is the **Pötting Palace** (Pöttingovský palác), an elegant 18thC building.

The house at #4 with some half-lost *sgraffiti* was the home of Johannes Kepler from 1607–12, the period in which he formulated the laws of planetary motion. The N side of the street in this part is occupied by the imposing complex of the CLEMENTINUM.

LESSER SIDE SQUARE (Malostranské náměstí) ★
Map 3C3. Metro: Malostranská.
The town square of the Lesser Side is divided into two disjointed halves by the monumental bulk of St Nicholas and the ex-Jesuit college adjoining it. While it cannot boast the spacious proportions of the Old Town Square, it is as thickly woven with history and romance as any in Prague.

The **Trinity Column** in the upper square, like its counterparts in every town and hamlet in the Habsburg lands, marked the conclusion of the plague of 1715. Giovanni Alliprandi's design shows the four patron saints of Bohemia with the Virgin and the persons of the Trinity under an obelisk surmounted by the Divine Eye.

St Nicholas (kostel sv. Mikuláše) ★
Open daily: May–Sept 9am–6pm; Oct, Mar–Apr 9am–5pm; Nov–Feb 9am–4pm.
The crowning work of the Dienzenhofers father and son is the most astounding example of Baroque religious architecture in Prague. The overall plan (1704) and the facade (1711) belong to Christoph; his son Kilian Ignaz added the 75-meter-high dome (1737–53), and Anselmo Lurago built the belfry and saw through the interior decoration (1755). The church stood under the jurisdiction of the Jesuits, who had already built the grim **college** on the adjoining plot in 1663–90. Count Kolowrat supplied the funds and thereby gained the right to put his **family crest** above the main gate.

The interior manifests the characteristic Baroque preoccupations with drama, illusion and ornament at a level of intensity matched by few other churches in Europe. The ceiling is covered with an extravagant *trompe-l'oeil* **fresco** by J.L. Kracker, with a surface of 1,500 square meters (16,150 square feet) that reportedly makes it the largest in Europe.

It details the life of St Nicholas, a 4thC bishop from Asia Minor who in time grew into Santa Claus the bringer of gifts, and patron of children, sailors, innocent prisoners and unmarried girls. Four larger-than-life figures representing the worldly powers beckon with subtle choreography toward the choir, where four church fathers — Sts Basil, John Chrysostom, Gregory of Nazianzen and Cyril of Alexandria — stand guard with a muscularity perhaps born of their epic struggle against heresy. The Jesuit saints Ignatius and Francis Xavier flank the main altar. The **chancel** is crowned with an astonishing *Beheading of John the Baptist* by sculptors Richard and Peter Prachner.

Contrary to appearance, the interior contains not a trace of genuine marble. What looks like marble is in reality *scagliola,* a painted mixture of plaster and glue that was much cheaper than the real thing in the marble-poor Habsburg lands.

Around the square ☆

The square dates back to the early 13thC, and so do the origins of most houses around it, although they have been buried under a bewildering variety of later accretions. Two watersheds have left their mark: the fire of 1541, which occasioned a general overhaul of the square in Renaissance style, and the social revolutions of the following century, which saw many old burghers' houses being taken over by nobles and converted into their town palaces, often in twos and threes.

Moving clockwise from the NE corner:

The former **Town Hall of the Lesser Side** (Malostranská radnice, at #21) received its current exterior in 1616–20 and its crested portal in 1660; it is now occupied by a touristy beerhall/nightclub (see MALOSTRANSKÁ BESEDA, page 153). The **Kaiserstein Palace** (#23), also called U Petzoldů, was redone in Baroque style in 1699–1700 by Alliprandi; the elaborate stucco work and the statues of the four seasons on the gable originate from that time. The bust outside the house is that of Ema Destinová (1878–1930), the national soprano: when she sang on the hill of Vyšehrad, legend says, admirers could hear her voice clearly in riverboats more than 100 meters below.

The **Grömlingen Palace** (Malostranská kavárna), a Rococo structure from 1773, was once the setting for the Kleinseitner Café, the legendary haunt of Franz Kafka, Max Brod and Franz Werfel in the 1920s; a touristy *kavárna* bearing the same name now searches for *le temps perdu*. The **Kaunitz Palace** (Kaunický palác) at Mostecká 15, now the Yugoslav Embassy, was built in 1775 for Wenzel von Kaunitz, Chancellor of Austria through the reigns of Maria Theresa and Joseph II.

In the courtyard of the **U Petržílků** (at #1; 13thC cellar, 16thC balcony, late 18thC facade) is a statue of St John Nepomuk from the Brokoff workshop. The **Six Columns and Three Bears** (#2) incorporates the 15thC town jail and parts of the medieval town wall. The **U Glaubiců** (#5) features an arcaded courtyard from the 16thC. The **U Palliardů** (16thC body, late

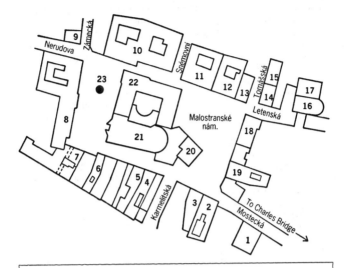

18thC facade) counts among its former residents a man who built the organ of St Vitus, and I.J. Palliardi, the leading architect of the Josephine era. The **Golden Lion House** (#10), a 16thC house with a 13thC cellar, is occupied by the famous wine tavern U MECENÁŠE (see page 136). The **Hartig Palace** (Hartigovský palác, at #12) originally consisted of two houses on either side of a street that were joined with an overpass in 1645.

The **Liechtenstein Palace** (Lichtenštejnský palác, at #13) was created out of five earlier houses by one of the 16thC Lobkowiczes and later acquired by Prince Johann Adam of Liechtenstein, the founder of the first state bank of Austria and the only man in modern history besides Ibn Saud after whom a sovereign state is named. The Classicist facade was added in 1791. Restituted to the principality in 1991, the palace is being restored into a Center of European Musical Culture.

On the corner of NERUDOVA ULICE is the former **Jesuit Gymnasium**

(Jezuitské gymnasium, at #17), originally another of the Lobkowicz palaces. Its splendid portal on Sněmovni ul. dates from 1726. At the **Smiřický Palace** (Palác Smiřických, at #18: Renaissance oriels from 1605, Baroque remodeling 1763), the Protestant conspirators met on May 22, 1618 to plan the defenestration that took place in the castle the next day. A recent bid by a Boston realtor to convert it, along with the next-door **Sternberg Palace** (Šternberský palác, at #19), into a posh hotel came to grief when the Czech National Council decided to take over the entire block to use for the offices of the new Czech state.

The **Velikovský House** (Dům Velikovský) traces its body to before 1354, its Renaissance oriel to 1584, its Baroque gable to 1652 and its Aleš-style *sgraffiti* to 1899; the U SCHNELLŮ beerhall (see page 137) has occupied its ground floor since 1787. The next house in the street, the **Golden Deer House**, carries over its mantelpiece an astonishing statue by F.M. Brokoff (1726), which shows St Hubert, the patron of hunters, being stared down by an angry deer.

St Thomas (kostel sv. Tomáše) ☆

An outstanding example of Baroque pyrotechnics hides in a cul-de-sac off the NE corner of the square *(map 4 C4)*. The bulk of the church of St Thomas is Gothic (choir 1285–1316, nave and belfry completed in 1379), but the real eye-poppers — the **facade** by Kilian Ignaz Dienzenhofer and the **ceiling fresco** by Václav Reiner — date from a remodeling carried out in 1723–31. The former is a tempest of pilasters, broken gables and volutes, which seem to float loose from all Classical restraint; the latter depicts the lives and deeds of the philosophical saints Augustine and Thomas Aquinas. The altar painting of St Sebastian (left of the chancel) is a work by Bartholomaeus Spranger. The original altarpiece by Rubens, showing the *Martyrdom of St Thomas*, is exhibited in the National Gallery at the STERNBERG PALACE (see page 85).

The former **abbey** of the Augustinian friars next door, now an old-people's home (look for the sign *Důchodků domov*), was a popular retreat for members of Rudolf II's eccentric court. Among those buried in its cloister is an Englishwoman, Elizabeth Jane Weston (1582–1612), who was viewed in her lifetime as one of Europe's leading humanist poets. The next courtyard *(entrance on Letenská ul.)* belongs to the famous St Thomas beerhall whose roots go back to the brewery the friars set up in 1358 (U SV. TOMÁŠE, see page 144).

LESSER SQUARE

A smaller space just off the OLD TOWN SQUARE.

LETNÁ GARDENS (Letenské sady)

*Letná (Prague 7). Map **4**A5. Trams 1, 8, 12, 17, 18, 22, 25, 26.*

The second-largest park in central Prague is less pretty than PETŘÍN but commands a superior view. The plateau on its summit was once the stage for a colossal statue of Stalin that towered over the Pařížská ul.-to-Old Town Square axis from 1955 until changing ideological winds blew it off its feet in 1962 (the fragments are said to be still in the cellar beneath the platform; the sculptor committed suicide). Since the revolution the site has been occupied by a red metronome, which will reportedly be replaced by an even more curious device by a Californian, involving a giant cube full of water, a wood-burning fire and 49 totem poles brought from different countries.

A short stroll from the platform leads to the **Hanau Pavilion** (Hanavský pavilón ✭), a cast-iron industrial gem of unclassifiable architecture and strange charm. It was built for the Jubilee Exposition of 1891, held in the Výstaviště fairgrounds nearby, then taken apart and reassembled here. The nightclub and café/restaurant on the premises are worth a visit for their lovely view.

LORETO (Loreta) ✭
Loretánské nám. 7, Hradčany. Map 3C2 ☎53 62 28 ▇ Open Tues–Sun 9am–noon, 1–5pm.

Over 500 Loreto shrines were built around Bohemia in thanksgiving for the Virgin's help in granting a Catholic victory at the battle of the White Mountain. Princess Benigna Catharina of Lobkowicz instituted in 1626 the famous one in Prague, which grew over the next 100 years into one of the most fascinating embodiments of Baroque piety.

A famous pilgrimage has taken place in Loreto, a town in central Italy, ever since the house of the Holy Family miraculously appeared there in AD1294, having apparently been flown there from Nazareth by some angels. Bramante rebuilt the original cottage in the 16thC into a masterpiece of the Italian Renaissance.

The shrine is preceded by a gallery of baby angels, beneath an elegant white **spire** (1694) with a carillon that plays *Hail thee Mary a Thousand Times* on the hour. Past the gate is a cloistered **arcade** (1634–40) containing two cherub-infested fountains (1740) and surrounded by many astonishingly over-decorated chapels.

At its center stands the **Casa Santa** (✭) of 1626, a quasi-Roman temple of white stone that replicates Bramante's vision of what a Nazarene carpenter's hut should look like. Inside it, a series of frescoes depict the Virgin and a retinue of female saints suffused with an extraordinary aura of suppressed sexuality. The **Church of the Holy Nativity** (kostel Narození Páně ✭), designed by the Dienzenhofers in 1717–34, possesses a stupendous interior with over 120 sculpted angels in evidence, frolicking, twirling, playing at various instruments or tumbling in free fall.

Note the bearded figure in fancy robes in the corner chapel to the right of the entrance of the cloisters. She is St Wilgefortis, a Portuguese girl, who grew a full beard after praying to God to save her from marrying the heathen king of Sicily. The king had second thoughts, and her father crucified the unfortunate girl, who became the protector of all unhappily married women. She was known in medieval England by the name of Uncumber.

Upstairs is the **treasury** (✫), a small collection of gold-and-silver reliquaries, chalices, monstrances, and votive gifts of exquisite workmanship and mind-boggling value.

Vicinity

The W side of Loretánské nám. is occupied by the stately bulk of the Foreign Ministry, the former **Czernin Palace** (Černínský palác, 1669–97). To the N are the tiled roofs of the low-lying **Capuchin Monastery** (Kapucínský klášter), founded in 1600 by Spanish monks who set up in Prague at the request of Rudolf II.

A steep alley on the N leads down into the **New World** (Nový svět ✫), a semi-rustic area of idyllic old houses and cobblestone lanes. It remains so far undiscovered by the hordes overrunning the Golden Lane (see page 75), though the anomaly is unlikely to last for long.

MALTÉZSKÉ NÁMĚSTÍ (Maltese Square) ✫
*Malá strana. Map **4C4**.*

The calm and attractive square in the Lesser Side is named after the Maltese (Hospitaler) Knights, who had their Prague headquarters here from the 12thC on, and have again since 1991.

> *The Order of the Knights Hospitalers of St John was founded before the First Crusade to supply medical aid to pilgrims in the Holy Lands, though it quickly grew into a fighting force that was not averse to a spot of piracy and hostage-taking when the occasion arose. Members were drawn from noble European families, and took vows of celibacy, poverty and obedience to a Grand Master. In their heyday they held the island of Rhodes, which became a naval fortress dreaded across the Mediterranean world. Expelled by the Turks in 1522, they moved on to Malta, from which they were expelled in turn by Napoleon in 1799.*
>
> *The Order has seen a certain revival under the papacy of John Paul II. The Maltese Cross, its insignia, is formed of four equal triangular sections.*

The statue in the middle of the square, by F.M. Brokoff (1715), shows John the Baptist, the knights' patron saint.

The church of **Our Lady Under the Chain** (kostel Panny Marie pod řetězem) retains the walls of the first (Romanesque) church that the Order built, in 1169, and two monumental towers from the second church, which it began in the 1370s. The latter was very much incomplete when 40 years later the Hussites chased the knights out, burned their church and looted their treasury, so an open yard instead of the usual nave separates the towers from the walled-up rump of what was to have been the choir of a gigantic Gothic edifice.

The **Palace of the Grand Prior** (Velkopřevorský palác) was built in 1726–38, when a gentleman named Gudanka Poppo von Dietrichstein was Grand Prior of the Maltese Knights. After rotting gently for decades as a music archive and museum, it has been restored by the returned knights into the sparkling Baroque creamcake that it ought to be. But for younger people, its salient part is still the garden wall known as the **John Lennon Wall**, the holiest shrine of Prague's counter-culture since the Beatle-hero's murder in 1980. Covered with a fantastic array of doodles and graffiti, the wall was the site of a decade-long battle between Lennonists and the Czechoslovak security police. The fun has mostly gone since the revolution, but a mini-Woodstock is still held at the wall on December 8 each year.

The **Buquoy Palace** (Buquoyský palác, 1682), facing the wall across a very Parisian row of chestnuts, houses the French Embassy. Nearby, the **Nostitz Palace** (Nosticky palác, 1660–70) rears its Baroque head crowned with Brokoff's statues of the Roman Caesars. The building is shared between the Education Ministry and the Dutch Embassy, and contains the private library of the Counts Nostitz, a rich source of 18thC and early 19thC musical rarities. Concerts are frequently held in the elegant ballroom.

Two restaurants on the square deserve notice. The **Painter** (U MALÍŘŮ: see page 140) features lovely painted vaults from the 16thC, though it takes a powerful wallet to dine under them. The **Golden Acorn** (U zlatého helmu), inexplicably, has nothing to show that Mozart stayed twice in the inn of the same name which used to be upstairs.

NA PŘÍKOPĚ ☆

Staré město/Nové město. Map 5C6. Metro: Můstek, nám. Republiky.

This is the glitziest of the three arteries that intersect at the so-called **Golden Crossing**, the hub of modern Prague: the others are WENCESLAS SQUARE and Národní třída. It follows the course of the former Old Town moat *(příkop)*, which was filled up in 1760, and developed into the poshest address in town.

The architecture originates mostly from the end of the 19thC and displays the ostentatious eclecticism of that period. An exception is the **Sylva-Taroucca Palace** (Palác Sylva-Tarouccovský) at #10, a Rococo residence (1747–51) recently converted into a gambling casino and inexplicably rebaptized as Palais Savarin. Its neighbors include the headquarters of nearly all of Czechoslovakia's banks, travel and airline companies as well as **Ubiquity**, the most outrageous music club in post-revolutionary Prague. The **Slavic House** (Slovanský dům) lives down a past when it went by the name of "German House" and served as the headquarters of the pre-1939 Sudeten–German nationalist party. The **Národní banka headquarters** at #24 replaces the former Blue Star Hotel where Austria and Prussia signed the 1866 peace treaty, which in effect gave birth to modern Germany.

Powder Tower and Municipal House (Prašná brána and Obecní dům) ☆

Not to be confused with the other Powder Tower (Prašná věž) in the CASTLE (see page 74), this defense tower of what used to be the main gate of the Old Town stands at the NE end of Na příkopě. It was built under Vladislav II in 1475–1500, though it owes the thicket of Gothic arabesquery and figural decoration covering its sides largely to the medievalist nostalgia of the 19thC. One of the stock sights of Prague, it has been hidden under scaffolding for some years, to reappear bright and sharp sometime soon.

The block to the N of the Powder Tower once carried the Royal Court, the residence of Bohemian kings from the time the Old Towners forced an embattled Wenceslas IV to settle in their city in 1394 until Vladislav II managed to slip their leash almost 100 years later. The **Municipal House** (Obecní dům; also called the Representation House) was built in its place in 1905–11, and counts as one of the finest products of Bohemian Art Nouveau. The bottom floor contains a very popular *kavárna* and a restaurant of slightly dusty elegance. Upstairs are **Smetana Hall**, a venue for Czech Philharmonic concerts, and **Primator's Hall**, a public function room decorated with frescoes by Alfons Mucha (1910).

A National Resistance Council met in the Municipal House during the final days of World War I, and Czechoslovakia's independence was proclaimed here by Tomáš Masaryk on October 28, 1918. The **náměstí Republiky** (Republic Square), outside, receives its name from that occasion.

NATIONAL GALLERY

There are three branches of the National Gallery in Prague: the **Old Bohemian Collection** (see CASTLE), the **European Collection** (see HRADČANSKÉ NÁMĚSTÍ) and the **Collection of Modern Czech Paintings** (see ST AGNES). The **Collection of Modern Czech Sculpture** is located in ZBRASLAV, 10km (6 miles) S of Prague (see under EXCURSIONS).

NATIONAL THEATER (Národní divadlo)

Národní 2, Nové město (near Most Legií). Map 4D5. Metro: Národní třída.

The massive Neo-Renaissance temple of the arts was the crowning achievement of the Czech national revival of the late 19thC, so much so that a generation of artists who took part in designing, building and decorating it were remembered collectively as the "National Theater school."

After 13 years in construction, the theater opened in 1881 to the patriotic tunes of Smetana's opera *Libuše*. A month later it burned down, and had to be rebuilt from scratch by a pupil of the original architect who meanwhile had died of chagrin. It became the breeding ground of Czech opera during the golden age of that not always appreciated genre. (Prague's Germans ran their own show at the Neue Deutsche Theater, which was renamed Smetana Theater after 1945 and the **State Opera** [Státní opera] in 1991.) See also THE PERFORMING ARTS, page 150.

Next to the National is the squat glass block of the **New Theater** (Nová scena), the outstanding example of 1970s architecture in Prague. It is one of the regular venues of the Laterna Magica multimedia show (see page 149).

NERUDOVA ULICE ☆

Malá strana. Map 3C3. Closed to vehicle traffic.

A picturesque old street in the Lesser Side sloping between the LESSER

SIDE SQUARE and the base of Hradčany Square (HRADČANSKÉ NÁMĚSTÍ), with an unbroken row of historic townhouses, many quaint and curious shops, and a lovely view over the orange-tiled roofs of the Lesser Side.

Nerudova abounds in old house signs (✪), the medieval cousins of today's street numbers. Note the Red Eagle at #6, which seems to have started out as a vulture. The Three Fiddles (pictured) at #12 mark the former home of the Edlinger family of violin-makers; the Golden Cup (#16) and Golden Key (#27) may have been goldsmiths, while the Golden Horseshoe (#34) suggests a smithy. St John Nepomuk, who is recognizable by his five stars, guards #18. No clues exist for the meaning of the Donkey in the Manger (#25), the Green Lobster (#43) or the Two Suns (#47).

This last was the house of Jan Neruda (1834–91), the writer of Dickensian short stories, who has been a godfather to the street.

Pablo Neruda, the Chilean poet (1904-73), adopted his surname at the age of 16 after reading the Czech author's Lesser Side Stories. *Several of the stories are set in specific houses on Nerudova ulice.*

Two noble residences stand out in a street of predominantly burghers' houses. The **Morzin Palace** (Morzinský palác) at #5, which is now the Romanian Embassy, is held aloft by two magnificent Moors by Brokoff, signaling the fact that Morzin is a Germanization of the Czech word for "Moor"; their curious placement — flanking a minor window instead of the portal — solves the problem of how to make a palace out of three existing townhouses. The **Thun-Hohenstein Palace** (Thun-Hohenštejnský palác) at #20, now the Italian Embassy, competes for attention with a pair of grotesquely contorted eagles by Matthias Braun. One of the most original architects of 18thC Prague, Jan Blasius (or Giovanni) Santini-Aichl, designed both palaces in the course of the systematic Baroque restyling of the street that he carried out c.1710–23. The church of **St Cajetan** (kostel sv. Kajetana) dates from the same period.

Vicinity

The alleys on the hillside below Nerudova hide some of the quaintest nooks and crannies of old Prague. They descend at the base of the valley into the quiet aristocratic zone of Vlašská ("Italian") and Tržistě ("Market") streets.

The **Italian Hospice** (Vlašský Špitál) that gives Vlašská its name is a complex of institutions (chapel, hospital, arcade) established in 1573 for the Italian craftsmen who came to work in Prague. It continues to serve in part as the cultural center of the Italian Embassy.

The Czech word for "Italian" (vlách/vlášsky) derives from the medieval German word for "foreigner"(welsch). The English word "Welsh" for their Celtic neighbors appears to have originated from a similar Anglo-Saxon root.

The **Lobkowicz Palace** (Lobkovický palác: by Giovanni Alliprandi, 1703–7), now the German Embassy, owns a sumptuous garden which made the headlines in September 1989 when a horde of wall-jumping East Germans took refuge in the embassy. Their flight triggered the chain of events that led to the collapse of the Berlin Wall, and ultimately of the Czechoslovak regime. The diplomats' favorite restaurant, LOBKOVICKÁ VINÁRNA (see page 135), is here.

The US Embassy is housed in the former **Schönborn Palace** (Schönbornský palác) at Tržiště 15 (1643–56, facade by Santini-Aichl 1715). Franz Kafka lived in this building during a short stint it had as a housing estate, and developed his ultimately fatal case of tuberculosis while here. A later tenant was Shirley Temple Black, the former actress who was US Ambassador to Czechoslovakia under Presidents Reagan and Bush.

OLD TOWN SQUARE (Staroměstské náměstí) ★
Staré město. Map 4C5. Metro: Staroměstská, nám. Republiky or Můstek. Closed to vehicle traffic.

"Fairytale" may be a tired phrase, but it leaps to mind with unusual vigor when describing the main square of Prague's Old Town, a lovely old piazza with the right proportions (125 x 93 meters/137 x 102 yards) to balance intimacy with grandeur. The tone is set by the spires of the Týn Church, looking like a cross between Klingsor's castle and a fantasy spaceship, and enhanced by the identical hood of the Town Hall opposite. There is a cuckoo clock with stars, planets, marching apostles, a rattling skeleton and a dancing Turk, and houses all around painted with unicorns, charging knights and rows of nubile fairies.

History
The appearance of the square has changed little since the late Middle Ages. Most of the houses on the E and SE sides were built in the 1230s when the floor of the square was raised to its current level. The Town Hall tower was built in the 1360s, and the Týn Church took its present shape by about the end of the 15thC.

Grave and curious incidents of Bohemia's history took place against their background. A famous one is commemorated by the **27 crosses** marked in the pavement outside the Town Hall, the spot where 27 leaders of the Protestant nobility of the kingdom faced the executioner on June 21, 1621. Their crime (lest their halo of martyrdom makes you forget) had been to plunge Europe into the worst bloodbath in its history before our century. The decapitations were performed, according to an Englishman who was present, "with great dexterity, not missing one stroake, as if the winde had blowen their heads from their shoulders." One to lose his head so was Dr Jessenius, the sharp-spoken rector of the Carolinum, who was singled out for special treatment and had his tongue lopped off before

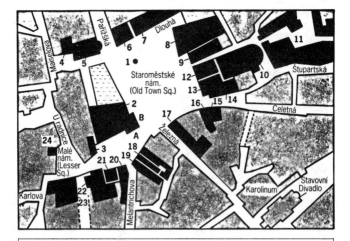

OLD TOWN SQUARE: KEY

1 Jan Hus monument
2 Staroměstská radnice (Town Hall)
  A Orloj (astronomical clock)
  B 27 Crosses
3 U minuty
4 Kafka's birthplace
5 Kostel sv. Mikuláše (St Nicholas)
6 Oppelt House (Ministry of Culture)
7 Ministry of Trade
8 Palác Kinských
9 U kamenného zvonu (Stone Bell House)
10 Kostel Panny Marie před Týnem (Týn Church)
11 Týnský dvůr (Týn Court)

12 Týnská škola (Týn School)
13 U bílého jednorožce (White Unicorn House)
14 U tří králů (Three Kings House)
15 U Sixtů
16 U Storchů
17 U zlatého jednorožce (Golden Unicorn House)
18 U modré hvězdy (Blue Star House)
19 Na kamenici
20 U vola (Ox House)
21 Former Servite Abbey
22 U zlatého anděla (Golden Angel House)
23 American Hospitality Center
24 U Rottů

he was hanged, beheaded and quartered. By a strange twist of fate, he had performed the world's first public dissection in the same square 20 years earlier.

> *Mydlář the Executioner was instantly transformed into a Prague legend. His favorite restaurant (the Green Frog, U ZELENÉ ŽÁBY, behind the Town Hall tower) and wine pub (U MECENÁŠE, on the Lesser Side Square) are still shown to visitors. (See pages 142 and 136.)*

On a snowy morning on February 25, 1948, Klement Gottwald announced the birth of socialist Czechoslovakia from the balcony of the Kinský Palace.

The square

The **Jan Hus monument**, in the center of the square, shows the reformer in Art Nouveau'ish elongation, accompanied by two groups representing the defeated and the defiant. The memorial was installed in 1915 for the 500th anniversary of Hus's martyrdom and represented a veiled protest against Austrian rule, then entering its terminal phase. The sculptor was Ladislav Šaloun.

A copper plate near the middle of the square marks the **Prague meridian**, formerly the basis for calculating the time in Bohemia.

Týn Church (kostel Panny Marie před Týnem) ★
Visits Tues–Fri 1–4pm, Sat–Sun 2–5pm.

Prague's best-known visual emblem, the 18-spired Gothic church of Our Lady Before Týn, was begun under Charles IV (1365) as the parish church of the Old Town, continued by Peter Parler & sons from 1390, left incomplete at the outbreak of the Hussite crisis c.1410, and resumed with the erection of the N tower (1457–63) under George of Poděbrady. Vladislav II (c.1490) added the s tower and the jaunty concatenation of turrets that lend the church its unmistakable profile. The four quadruplets of secondary towers were intended to act as observation posts.

The towers may eventually be opened for sightseeing as restoration work, now in its second decade, winds down.

The main gate hides behind a decidedly unmonumental corridor between two old houses facing the square: the former **Týn School** (Týnská škola: 12thC cellar, 13thC body, curious late 16thC gable) and the **White Unicorn House** (U bílého jednorožce: 12thC cellar, 13thC structure, 14thC arcade, 18thC facade, 19thC upper story).

The Baroque and Neo-Gothic interior of the church, all black and gold, fails to swamp the Gothic simplicity of the architecture. Two outstanding works of carved-wood sculpture deserve notice: a *Crucifixion* from c.1500, in the left side-altar, and a 16thC *Baptism of Christ*, near the penultimate pier on the right, signed by master I.P., whose other work is exhibited in St George's Abbey in the CASTLE. More popular among sightseers is the pink **tombstone of Tycho Brahe**, beneath the last pier on the right, with a relief showing Rudolf II's court astronomer wearing his artificial nose (see page 29).

The church takes its name from the **Týn Court** (Týnský dvůr; Ungelt in German, by which name it is often known), a complex of buildings around a court (*Týn* actually means a court) in the very ancient district behind. The compound was already in existence in the 11thC, before there was an Old Town, serving as a warehouse-cum-residence for foreign businessmen. It incorporated workshops, an inn, a clinic and a chapel: any foreigner who imported goods into Prague paid a duty (the *Ungelt*), which entitled him to storage space and board in the Týn. The court has been closed for restoration for more than a decade.

The **Storch House**, on the right near the entrance of CELETNÁ ULICE (next door to the **Sixt House**: see page 76), bears a flamboyant fresco by Mikoláš Aleš (1898) showing St Wenceslas on his horse Ardo.

The **Týn Church**

Stone Bell House and Kinský Palace (U kamenného zvonu and Palác Kinských) *Staroměstské nám. 13 and 12. Kinský Palace* ☎ *231 51 35* 📷 *open Tues–Sun 10am–6pm.*

The **Stone Bell House** is one of the oldest buildings on the square, although one would scarcely know it if one came ten years ago. All the Gothic arches and pointed windows you see now were discovered under a Baroque skin in the mid-1980s and subsequently restored to their pristine form of c.1330. The house is used for exhibitions of contemporary art and occasional concerts. The interior possesses two chapels and some lovely painted ceilings, but is otherwise quite blank.

The **Kinský** (or Goltz-Kinský) **Palace** displays the dainty elegance of the transitional style from Baroque to Josephine Classicism, known for lack of a better term as Rococo. It was designed in 1755–65 by Anselmo Lurago, acquired by Prince Kinský shortly afterward, and owned by his descendants until confiscated by the government in 1945. At one point it housed a German grammar school, organized under Kinský auspices when the nationalist fever of the 1880s had banned German-language instruction from public schools. Its pupils included Franz Kafka, whose father owned a little shop in the building. Recently restored, the palace houses the National Gallery's collection of prints, drawings and graphic art. Modern Czech artists predominate.

On the left, across Dlouhá ul., is the Baroque former **Paulist Abbey** (Paulánský klášter), adjoining the florid facade of the **Ministry of Trade** building. The latter was designed in 1898 by Osvald Polívka, a prominent architect of the Czech Art Nouveau movement.

Pařížská ulice (Pařis Street) ★

Pařížská ul. presents a rich and joyful lineup of turn-of-the-century residential architecture, one of the most charming of its kind in any major European city. The houses combine the free license of historicism (one can count two dozen Gothic turrets, nearly as many Romeo–Juliet balconies and 16 onion-domes within a six-block area) with the stricter elegance of Art Nouveau. A majority of them lie in the former JEWISH QUARTER, which made the dizzying leap in the 1890s from ghetto to middle-class fashionableness. Self-confidence and humor are almost palpable — contrast the insecure world of Kafka, a child of the time and the neighborhood, who lived on the top floor of the **Oppelt House** at #1 (now the Ministry of Culture) while he wrote *Metamorphosis*, the story of a man who wakes up one day to find himself transformed into a cockroach.

St Nicholas (kostel sv. Mikuláše) ★

K.I. Dienzenhofer's sparkling Baroque church at the NW corner of the square (1732–37) encloses a small interior, delicate rather than overwhelming, and very well suited for the chamber concerts that are held in it daily during the tourist season. Since 1920 the building has been the property of the Czechoslovak Church, a Hussite sect that was revived at the time of Czechoslovakia's independence and enjoyed official support under the communist regime.

Kafka was born in the next house *(Kaprova 1),* where a souvenir store designating itself as a **Kafka Museum** has operated since 1991.

Town Hall of the Old Town (Staroměstská radnice) ★

Tower and chapel ▨ *open daily 8am–6pm. Other rooms* ✗ *every hour on the hour.*
The town hall was the seat of the self-governing burgherdom of Old Prague in its age-long tug-of-war against the authority of Hradčany. It reached the peak of its fortunes in the 14thC, becoming powerful enough in the 1390s to jail the king when it disliked his policies. It took the lead both in starting the Hussite revolution and defeating its fanatic fringe, usurped the right to choose the country's kings during a lucky streak that ran until 1526, and led a number of revolts when the Habs-

burgs began to claw back the royal prerogative. Its decline took a precipitous turn after the White Mountain. It came to rest on a whimper when Joseph II abolished the Old Town in 1783.

The actual building dates back to a decree of John of Luxemburg (1338) authorizing the city to buy two existing houses and to levy a wine tax to finance the purchase. Two more houses were incorporated at later dates, and a tall tower was built in 1364 to cap them all (it did not receive its multiturreted cap until some 100 years later). With parts and patches added on over the following 600-plus years, the ensemble presents even more of an architectural hodgepodge than is usual for Prague.

EXTERIOR: Go left to right for the highlights: the **Cock House** with an early 19thC facade; Renaissance windows (1520) over the modern entrance; the Late Gothic (1475) **main portal** (✰) surmounted by the coat-of-arms of Prague (1649; see page 33); and the **astronomical clock** (Orloj, c.1480) with Gothic frame, niche figures from the 17thC, marching apostles from 1864, and a dial that is a modern copy. The Gothic **oriel** (✰) protruding from the second story of the tower belongs to the Town Hall chapel, which was originally built in 1381. It and the adjoining Gothic

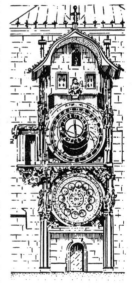

house on the right were bombed to pieces by the Wehrmacht on the last day of German occupation (May 8, 1945) and rebuilt only recently.

THE CLOCK: The **astronomical clock** (★ ✷) delights its viewers as each hour strikes, with a morality play performed by a 17-puppet cast. The 12 Apostles parade out of their window, a skeleton representing Death reverses an hourglass, Greed (until lately called the Jew) and the Turk (not yet euphemized) mock him, and the Cock crows when it is all over.

Quite apart from Punch-and-Judy antics, the clock is also a wonder of technology in its own right. The upper dial shows the hour in the usual way (Roman numerals), as well as the hour calculated from sunset to sunset (Arabic numerals), the current phase of the sun and the moon (the inner dial with zodiac signs), and the position of the planets (the arched lines on the main dial). The lower dial is divided into 365 ticks, which make a full circle each year, keeping track of leap years as well.

The clock was rebuilt in its current form by a certain Master Hanuš in 1490. Legend has it that the Town Hall failed to pay him per contract (others say he was blinded to make sure he did not build a copy of his clock elsewhere), so he scaled the tower, threw a spell in the works, and died on the spot. No one was able to fix the bug until 1572.

INTERIOR: You pay separately for the tower, the chapel, the art gallery and the guided tour of the ceremonial rooms. The **tower** (★) offers a fascinating view from the top. An elevator goes only part way up, leaving many rounds of ramp to climb on foot. The **chapel** is a memorial to the victims of two world wars, with the ostentatious emptiness that is a common characteristic of such places. The tour features the old **Council Chamber** (c.1470 ★) and two rooms with immense patriotic tableaux *(Charles IV Founding Prague University, The Trial of Jan Hus, The Election of King George of Poděbrady)* by 19thC painter Mikoláš Aleš.

Malé náměstí (Lesser Square) ★

The cartoon-strip panels of the medieval **Minute House** (U minuty) (★) set off Malé náměstí ("Lesser Square"), a cozy little space off the sw corner of the larger one. The *sgraffiti* mix the barely-clad Seven Graces and other pagan deities with Biblical figures; they date from 1610, but lay hidden under layers of plaster until rediscovered by accident during the 1920s. Kafka lived in the house as a child in 1889–96.

The more colorful exterior of the **Rott House** (U Rottů) at #3 belongs to the school of Aleš (1890s). At #13 is a **historic apothecary** *(open Mon-Fri 8am-3pm),* guarded by statues of Apollo and Asclepius, the medical divinities. The **American Hospitality Center** next door popped up a few weeks after the 1989 revolution to introduce Praguers to the joys of Western democracy, pizza and Sky TV.

OUR LADY OF VICTORY (kostel Panny Marie vítězné)
Karmelitská ul., Malá strana. Map 3C3. Tram 12, 22.

The **Baby Jesus of Prague** (Pražské Jezulátko, Bambino di Praga, Jesus Niño de Praga ★) is a wax doll with a reputation that modern medicine can only envy for healing the sick, the lame and the blind. His cult spreads across the Catholic world and especially Andean South America, where pious Indians are said to imagine *Praga* to be a place of the fullness of divine grace. He lives in a silver house of undescribable Baroque splendor, and owns 39 sets of clothes, changed daily, that include one made of the finest silk of Shanghai and another that was embroidered by Empress Maria Theresa herself. He holds the rank of Count Palatine of the Austrian Empire and wears the Order of the Golden Fleece granted by the King of Spain.

The *niño* was born in Spain, where he belonged to Princess Manriques de Lara, née Habsburg. He came to Prague with the trousseau of her daughter Polyxena, who married a Lobkowicz. In 1628 she donated the baby to the Carmelite nuns who had just taken over the church of Our Lady of Victory, formerly the Lutheran parish church of the Lesser Side. Four years later he saved the city from Swedish invasion, and (although he failed to repeat the feat when the Swedes came back in 1648) his miracle-working career was secure thereafter.

Built in 1611–13, the church itself has the distinction of being the oldest Baroque ecclesiastical building in Prague. The Maltese Knights took it over when the Carmelite order was abolished by Joseph II. This explains the prominent Maltese Cross over the facade.

PETŘÍN

Malá strana. Map 3D3. Trams 6, 9, 12, 22.

The steep forested hill that rises to the s of Hradčany was where the ancient Slavs made sacrifice to their gods. Here ended the history of the mighty tribe of the Vršovici who were defeated by the Přemysls in the year 1107 and massacred to a man. Their ghosts are said to lurk in the fog that shrouds the hill on most mornings.

The church of **St Lawrence** (kostel sv. Vavřince) was erected shortly after the massacre, in the field where it took place (the current structure dates from 1770). Later, the hill was divided up into the private gardens of four noble houses (the Kinský, Lobkowicz, Schönborn and Vrtba) and three ecclesiastical bodies. Collectively, these now form the most attractive public **park** in central Prague. Its features include the ever-popular **funicular** (✪ ☀), the panoramic restaurant NEBOZÍZEK (see page 138), a cast-iron tower optimistically named the Little Eiffel, an observatory and planetarium, a mirror labyrinth *(bludiště)* and a 10-meter-wide (33-foot) diorama re-creating the battle of Prague's students against the Swedes in the year 1648.

POWDER TOWER

There are two Powder Towers: visually the best-known one — the **Prašná brána** — in NA PŘÍKOPĚ (see page 97), and the **Prašná věž** in the CASTLE (see page 74).

ST AGNES MONASTERY – NATIONAL GALLERY MODERN CZECH PAINTINGS (Anežsky klášter)

U milosrdných 17, Staré město. Map 5B6 ☎231 42 51 ▨ Open Tues–Sun 10am–6pm.

The twin monasteries of St Agnes (see page 27), established c.1234, around the same time as the Old Town itself, constitute the most important example of Early Gothic architecture in Prague. Little actually remains of the Franciscan (Minorite) monastery, now under restoration, while the convent of the Poor Clares has been fully, perhaps too fully, reconstructed into a 20thC approximation of the medieval original.

The cohabitation of monks and nuns in a single compound was unusual for the time. It was ended by Joseph II (1782), and the site was abandoned to a swarm of poor squatters that included, at various times, many of the penniless artists of 19thC Bohemia. Restoration was taken up as a public cause at the end of the century, although it was the communist government that actually carried it through. In 1963, the National Gallery's collection of modern Czech painting art was installed in a restored wing of the convent. A second wing opened in 1980.

The **gallery** (✪) documents the progress of national Czech art from its tentative beginnings in the early 19thC through the emergence of increasingly individual voices in the first decades of the 20thC. A room is devoted to Josef Mánes, the dominant figure of Czech painting in the Romantic generation of 1848. Jaroslav Čermák (1830–78) stands out with a sensuous elegance akin to Ingres, while Karel Purkyně (1834–68) achieves a high level of psychological intensity. Mikoláš Aleš (1852–1913) and Maximilián Pirner (1854–1924) come up with some admirable work in the framework of the NATIONAL THEATER generation.

Vicinity

The monastery stands in a quietly beautiful district of the Old Town. On the corner of U milosrdných and Dušní is the **Church of Sts Simon and Jude** (kostel sv. Šimona a Judy), a 14thC structure with some impressive Gothic vaulting behind its Baroque facade. Mozart and Haydn both played its organ.

ST JAMES (kostel sv. Jakuba) ☆

Malá Štupartská, Staré město (near Old Town Square). Map 5C6.

One of the pinnacles of Baroque church decoration in Prague, easy to miss in the tangle of rundown alleys behind the TÝN CHURCH. The building is actually High Gothic (1318–74), but you would not notice it under the layers of stucco and trick-architecture filling the interior. The Baroque styling took place in 1736–39. It may lack the manic intensity of St Nicholas, but for sheer elegance it has no rival in the city.

The relief figures leaping out of the facade belong to St James flanked by the Franciscan saints Francis of Assisi and Antonius of Padua. Inside, two rows of magnificent wood-cut side altars compete for attention with the **main altar** (☆), carried aloft by three pairs of uncharacteristically lean and athletic angels.

A bay on the left contains the **Mausoleum of Count Vratislav of Mitrowicz** (☆), a joint work by the two greatest artists of the Habsburg Baroque, J.B. Fischer von Erlach and F.M. Brokoff (1716). The corpulent count is shown rising from his coffin as from a pleasant nap. Sorrow is left behind, mighty Death hesitates in an ambivalent gesture, while the Angel of Record flutters in mid-sentence.

> *Note the grizzled human forearm hanging from a chain on the left of the high altar. It belongs to an ill-advised thief who tried to rob the Madonna of St James of her jewels in the year 1400. The Virgin grabbed his hand and would not let go despite the prayers of priests and laity. A meat cleaver finally did the job.*

The adjacent **Franciscan Monastery** (13thC) now houses a school of music.

ST MARGARET, ABBEY AND CHURCH OF (Benediktinský klášter a kostel sv. Markety) ☆

Markétská 28, Břevnov (Prague 6), 5km (3 miles) w of city center. Map 1C3.
Metro to Hradčanská, then tram 8 or bus 108, 174, 235; or tram 22 from Karlovo nám.

The earliest abbey in Bohemia, dedicated to St Margaret, was founded in 993 in the Prague suburb of Břevnov (an earlier convent for noble nuns had been established 20 years before in Hradčany: see St George's Convent under CASTLE. A pre-Romanesque crypt, the oldest fragment of Bohemian architecture in existence, survives under the impressive Baroque compound that replaced the original buildings in 1708–40. The Benedictine friars have returned to the abbey since the revolution.

The chief points of interest are a lofty outer **portal** and the **church of St Margaret**, both by the great Christoph Dienzenhofer. The **monks' quarters** (✗ *available*) include some stupendously decorated Baroque rooms, notably the **Prelates' Hall** (✪), which features a ceiling fresco by the Bavarian master Cosmas Damian Asam (1729) depicting *The Miracle of Blessed Gunther*.

> *Gunther was an ambitious and pleasure-loving Bavarian gentleman before he changed his ways and began to practice severe asceticism. Late in life he came to Břevnov, where he is buried under the altar of St Margaret. Here, according to legend, he was invited to a banquet by the prince of Bohemia and served a roast peacock on a day on which monks could eat no flesh. Gunther prayed to God to save him from sin without offending the prince, so the peacock suddenly came to life and walked away from the table. Suitably impressed, the prince agreed to abandon his life of excess.*

ST NICHOLAS

The outstanding achievement of Baroque architecture in Prague is the Dienzenhofers' church in the LESSER SIDE SQUARE. The younger K.I. Dienzenhofer's smaller church of the same name is in OLD TOWN SQUARE.

ST VITUS'S CATHEDRAL

There is a plan of the cathedral on page 70 (see CASTLE).

STAR CHÂTEAU (Letohrádek Hvězda)

6km (4 miles) w of city center 🖼 *Open Tues-Sun 10am-5pm. Metro: Hradčanská, then tram 1, 2 or 18 to Heyrovského nam. terminal, then walk or bus 179.*

Obora hvězda, a former royal hunting preserve, is one of the most attractive parks in the Prague area. At its center lies a remarkable piece of Renaissance architecture: a hunting lodge that consists of six acute-cornered sections combining to form a six-pointed star. The lodge (built 1555) once belonged to Ferdinand of Tyrol, a son of Ferdinand I of Habsburg, a famous dilettante who is also credited with Château Ambras near Innsbruck, in Austria. The interior is decorated with some superb Italian stucco, and houses a **museum** dedicated to the 19thC writer Alois Jirásek and his contemporary, the painter Mikoláš Aleš (🖼 *open Tues–Sun 10am-5pm).*

The park abuts in the s on the **White Mountain** (Bílá hora), the scene of the most traumatic moment in Czech history. On this hill on November 8, 1620, Catholic forces led by Maximilian of Bavaria destroyed the rebel Protestant army of Frederick the Winter King, so wiping Bohemia off the European map for nearly 300 years. A small 17thC church near the base of the hill, dedicated to **Virgin Mary Victorious**, commemorates the Habsburg victory. A **War Memorial** set on the hilltop reflects the different view taken by modern Czech nationalism.

STRAHOV ABBEY – NATIONAL LITERATURE MEMORIAL (Strahovský klášter; Památník národního písemnictví) ☆

Strahovské nádvoří 1, Hradčany (entrance at Pohořelec 8). Map 3C1 ☎53 88 41 ☒ Open Tues–Sun 9am–4.30pm. Tram 22 from metro Malostranská, or 23 from metro Hradčanská

The sprawling monastic complex was established outside the western approaches of Hradčany in 1148, in part with defensive considerations in mind (*strahovati* means "lookout"). It rewards a visit with its tranquil setting and the magnificent halls of its Baroque library.

> *Strahov was already a center of bookishness from the oldest times, and the Premonstratensian monks were known for their traditional devotion to scholarship. Their great Philosophical Library, however, was only put together in 1780 to persuade the monk-hating Joseph II that this particular establishment served a useful social purpose. Much of the collection came from monasteries that Joseph was abolishing by the dozen. The communists eventually evacuated the monastery in 1951 and converted it into a Monument of National Literature. The monks returned after the revolution, and parts of the compound are now off-limits to visitors.*

The small **church of St Roch** (kostel sv. Rocha, 1603–17), near the main entrance, was built by Rudolf II in payment for the saint's help in saving Prague from the plague of 1599. The main **church of the Assumption** (kostel Nanebevzetí Panny Marie ☆) buries its 12thC structure — a Romanesque basilica — under a surfeit of Baroque accretions. Notable among these are the superbly expressive *Immaculata* by J.A. Quittainer (over the main gate) and an 18thC organ that is considered the finest in Prague. Two rows of sumptuously dressed skeletons, of former abbots, assist divine service on either side of the choir. A passage through the church leads to the Romanesque core of the monastery, which holds the permanent displays of the **Czech Literature Museum**. Except for some illuminated medieval manuscripts, they are unlikely to excite a non-Czech-speaker.

The **Library** (☆), entered separately, consists of a **Theological Hall** (1671, frescoes 1723–27) of almost frivolous ornateness, and the more impressive **Philosophical Hall**, one of the most successful products of Josephine Classicism in Prague (1780–82). The vast ceiling composition depicting *Mankind's Efforts to Achieve Enlightenment* is the last major work by Franz Anton Maulpertsch, the outstanding painter of the Viennese Rococo. Finished five years after the French revolution (1794), it avoids virtually all reference to religious subjects — a radical break with the previous century-and-a-half of Baroque painting.

Behind the monastery is a vast orchard of apple and pear trees, with a path leading through it to the park of PETŘÍN.

TROJA CHÂTEAU (Letohrádek Troja) ☆

U trojského zámku, Troja (Prague 7). 3km (2 miles) N of the center. Map 2B4 ☒ ≡ Open Tues–Sun 10am–8pm (no admission after 5pm). Bus 112 from metro

*Nádraží Holešovice. Boats from Palackého most (Palacky Bridge) at 8.30am,
9.30am, 1.30pm, 3pm.*

A stately country house on the Vltava, with formal gardens, now used
as a gallery of 19thC Czech art. The builder was Count Wenceslas
Adalbert of Sternberg, whose dearest hope was to host the Habsburgs
in the event that they should come to hunt in the royal game reserve
across the river (now STROMOVKA Park: see page 123). The architecture
(1679–85, by Jean-Baptiste Mathey) echoes Roman villas of the period;
the name *Troja* (Troy) is a reference to Aeneas, the Trojan hero who
founded Rome, thus counting as an ancestor of the Habsburgs in their
capacity as Roman emperors.

An outstanding sight is the **ceiling fresco** (✮) of the Great Hall, a
masterpiece of illusionistic painting by the Flemish artist Abraham Godyn
(1690). Floating in the sky above pilasters that defeat the eye whichever
way one looks at them, the w wall shows Rudolf I of Habsburg, the actual
founder of the family's fortunes, lending his horse to a priest and being
promised an empire in return.

The E wall depicts the triumphal march of Leopold I after his victory
over the Turks in 1683. The barbarous figure in mustache and helmet is
Jan Sobieski, the Polish king who ran to his rescue. The Turkish pasha is
flung down from the ceiling as Imre Tököly, the Hungarian–Protestant
turncoat who joined him in the siege of Vienna, awaits his turn.

Vicinity
The neighborhood of the château, once a favorite suburb of the communist elite, is filled with villas that seem quaintly middle-class by
Western standards. Next to the château is Prague's **Zoo** (Zoologická
zahrada ✱), containing 2,000 animals of 600 different species *(◩ open
daily from 9am-sunset).* The **New Botanical Garden** (Nová botanická
zahrada) opened its gates to the public in 1992 after having served
many years as a private retreat for party officials and their families
(Nádvorní 134 — walk up Trojská ul. and turn right).

TÝN CHURCH
Illustrated on page 103, this is the Old Town's most impressive Gothic
structure. See OLD TOWN SQUARE.

VYŠEHRAD ✮
*Prague 2 (2.5km/1½ miles s of the center). Map 1D3. Metro Vyšehrad (then
15min walk to upper entrance) or tram 3, 17 (to lower entrance).*

Nowhere in Prague is so steeped in patriotic lore as Vyšehrad, the
ancient fortress facing the city on a steep rock on the right bank of the
Vltava. Here the earliest Czech chiefs had their stronghold. Here Libuše
prophesied the future glory of Prague, and here, in a bath that is still
shown to tourists willing to suspend disbelief, she frolicked with her
lovers before tossing them in the river (see page 26). A few of her
medieval descendants held court here in preference to Hradčany, and

Charles IV, ever the romantic, insisted on starting his coronation rites in Vyšehrad. In 1420, a Hussite army destroyed the royal castle after one of the most epic battles of the wars of religion.

Vyšehrad had long fallen into oblivion when 19thC Romantics stumbled upon it in their search for national roots: the old tribal hearth became a symbol of the Czechs' semi-forgotten Slavic origins. Great patriotic fêtes were held on the hill; Smetana devoted the opening piece of *My Fatherland* to Vyšehrad, and set his opera *Libuše* there. In the 1880s, a National Cemetery was established in Vyšehrad to collect the graves of the nation's great and good. The little church of **Sts Peter and Paul** (kostel sv. Petra a Paula) was rebuilt in 1885–1902 into a giant Gothic pseudo-cathedral, echoing the spires of St Vitus across a distance of two miles.

An attractive park commanding an excellent **view** (★) of the river and the city now occupies the hill. The fortifications date from the time of Leopold I (1655 and 1670); of medieval Vyšehrad, only the Romanesque **Rotunda of St Martin** (Rotunda sv. Martina, c.1100) and some ruins of Charles IV's castle remain.

The real highlight of the site is the **National Cemetery** (Vyšehradský hřbitov ★), a matchless collection of *fin de siècle* funereal elegance that will delight any lover of Art Nouveau design. The Pantheon (Slavín) dates from 1889; the memorial arcade from 1890–98. Among luminaries buried in them are the leading writers (Jan Neruda, Karel Čapek), painters (Mikoláš Aleš, Alfons Mucha), musicians (Bedřich Smetana, Antonín Dvořák) and scientists of pre-World War II Czechoslovakia.

WALLENSTEIN PALACE AND GARDENS (Valdštejnská palác a zahrada) ★

Valdštejnské nám. 1, Malá strana (gardens on Letenská ul.). Map 3C3 ▨ *for gardens. Open daily May–Sept 9am–7pm. Closed Oct–Apr. Metro: Malostranská.*
The residence of the generalissimo of the Thirty Years' War (see page 30) constitutes the most outstanding example of Late Renaissance (or Early Baroque) architecture in Prague. Its garden is one of the city's gems.

> *Wallenstein was rewarded for his services with huge tracts of land in northern Bohemia, which he ruled virtually as an independent monarch; in the end he was vastly richer than his employer, the emperor. Golo Mann describes his palace as "an independent territory, a miniature kingdom amid the hustle of the city, enclosed by secondary buildings and a fortress-like garden wall."*

Wallenstein employed the Milanese Gian-Battista Marini to construct the palace (1623–29), directing him with the same manic attention to detail with which he drilled his mercenary army into the most formidable war machine on the continent. The ceiling fresco of the main hall portrays him as Mars, the god of war, riding his carriage in triumph. In the majestic **Sala Terrena** (★), or garden terrace, he is depicted in turn as Achilles, presiding over the assembled gods and heroes of the Trojan war. Hercules stands alone on the island of the artificial pond in the rear garden, pursuing the theme of self-glorification.

The garden is lined with a series of splendid bronze **statues** (★) by

Adriaen de Vries, the Mannerist genius of the court of Rudolf II who entered Wallenstein's service after the mad emperor's death; they stand on the watershed between the Renaissance ideal of harmony and the Baroque preoccupation with emotional extremes. The original statues were carted off by the Swedes during their occupation of the city in 1648, and are now in Stockholm's Drottningholm Palace. These ones are copies made at the beginning of the 20thC.

Other reminders of Wallenstein include the two peacocks of the aviary, said to be descendants of the generalissimo's own brood. A passage *(currently closed)* in the fake-grotto wall leads to his private observatory where Johannes Kepler was employed until his death in 1630. The **Riding School** (Valdštejnská jízdárna) is used for exhibitions of contemporary art. The main part of the palace, formerly occupied by government offices, is closed to the public pending restoration.

Vicinity
Valdštejnská ulice (Wallenstein Street) preserves the atmosphere of Baroque Prague in a purer fashion than any other part of the city. At #14 is the Palffy Palace (Pálffyho palác). Between it and the Kolowrat Palace (Kolovratský palác) at #10 one finds the entrance of the Ledebur Gardens (Ledeburská zahrada), a terraced park in the Italian style affording beautiful views over the city. The Fürstenberg Palace (Fürstenberský palác) at #8 serves as the Polish Embassy.

WENCESLAS SQUARE (Václavské náměstí) ✭
Nové město. Map 5D6. Metro: Můstek, Muzeum.
Prague's response to the Parisian Champs-Élysées and the Viennese Ringstrasse has invariably supplied the stage for the great events of modern Czech history. An open-air mass celebrated here on June 16, 1848 formed the high point of the nationalist revolution which served to put the Czech nation back on the European map after a break of two centuries. On August 21, 1968 the world was treated to images of Warsaw Pact tanks rolling through taunting crowds against the backdrop of St Wenceslas and the angels of the National Museum. In the week of November 17, 1989, the same backdrop surrounded the makeshift platform on which much of the spine-tingling drama of the vanishing days of communism was played out.

> *The square was in fact laid out in the 14thC as part of Charles IV's New Town, and bore the name of "Horse Market" until a more suitably patriotic title was found in 1848. Nearly all of its architecture, however, dates from the period 1885-1930.*

National Museum (Národní muzeum)
Václavské nám. 68 ☎ 26 94 51-7 ▨ Open Mon, Wed–Fri 9am–5pm; Sat–Sun 10am–6pm. Closed Tues.
The monumental dome of the National Museum looms over the entire square above an elevation at the SE end. The museum is more distin-

guished for what it symbolizes than what it contains. Its foundation in 1818 formed the first modern manifestation of Czech national sentiment in Austrian-ruled Bohemia. The current Neo-Renaissance palace–temple was designed by the architect Josef Schulz and erected in 1885–90. The magnificently ostentatious **central hall** (★) is painted with various legendary and patriotic scenes. A **Pantheon** holds the statues of 48 of the nation's most distinguished sons and daughters. There are the usual rocks, fossils and stuffed animals.

A section is devoted to the fossil collection of Joachim Barrand (1799-1883), the French geologist who used 6,000 pages to publish his studies of the Prague region. The trilobites, which he was the first to identify and name, have become a symbol of Prague's antiquity.

Wenceslas monument and Palach memorial

The statue of the patron saint of the Czechs was commissioned in 1873, but it took nearly 40 years of political quarreling before it could finally take its place at the head of Wenceslas Square. Josef Myslbek's composition shows the Good Prince surrounded by other native saints, Ludmila, Prokop, Agnes and Adalbert.

A plaque marks the place, near the statue, where young Jan Palach put himself to the torch in 1969 to protest against the invasion of his country by Soviet troops. The spontaneous shrine which was formed there during the demonstrations of November 1989 has been converted into a Memorial for the Victims of Communism, and carries a fresh commemorative pile of carnations on most days.

Palach was one of 14 philosophy students at the Charles University who drew lots to set themselves on fire successively until press freedom was restored in Czechoslovakia. He became the first to die. A crowd of 800,000 attended his funeral, during which demonstrators changed the name of the space outside the Philosophy Faculty from Red Army Square to Jan Palach Square;

in 1990 it was again renamed nám. Jana Palacha (map 4C5). In February 1989, Václav Havel was sentenced to four months in prison for attempting to place flowers at the site of Palach's self-immolation.

Around the square

Measuring 680 by 60 meters (750 by 65 yards), the *náměstí* is actually more boulevard than square. Its buildings display the ostentatious eclecticism of turn-of-the-century boulevard architecture, while the Guccis, Cartiers and McDonalds that have now almost completely taken over from the state-shop tawdriness of yore make Wenceslas Square as glamorous a Main Street as that of any modern European metropolis.

Keep an eye open for the **Grand Hotel Evropa** at #25–27, an Art Nouveau jewel from 1903–6 with a magnificently old-fashioned café at street level. The Three Graces spinning their golden thread on top of #19 date from the same period.

The **Lucerna** building at the corner of Štěpánská, enclosing a sumptuous ballroom and cinema, was designed by Václav Havel Sr., grandfather of the President. The *sgraffiti* covering the **Wiehl House** at #34 are by the ubiquitous Mikoláš Aleš.

There was an emotional homecoming when the **Bata Shoe Company** returned in 1991 to its headquarters at #6. The company was born in Czechoslovakia and grew there into the world's largest manufacturer of shoes before it was forced into exile in Canada by the Nazi takeover in 1938. A nonagenarian Tomáš Bata returned to his native country to receive the highest medal of the republic from President Havel.

Churches in Prague

More than 30 churches and chapels have been mentioned under various entries earlier in this chapter. On the following pages we list them all with their page- and cross-references, and add notes on a few additional churches of historical or artistic significance.

ASSUMPTION AND CHARLES THE GREAT   See KARLOV, page 90.

BETHLEHEM CHAPEL (Betlémská kaple)
Betlémské nám., Staré město. Map 4D5.
A place of great patriotic interest. The original Bethlehem chapel was founded in 1391 for the purpose of conducting ministry in the Czech language, and became a fountainhead of reformist agitation. Jan Hus was appointed preacher in 1402 and lived in the pastor's house next door. The chapel was pulled down in the 18thC; the communist government rebuilt it from scratch on the pretext that the 16thC revolutionary leader Thomas Müntzer had once preached from its pulpit.

EMMAUS   See CHARLES SQUARE, page 82.

HOLY CROSS CHURCH (kostel sv. Kříže)
Na příkopě. Map 5C6.
The only church in Prague in the Empire (early 19thC Neoclassical) style, built in 1816–24 for the Piarist order.

HOLY CROSS ROTUNDA (Rotunda sv. Kříže)
Ul. Karoliny Světlé, Staré město. Map 4D5.
Circular Romanesque structure from c.1100, one of Prague's oldest buildings along with the similar rotundas of **St Martin** in VYŠEHRAD and of **St Longinus** in Nové město. Completely restored in the 19thC, with the interior repainted on the basis of surviving medieval frescoes.

HOLY SPIRIT, CHURCH OF THE (kostel sv. Ducha)
Elišky Krásnohorské/Dušní, Staré město. Map 4B5.
A small Gothic church in the midst of the Jewish Quarter. Built 1346; Baroque restoration after 1689. Excellent 14thC *Pietà* inside; statue of St John Nepomuk by F.M. Brokoff outside.

ITALIAN CHAPEL   See CLEMENTINUM, page 83.

LORETO   See entry on page 95.

OUR LADY BEFORE TÝN (Týn Church)   See OLD TOWN SQUARE, page 102.

OUR LADY OF THE SNOWS (kostel Panny Marie sněžné)
Jungmannovo nám., Nové město. Map 5D6.
Founded by Charles IV in 1347 with plans to make it the largest Gothic cathedral in the city; left incomplete at the outbreak of Hussite wars, leaving an empty courtyard where the nave was supposed to be, between a colossal choir and the blank front gate. Magnificent early Baroque altar (1641) inside. Charming wine cellar and pleasant park within the adjoining Franciscan abbey.

OUR LADY OF VICTORY   See entry on page 106.

OUR LADY UNDER THE CHAIN   See MALTÉZSKÉ NÁMĚSTÍ, page 96.

SACRED HEART CHURCH (kostel Srdce Páně)
Nám. Jiřího z Poděbrad, Vinohrady (Prague 3). Map 2C4.
One of the most interesting, successful works of modern religious architecture in Prague (1933). Architect Jože Plečnik's design combines a Neoclassical pediment with Art Nouveau ornamentation and many historical references.

ST AGNES   See entry on page 107.

ST BENEDICT   See HRADČANY SQUARE, page 85.

ST CAJETAN   See NERUDOVA ULICE, page 99.

ST CATHERINE (kostel sv. Kateřiny)
*Kateřinská ul./Viničná ul., Nové město. Map **5F6**.*
The original Gothic church (1355) was destroyed during the Hussite wars and rebuilt in Baroque format in 1737–41. Now used as the sculpture depository of the Prague City Museum, it holds a fascinating collection of worn-out Baroque statues, broken fragments and architectural details. A mine for photographers.

ST CLEMENT   See CLEMENTINUM, page 83.

STS CYRIL AND METHODIUS   See CHARLES SQUARE, page 82.

ST FRANCIS SERAPHICUS   See CLEMENTINUM, page 83.

ST GALLUS (kostel sv. Havla)
*Havelská ul., Staré město. Map **5C6**.*
Built in 1232–65 in Early Gothic style; powerful Baroque facade added in 1722–23. Woodcut statues of the Evangelists by F.M. Brokoff and the impressive tomb of Karel Škréta, the prominent 17thC painter, inside. The neighborhood of Gallus-town (Gallistadt) was formed around the church by German immigrants in early 13thC. Their traditional street market lives on.

ST GEORGE'S BASILICA   See CASTLE, page 73.

ST GILES (St Aegidius; kostel sv. Jiljí)
*Husova ul., Staré město. Map **4C5**.*
An imposing Gothic structure in the Old Town (1339–71) with a simple and severe exterior. Dominican friars have been back in possession of the church and the adjoining abbey since 1991. The interior was given the Baroque treatment in 1733–35 with some splendid ceiling frescoes *(St Thomas Aquinas, The Legend of St Giles, The Founding of the Dominican Order)* by Václav V. Reiner, the 18thC painter who is buried inside. The abbey encloses a delightfully romantic **cloister** (✮), which is sometimes used for concerts.

ST HENRY (kostel sv. Jindřicha)
*Jindřišská ul. and Jeruzalémská, Nové město. Map **5D7**.*
Gothic church established in 1348–51 as the parish church of the New Town. The interior is mostly Baroque: there are several splendid 18thC altarpieces by V.V. Reiner in the chapel of the Mater Dolorosa.

ST IGNATIUS   See CHARLES SQUARE, page 81.

ST JAMES   See entry on page 108.

ST JOHN AT THE LAUNDRY   See KAMPA, page 90.

ST JOHN NEPOMUK (kostel sv. Jana Nepomuckého)
Kanovnická ul., Hradčany. Map 3C2.
The first church (1720–29) designed by Kilian Ignaz Dienzenhofer, completed in the course of a Jesuit-inspired campaign to get the 14thC martyr canonized (his sainthood was confirmed in 1729, in time for the consecration of the church). Three other churches are dedicated to St John Nepomuk in Prague, including Dienzenhofer's own masterpiece near CHARLES SQUARE (page 82).

ST JOHN OF NEPOMUK ON THE ROCK   See CHARLES SQUARE, page 82.

ST JOSEPH (kostel sv. Josefa)
Josefská ul., Malá strana. Map 4C4.
Small early Baroque church from 1686–89 with statues by Václav Jaeckel and an attractive overgrown courtyard. Used by the English-speaking Roman Catholic community of Prague.

ST LAWRENCE   See PETŘÍN, page 107.

ST MARGARET   See entry on page 108.

ST MARTIN, ROTUNDA OF   See VYŠEHRAD, page 112.

ST MICHAEL (kostel sv. Michala)
Michalská ul., Staré město. Map 4C5.
A semi-ruined Baroque church (c.1740) hidden in a courtyard off Melantrichova ul. in the Old Town. Beneath the crumbling walls are traces of details from an earlier church on the site.

ST NICHOLAS (IN THE LESSER SIDE)   See LESSER SIDE SQUARE, page 91.

ST NICHOLAS (IN THE OLD TOWN)   See OLD TOWN SQUARE, page 104.

STS PETER AND PAUL   See VYŠEHRAD, page 112.

ST ROCH   See STRAHOV ABBEY, page 110.

ST SALVATOR   See CLEMENTINUM, page 83.

ST SALVATOR (kostel sv. Salvátora)
Salvátorská, Staré město. Map 4C5.
Church of the Bohemian Brethren. It was built in 1611–14 as a Lutheran church and later acquired by the Catholics, and became the first Protestant church in Bohemia allowed under the reforms of Joseph II in the 1780s.

STS SIMON AND JUDE   See ST AGNES, page 108.

ST STEPHEN (kostel sv. Štěpána)
Štěpánská ul., Nové město. Map 5E6.
Gothic church founded by Charles IV in 1351; tower added early 15thC. Splendid interior with three altar paintings by Karel Škréta and an excellent late Gothic altarpiece *(Madonna with St Stephen)* from 1472. Across the street is the Romanesque rotunda of St Longinus (see HOLY CROSS ROTUNDA, page 116).

ST THOMAS   See LESSER SIDE SQUARE, page 94.

ST URSULA (kostel svaté Voršily)
Národní třída 8, Nové město. Map 4D5.
The Baroque church of the Ursuline sisters (convent next door) was built in 1702–4 by Marcantonio Canevale. The statue group outside (*St John Nepomuk with Cherubs,* 1747) is by Ignaz Platzer.

ST VITUS'S CATHEDRAL   See CASTLE, page 68.

Museums in Prague

The top museums — the European, Old Bohemian and Modern Czech collections of the National Gallery, and various exhibits in Hradčany — have been described in the preceding pages. Many others have been affected by revolution and privatization. The **Ethnographical Museum** in the Kinský Garden Palace in Petřín is closed pending an overhaul. The **Museum of Musical Instruments**, formerly in the Grand Prior's Palace on Maltézské nám., has been left homeless by the return of the palace's former owners. The **Museum of National Security and Interior Ministry**, which once graced the Charles Court (Karlov), is probably gone for good.

On the following pages we list all these major museums with their page- and cross-references, and add notes on a number of other museums likely to be of interest to non-Czech visitors.

BÍLEK HOUSE (Bílkův dům)
Miczkiewiczova 1, Hradčany. Map 4B4 ▨ Open May 15–Oct 15 Tues–Sun 10am–noon, 1–6pm. Closed Oct 16–May 14.
The work of František Bílek (1872–1941), one of the most creative figures of modern Czech sculpture, exhibited in the villa he designed for himself.

CZECH LITERATURE MUSEUM   See STRAHOV ABBEY, page 110.

DECORATIVE ARTS, MUSEUM OF (Uměleckoprůmyslové muzeum; UPM)
17. listopadu 2, Staré město. Map 4C5 ▨ Open Tues–Sun 10am–6pm ☎ 232 0051.

Handicrafts and applied art from the 16thC onward; substantial collection of modern posters and photographs. A highlight is the **glass collection** (★), said to be the world's largest, containing a splendid range of Bohemian crystal. The museum was formed in 1897–1901 when industrial art and crafts were in worldwide vogue. The building itself is a nice example of Art Nouveau, with some excellent tiles decorating the interior.

Further exhibitions connected with the museum take place in the neighboring **Rudolfinum** (Artists' House/Dům umělců): see also page 123.

DVOŘÁK MUSEUM (Muzeum Antonína Dvořáka)
Ke Karlovu 20, Nové město. Map 5F6 ☎231 00 51 ☒ Open Tues–Sun. Metro: I.P. Pavlova.

The composer's memorabilia are housed in **Villa Amerika**, a dainty Baroque mansion which K.I. Dienzenhofer designed for the Michna family in 1717–20. The interior of the building is decorated with 18thC frescoes by Johann Ferdinand Schor. The name of the villa refers to a restaurant that once existed on the premises. Dvořák never lived here.

Antonín Dvořák (1841-1904) was one of the two founders, along with Bedřich Smetana, of the modern Czech musical tradition. His Symphony no. 9 ("From the New World") reflects impressions of his long visit to the USA, where he worked as the director of the National Conservatory in New York. He composed large-scale choral works (such as Stabat Mater and Requiem) and ten operas (including Rusalka) under strong Wagnerian influence.

JEWISH MUSEUM   See JEWISH QUARTER, page 87.

JIRÁSEK AND ALÉŠ MUSEUM   See under STAR CHÁTEAU, page 109.

MILITARY HISTORY MUSEUM (Schwarzenberg Palace)   See HRADČANY SQUARE, page 84.

MOZART MUSEUM   See BERTRAMKA, page 64.

NÁPRSTEK MUSEUM (Náprstkovo muzeum)
Betlémské nám. 1, Staré město. Map 4D5 ☎22 76 91 ☒ Open Tues–Sun 9am–noon, 1pm–5.30pm.

Curious collection of objects from Amerindian cultures, Africa, Australia and Oceania. A branch housed in the **Liběchov Castle** in northern Bohemia *(7km/4½ miles N of MELNIK, see page 176)* holds the museum's Asian collections.

- **NATIONAL GALLERY EUROPEAN COLLECTION** (Sternberg Palace)
  See HRADČANY SQUARE, page 85.
- **NATIONAL GALLERY OLD BOHEMIAN COLLECTION** (St George's Convent)   See CASTLE, page 74.

- **NATIONAL GALLERY MODERN CZECH PAINTINGS** (St Agnes's Convent)   See ST AGNES, page 107.
- **NATIONAL GALLERY MODERN CZECH SCULPTURE**   See ZBRASLAV, page 179.
- *All exhibitions open Tues–Sun 10am–6pm. Zbraslav Château open May–Oct; closed Nov–Apr.*

See under SIGHTS A TO Z for the first three and under EXCURSIONS for the fourth. The National Gallery also mounts circulating exhibitions from its vast store of contemporary Czechoslovak art at various venues, including the **Municipal Library** (Městská knihovna) *(Mariánské nám. 1, Staré město, map 4C5* ☎ *232 25 77)*, the **Riding School of the Wallenstein Palace** (Valdštejnská Jízdárna) *(Valdštejnská 3, Malá strana* ☎ *53 68 14)* and the **Riding School of Prague Castle** (U prašného mostu) *(Hradčany* ☎ *3337 ext. 3532)*.

A permanent museum of contemporary art is planned for the Výstavyště fairgrounds in Holešovice (Prague 7).

The **Kinský Palace** (see OLD TOWN SQUARE, page 103) holds the National Gallery's collections of old and modern graphics.

NATIONAL HISTORY MUSEUM (Lobkowicz Palace)   See CASTLE, page 75.

NATIONAL MUSEUM   See WENCESLAS SQUARE, page 113.

NATIONAL TECHNICAL MUSEUM (Národní technické muzeum)
Kostelní 42, Letná (Prague 7). Map 5A6 ☎ *37 16 51* 🚅 *Open Tues–Sun 9am–5pm. Bus 125.*
The colossal main hall holds a collection of historic automobiles, a royal railway carriage used by the Habsburgs, and 12 old airplanes suspended in the air. There is a hall devoted to the history of clocks, and an astronomical collection on the second floor that includes instruments used by Tycho Brahe and Johannes Kepler. Deep under the ground level is a **model coalmine** (✸), which can be toured in guided groups (✗ *departures at 11am, 1pm, 3pm*).

POSTAGE STAMP MUSEUM (Muzeum poštovní známky)
Nové mlýny 2, Nové město. Map 5B6 ☎ *231 20 60* 🚅 *Open Tues–Sun 9am–5pm. Metro: nám. Republiky.*
Collections of Czechoslovak and European stamps; old prints. The setting is an attractive Biedermeier house with original period decorations from the 1840s.

PRAGUE CITY MUSEUM (Muzeum hlavního města Prahy)
Na poříčí, Nové město. Off map 5B7 ☎ *236 24 49* 🚅 *Open 9am–noon, 1pm–5pm. Metro: Florenc.*
Worth a visit for the fascinating papier-mâché **model of old Prague** (★ ✸) constructed by an amateur named Anton Langweil in the years 1826–37. The model reproduces on a scale of 1:480 nearly all buildings in the historic center as they appeared at that time.

SMETANA MUSEUM (Muzeum Bedřicha Smetany)
Novotného lávka 1, Staré město (near Charles Bridge). Map 4C4 ☎ *26 53 71*
✉ *Open Wed–Mon 10am–5pm.*
Mementoes of Bedřich Smetana, the Czech national composer. The museum is set in an old water-tower and commands a good view of the river Vltava.

Smetana (1824-84), who spent nearly all his life in Prague, took an active part in the nationalist ferment of the 1840s. In 1848 he established a music school in the Golden Unicorn House on the Old Town Square. In 1866 he was appointed director of the National Theater Orchestra. His operas (The Bartered Bride, Libuše, Dalibor) made use of Czech folk tunes, and he dealt with patriotic subjects in his cycle of symphonic poems entitled Ma Vlast ("My Country" — most famous title: Vltava). He became deaf at the age of 50 and later went insane.

Other sights

A selection of sights that just missed making it onto our main list, but could make it onto yours.

BABA HOUSING ESTATE
Na Babě, sídl. Baba (Prague 7). Map 1B3.
Perhaps the most original product of Modernist architecture in Prague. Designed in the early 1930s, the community of two- or three-story houses was hailed as "a moral example and a little wonder." All major Czechoslovak architects of the interwar era took part in designing it, for example, Josef Gočár (#1), Pavel Janák (#6), Oldřich Starý (#7) and Ladislav Machoň (#11).

BOTANICAL GARDEN (Botanická zahrada)
Na slupi, Nové město. Map 5F6.
A park with a history of 600 years and a correspondingly well-rooted collection of native and exotic plants. Charles IV employed a Florentine herbalist by the name of Angelo to design the garden.

HOUSE OF THE LORDS OF KUNŠTÁT AND PODĚBRADY (Dům pánů z Kunštátu a Poděbrad)
Řetězova ul., Staré město. Map 4C5 ✉ *Open Tues–Sun 10am–6pm.*
A minor architectural wonder in the Old Town. Its two subterranean stories hide some of the oldest vestiges of early-medieval Prague. They hold a permanent exhibition about George of Poděbrady, the Hussite lord who lived here until he was elected king in 1458, and spent the rest of his life devising schemes to retake Constantinople from the Turks. Upstairs is a highly regarded art gallery.

HYBERNIAN HOUSE (U hybernů)

Hybernská 1, Staré město (corner of nám. Republiky). Map 5C6.

Originally a Baroque church and convent belonging to the Irish Franciscans, converted in the early 19thC into a customs post and warehouse. Recently restored into a splendid exhibition and market hall.

PALACE OF CULTURE (Palác kultury)

5. května ul., Nusle (Prague 4). Map 2D4.

An architectural monstrosity that is sometimes shown as the pride and joy of Modern Czechoslovakia. It contains a convention center, performance halls, a café, a nightclub and a gambling casino.

RUDOLFINUM/ARTISTS' HOUSE (Dům umělců)

Nám. Jana Palacha, Staré město. Map 4C5.

A monument of the nationalist architecture of the 1880s; recently restored, it contains a concert hall and exhibition areas.

STROMOVKA

Prague 7. Map 1C3.

A vast park with overgrown woods, duck ponds, a bicycle route and the remains of what was once a great botanical garden. Rudolf II built a mile-long tunnel here to feed an artificial lake, now a swamp protected by law as a nature preserve. Next to it are the **Výstaviště Fairgrounds** (✽ formerly the Julius Fučik Park of Culture and Recreation), a fabulous complex of Victorian-era cast-iron structures erected for the Jubilee Exposition of 1891. They feature a lunapark, a sports hall used for rock concerts, a planetarium, a diorama of the battle of Lipány, a 3-D cinema and a public swimming pool.

ŽIŽKOV HILL

Prague 3. Map 2C4.

On top of the hill stands the colossal monument (1950) of the Hussite commander Jan Žižka, the half-blind giant who led an army of peasants to victory on this spot (then called Mount Vítkov) in the first great battle of the wars of religion. It is said to be the largest equestrian statue in the world. Nearby are the mausoleum of the presidents of the Republic, a World War I memorial and the **Military Museum of the Czechoslovak Army**.

Where to stay

A hard choice

Guests should announce the abandonment of their rooms before 12 o'clock, emptying the room at the latest until 14 o'clock, for the use of the room before 5 at the arrival or after the 16 o'clock at the departure, will be billed one night more.
(Notice seen on Prague hotel bedroom door)

The dilemma is the same as in other ex-socialist countries: a handful of bureaucratico-capitalistic ziggurats for rich Westerners, and a chaos of little private hotels that pop up and sink as you blink your eyes.

Privatization has worked wonders: nearly all of the country's hotels that did not already belong to the multinational giants were privatized after the revolution, in the first place by outright restitution to previous owners where these could be found, otherwise by sale to anyone who would pay. Many then pulled out of the market for a while, to return brighter, newer and friendlier after some months in the restorer's cocoon.

However, not all new owners were experienced professionals, nor did all of them have enough working capital, and a certain amount of confusion has inevitably been the outcome. New hotels of every imaginable class and hue have been opening at a furious pace. Foreign investors have poured into the market by the score, either directly or through local proxies. We have tried our best, but a really satisfactory listing of hotels in Prague must probably wait for calmer days.

Gone, largely, are the nightmare times when all hotels were owned by the state and treated their foreign customers as either sheep to shear or vermin, or both. But old habits take time to die. A number of hotels remain, as of this writing, either unrepentant or still in the hands of semi-privatized conglomerates like Interhotel or Čedok whose bureaucratic hearts beats beneath their reformed veneer. Even where that is not the case, the best efforts of a well-meaning management can be wrecked by staff trained in the old system.

As a general guideline, we suggest the following: the smaller and the less professional the establishment, the better your chances of coming away thinking of your hosts as jolly and courteous fellows.

RESERVATIONS
Finding your jolly host may not be the easiest task in the world. With 10,000 beds added since the revolution, Prague is no longer the disas-

ter area that it used to be; but the capital still falls very short of meeting demand with its total of 36,000 beds against a burgeoning inflow of tourists (or 14,000 beds in the 3-star or better class, against an estimated daily demand of 24,000).

So it makes sense whenever possible to **reserve rooms at least a couple of weeks in advance**. To go without a reservation in the July–August peak season would be suicidal; at other times you should be able to find something satisfactory after two or three attempts.

HOTEL PRICES

Costs in the top categories approach Western European levels; but more modest places cost only about half (or less) of their Western (German or British) equivalents. Officially, hotels are classified according to a system of letters and stars, though the mad pace of change seems to have made this system somewhat obsolete. Our price categories are based on the high-season cost of a **double room with bath or shower, including breakfast**.

Symbol	Category	Current price	(US dollar amount)
☐	rock bottom	up to kč450	(up to $18)
☐	inexpensive	kč450–1,000	($18–40)
☐	moderate	kč1,000–2,400	($40–96)
☐	expensive	kč2,400–5,000	($96–200)
☐	very expensive	kč5,000 and up	($200 and up)

HOTELS — MEDIUM AND BETTER

Most of the comfortable hotels are located in the immediate vicinity of **Wenceslas Square** and other parts of the **New Town**. The **Old Town** has few of them (with the notable exception of the **INTER-CONTINENTAL**) and the **Lesser Side/Hradčany** virtually none.

A series of modern big hotels can be found around the edges of the city center, at **Nusle-Michle**, lower **Vinohrady**, **Karlín**, **Holešovice** and **Dejvice**.

Our list falls into two sections: a first-choice selection, which we describe in some detail, and a more concise listing of further hotels that meet our basic criteria of quality in this category.

ALBATROS

Nábř. Ludvíka Svobody, Nové město (on the Vltava). Map 5B6 ☎*231 36 00* ☐ *75 rms* 🚇 *Metro: nám. Republiky.*
The most centrally located of Prague's three "botels," floating hotels permanently moored on the Vltava: the others are **Admirál** *(* ☎ *54 86 85)* and **Racek** *(* ☎ *42 57 93).* Cabins are clean and functional if a bit small; all are doubles, and all have showers. The clientele is mostly young, as is the crowd at the

on-board nightclub, which stays open until 3am.

AMBASSADOR / ZLATÁ HUSA

Václavské nám. 5–7, Nové město. Map 5D6 ☎*214 31 11* ☐ *to* ☐ *140 rms* 🚗 *Metro: Můstek.*
A sumptuous pair of eclectic pseudo-palaces from the early years of the century (1912), situated at the head of Wenceslas Square, possibly the liveliest spot in the city. The lobby is a good

place to stop for a coffee and cake after your boulevard stroll. The **Ambassador** has the more comfortable rooms, some with pseudo-antique furniture; **Zlatá husa** (Golden Goose) is the uglier duckling of the two, but has somewhat lower prices.

ATRIUM

Pobřežní 1, Karlín (Prague 8). Off map 5B7
☎ 284 44 44 🖷 232 37 91 ⬛ 788 rms
🆎 ⊙ ⬛ ⬛ ₫ ⇌ ♈ 🛰 ⇝ Metro:
Florenc.

The newest, biggest and brightest of Prague's luxury hotels features a vast, glass-encased atrium where all is spick, span and sterile. The Austrian company that manages it is said to have built everything with imported materials. Good but mostly unchallenging restaurants (four of them). Excellent fitness center with swimming pool, massage parlor, indoor tennis courts and saunas. Wide range of services in lobby, including car rental.

DIPLOMAT

Evropská 15, Dejvice (Prague 6). Map 1C3
☎ 331 41 11 🖷 331 41 53 ⬛ 386 rms
🆎 ⊙ ⬛ ⬛ ₫ ⇌ ⬛ ♈ 🔲 ♪ Metro:
Dejvická.

The favorite hotel of Prague's budding business community, modern, comfortable, neat and impeccably run by Austrians. The gourmet restaurant **Loreta** has the distinction of being the official caterer to the president's office. The **Belvedere** serves buffet meals including an excellent Sunday brunch *(11.30am-3pm)* and daily Japanese breakfast. **Café Klimt** plays chamber music at teatime. The **Skyline** nightclub offers a floor show from 11.30pm. Relax-center with sauna, whirlpool, exercise room and massage. Secretarial services. Nonsmoking floor. Five rooms for handicapped guests.

EVROPA

Václavské nám. 25, Nové město. Map 5D6
☎ 26 27 48 🖷 236 52 74 ⬛ 104 rms, 3 suites ⇌ ♈ Metro: *Můstek.*

Justly famed for its elegant Art Nouveau architecture, the finest on Wenceslas Square, the Evropa is equally famous for its laconic management, which has so far resisted post-revolutionary improvement. The building dates from 1903–5, the service, assuredly, from 1948–89 — you get as much of it as you are willing to pay for . . . . Glamorous "French" restaurant, beerhall, and a street level café (see page 146), which is a major tourist attraction in its own right.

FORUM

Kongresová 1, Nusle (Prague 4). Map 2D4
☎ 419 01 11 🖷 42 06 84 ⬛ 531 rms
₫ ◀€ ⇌ ♈ ⬛ 🔱 🔲 ♈ 🔲 ♪ Metro:
Vyšehrad.

A glass-encased tower in the southern district of Nusle, with an excellent if somewhat distant view of Prague's skyline. Getting your tan at the solarium of the Forum is very much the in thing in Prague these days. That apart, the facilities are fairly standard 5-star stuff: television (CNN) in all rooms, two restaurants, a café, a cocktail bar, a nightclub with dance floor, a pub with bowling alley, fitness and conference facilities, secretarial services, a hairdresser, a travel office and a car rental bureau.

INTER-CONTINENTAL

nám. Curieových 43/5, Staré město. Map 4B5 ☎ 280 01 11 🖷 231 05 00 ⬛ 395 rms 🆎 ⊙ ⬛ ⬛ ◀€ ⇌ ⬛ 🔱 🔲 ♈ ⇝ Metro: *Staroměstská.*

The Inter-Continental boasts the best location among Prague's top-class hotels: it sits by the riverbank in the heart of the Old Town, just off the Jewish Quarter and a mere hop from the Old Town Square. Half the rooms face the Vltava, with a wonderful panorama of the Castle. Another asset is the ground-floor BRASSERIE (see page 135), which serves a superb breakfast/lunch/dinner buffet in a bright, attractive hall facing the river. There are a few gripes: a small lobby with only one shop, and too few extra services. On the plus side: there's CNN television in every room, and an elegant rooftop restaurant with a tremendous view.

INTERNATIONAL

Koulova 15, Dejvice (Prague 6). Map 1C3
☎*331 91 11* ⊠*311 60 31* ⚑ ◨ *Metro: Dejvická, then tram 20 or 25.*

A monument of 1950s Stalin Gothic, the only one of its kind in Prague! The proud socialist star has now gone from the spire, but other hallmarks of the workers' regime — receptionists whose eyes glaze over when you ask for a room, uncooperative waiters who turn into the jolliest chaps in the world once you decide to buy that can of contraband caviar — remained very much alive as of this writing. Entertainments: a nightly party in the beerhall with oompah band and floor show; parties in the wine garden with Gypsy band and "typical Slovak dishes"; the 12th-floor nightclub with strip show.

METEOR – BEST WESTERN

Hybernská 6, Nové město. Map 5C7
☎*235 8517* ⊠*22 47 15* ▥ to ▥ *90 rms* ⚑ ▣ ☐ *Metro: nám. Republiky.*

A pleasant old hotel reclaimed by its pre-1948 owners and reopened after full modernization. The Baroque exterior conceals a medieval house that was already registered as an inn in 1307, serving travelers who came to town after the city gates closed at night. Guests included Joseph II, who as a youth liked to check out the humbler inns of his future empire and enjoy the company of innkeepers' nubile daughters. It has been redecorated in the ruddy neo-rustic style favored by German tourists, with a wine tavern in the original 14thC cellar, and a garden courtyard.

OBORA

Libočká 1, Horní Liboc (Prague 6). Map 1C2
☎*36 77 79* ▥ ⊞ ⧉ *Tram 1, 18 from metro Hradčanská or tram 2 from metro Dejvická.*

An attractive little hotel run by a French group who also operate an excellent gourmet restaurant (see page 141) on the premises. The hotel is set in a tidy garden beside the wooded grounds of Letohrádek Hvězda (Star Château), a former royal hunting lodge on the outskirts of Prague. Somewhat far if you are without a car, but otherwise it's a very pleasant place.

PALACE

Panská 12, Nové město (near Wenceslas Sq.). Map 5D6 ☎*219 71 11* ⊠*235 93 73* ▥ *125 rms and suites* ⧉ ⧉ *Metro: Můstek.*

Thorough remodeling in 1991 has spared few of the former Art Nouveau details, but otherwise created one of the most comfortable (and most expensive) 5-star hotels in Prague. Special rooms for "lady travelers" feature pink decor, extra mirrors and a red rose. The salad bar is justly famous for its reasonable prices, well-prepared sauces and wide variety of trimmings (take-out available).

PAŘÍŽ

U obecního domu 1, Staré město. Map 5C6
☎*236 08 20* ⊠*236 74 48* ▥ *96 rms, 2 luxury suites* ⧉ *Metro: nám. Republiky.*

The building is a flamboyant mix of Neo-Gothic and Art Nouveau, with turrets, gables, spires, baldachins, pointed arches and gargoyles galore. It was built in 1907, declared a national monument in 1984, and is featured in the Parisian Musée National d'Art Moderne as an outstanding example of Central European Jugendstil. The management struggles gamely, so far with limited success, to shake the place out of its socialist miasma. The "French" restaurant mixes sumptuous turn-of-the-century decor with Brezhnevite-period paneling.

PRAHA (HYATT)

Sušická 20, Dejvice (Prague 6). Map 1C3
☎*333 8111* ⊠*312 1757. 124 rms, 4 presidential suites* ⧉ ⧉ ⚑ ⛱ ⚑ ⧉ ⧉ *Jacuzzi, tennis courts, bowling lane, jogging track, business facilities* ◨ *Metro: Dejvická, then take taxi.*

The exclusive former retreat of the Party Central Committee and its high-level guests was reclaimed for international tourism in 1990 and came under American management soon thereafter. The curvaceous block of glass and concrete overlooks manicured lawns and a fabulous view of the city. Main assets: functional, unexaggerated luxury; quiet, park-like setting. One of the best buys in town in the upper price range.

UNGELT

Štupartská 1, Staré město (off Old Town Sq.). Map 5C6 ☎*232 04 70* [Fax]*231 95 05* ▥ *16 suites. No cards. Metro: Staroměstská.*

The only hotel in central Old Town: it occupies a wing of the Týn Court, a medieval inn/warehouse, probably the oldest building in Prague. *Ungelt* was the tax that German merchants had to pay to get their wares and themselves into the defended compound, and Germans it is who who still seem to monopolize the 16 altogether cozy, functional, domestic suites. Breakfast in courtyard.

U RAKA (Lobster)

Černinská 10, Hradčany. Map 3B2 ☎*35 14 53* [Fax]*35 30 74* ▥ *to* ▥ *5 rms* [AE] *Tram 22 from metro Malostranská.*

You cannot get any more romantic than this: a log-and-plaster house from Hansel and Gretel, fireplace and all, tucked away in a totally quiet and provincial corner of Nový svět. It is renovated beautifully, has an amicable management, and is a mere 3-minute walk from Hradčany nám. You have to reserve long in advance if you want a room in summer, but may have better luck off-season. No restaurant.

U TŘÍ PŠTROSŮ (Three Ostriches)

Dražického nám. 12, Malá strana (near Charles Bridge). Map 4C4 ☎*53 22 38* ▥ *18 rms. No cards* ▤ *Metro: Malostranská.*

Possibly the most famous hotel address in Prague: a quaint Renaissance house with a 17thC attic situated directly by the hooded towers of the Charles Bridge. Past clients have included Barbra Streisand and Miloš Forman, and you have to wait a long, long time before you can join their illustrious company. Expensive gourmet restaurant downstairs.

ZLATÁ HUSA See AMBASSADOR.

MORE HOTELS — MEDIUM AND BETTER

- **Alcron** Štěpánská 40, Nové město. Map **5D6** ☎24 57 41 ▥ ▤ Metro: Muzeum. A 1930s building with marble staircases and wood-paneled dining room. Own parking garage.
- **Atlantic** Na poříčí 9, Nové město. Map **5C7** ☎231 85 12 [Fax]232 60 77 ▥ 60 rms ▤ ♈ ⚅ Metro: nám. Republiky. Modern and centrally located, with reasonable facilities.
- **Club Hotel Průhonice** In Průhonice, 16km (10 miles) SE of the center ☎643 65 01 [Fax]643 67 73 ▥ 100 rms. Čedok's new resort hotel, with a wide range of outdoor and indoor sport facilities (ten tennis courts, squash, bicycle rental, horses).
- **Esplanade** Washingtonova 19, Nové město (off Wenceslas Sq.). Map **5D7** ☎22 60 56 [Fax]231 05 00 ▥ 42 rms ▤ Metro: Muzeum. Strained elegance, sumptuous decor, excellent food and highly professional staff.
- **Flora** Vinohradská 121, Vinohrady (Prague 3). Map **2C4** ☎27 42 41 ▥ Metro: Jiřího z Poděbrad. Within short distance of the center. Remodeled in 1991.
- **Golf** Plzeňská 215, Motol (Prague 5). Map **1C2** ☎52 32 51 [Fax]52 21 53 ▥ ▤ Metro: Anděl, then tram 4,7 or 9. Located on the outskirts of the city near the main western highway. Features a golf course that until recently was the only one in Prague.
- **Hybernia** Hybernská 24, Nové město (near Masarykovo train station). Map **5C7** ▥ Metro: nám. Republiky. Although sleazy outside, it is acceptable inside.

- **Jalta**   Václavské nám. 45, Nové město. Map **5D6** ☎26 55 41 ☒26 53 47 ▥▥ Metro: Muzeum. Central location on Wenceslas Square. A highbrow lobby in an ugly 1960s building. Good place to meet old Party stalwarts or dream up a Cold War novel.
- **Karl-inn**   Šaldova 54, Karlín (Prague 8). Map **2C4** ☎232 25 51 ☒232 80 30 ▥▭ ⇶ Metro: Křižíkova. Modern, neat, functional hotel not far from the center.
- **Koruna**   Opatovická 16, Nové město. Map **4E5** ☎29 39 33 ▥▥ 20 rms. Metro: Karlovo nám. Clean, pleasant, and a stone's throw from the oldest beerhall in Prague.
- **Opera**   Těšnov 13, Nové město. Map **5B7** ☎231 56 09 ▥▭ 46 rms. Metro: Florenc. Elegant 19thC mansion at the edge of a busy highway. Excellent breakfast.
- **Parkhotel**   Veletržní 20, Holešovice (Prague 7). Map **2C4** ☎380 71 11 ☒38 20 10 ▥▥ 383 rms. Metro: Vltavská. Glass and concrete 1960s building. Trained and professional staff.
- **Pyramida**   Bílohorská 24, Střešovice (Prague 6), near Hradčany. Map **1C3** ☎311 32 41 ▥▭ 300 rms. No cards. Bus 132, 217. Socialist efficiency at its best: no frills, few smiles, good price. Huge glass block with park and sport facilities.
- **Splendid**   Ovenecká 33, Holešovice (Prague 7). Map **2C4** ☎37 33 51 ▥▭ 35 rms. Tram 1, 8, 25, 26. Comfortable small hotel in a pleasant street by the Stromovka Park.

HOTELS — INEXPENSIVE

Few of these existed before the revolution; dozens have opened since. You will look in vain for a comprehensive, or even extensive, listing. The accommodation agencies that clutter Prague's streets (see page 130) are very often your only way of reaching them. Expect to shop around, since most agencies hold a thin portfolio — often a single pension or short-rental property or a few private apartments.

None of the following accepts credit cards.

ADRIA

Václavské nám. 26, Nové město. Map **5D6** ☎*236 04 72* ▥▭ *Metro: Muzeum.*
The lovely 18thC facade promises more than it delivers. None of the rooms has private bath or shower, and there's no restaurant. In a conveniently central location.

AXA

Na poříčí 40, Nové město (near bus terminal). Map **5C7** ☎*232 44 67* ▥▭ *154 rms. Metro: Florenc.*
An inexpensive hotel favored by students and backpackers. The spartan rooms may be constructed of plywood and plastic, but the convenient location and helpful personnel are evident pluses.

BERÁNEK

Bělehradská 110, Vinohrady (Prague 2). Map **5E7** ☎*25 45 44* ▥▭ *200 rms. Metro: I.P. Pavlova.*
No frills, but very close to Wenceslas Square, and the new owner promises improvements. No reservations are taken, so in an emergency there may be a good chance of finding a room here.

EUROKONTAKT (TESLA)

Drahobejlova 17, Karlín (Prague 9). Map **2C4** ☎*683 12 07* ▥▭ *40 rms. Metro: Českomoravská.*
An apartment house hastily converted into a hotel, run with few hitches by a young and well-meaning staff. All rooms are in suites of two or three sharing a bath, WC and kitchen. Breakfast served.

POD LIPKAMI
Pod lipkami 8, Prague 5. Off map 3C1
☎ *52 20 28* ▥ *11 rms. Metro: Anděl,*
then bus 132, 191 or 217.
A small private hotel in a quiet suburban area that is not far from the center of the city. All rooms have bath, telephone and TV.

SOLIDARITA
Soudružská 14, Strašnice (Prague 10). Map
2C5 ☎ *77 80 41* ▥ *310 rms. Metro:*
Strašnická.
This enormous tower block is a well-

known destination for the intercontinental backpacking brigade. Lively night scene with singing, dancing, and horseplay in the corridors.

U BLAŽENKY
U Blaženky 1, Smíchov (Prague 5, near
Bertramka). Map 1D3 ☎ *53 82 66* ▥
13 rms. Metro: Anděl, then taxi or steep
15min walk.
An attractive 19thC villa in a quiet residential street on a wooded hill. It is run by a friendly couple who will go to great lengths to cater to your needs.

ACCOMMODATION AND ROOM SERVICES

Literally hundreds of these now invade Prague's streets, bus and train stations, highway approaches and newspaper pages. Their services are generally honest and well-meaning, if not always efficient. Their portfolio ranges from private rooms (with or without resident family), through dormitory and youth hostel beds to inexpensive hotels. Most of these hotels turn out to be perfectly acceptable places if you don't pay too much attention to the ad hoc character of the arrangements.

Finding a place in the historic center is everybody's dream, but it's not an easily fulfilled one — it would be a matter of luck in Staré město, a miracle in Malá strana. In the outer districts, the best guideline is to aim to stay within walking distance of the center, or at least near a metro stop. The best districts generally are Vinohrady (Prague 2/3), Nusle, Michle (Prague 4), Dejvice and Bubeneč (Prague 6).

A room for two will typically cost about kč500 (US$20) in the center and kč400 (US$16) in the outer districts. A dorm bed can go as low as kč150 (US$6).

ČEDOK
Panská 5, Nové město (off Na příkopě, near
main Čedok HQ) ☎ *22 56 57* ▨ *236 10*
62. Open Mon–Fri 8am–9pm; Sat–Sun
8am–4pm. Metro: Můstek.
The first place to go to if you are in Prague without a hotel room. The office lists currently available space in all of Prague's bona fide hotels, and also brokers a wide range of private rooms. Praguers who have room to offer but want to save the Čedok fee can generally be found on the sidewalk outside.

CKM
At Žitná 9, Nové město, map 5E6 ☎ *29 99*
49, metro Karlovo nám, open Mon–Sat
8am–6pm; and at Jindřišská 28, map 5D6,

metro Hlavní nádr. or nám. Republiky.
A specialist in student accommodation. The Žitná office lists available spaces in youth hostels and cheap hotels. The Jindřišská office offers beds in student dormitories. Student IDs and IYH cards can be purchased here at very low prices.

PRAGOTUR
U obecního domu 2, Staré město. Map 5C6
☎ *232 22 05–16. Metro nám. Republiky.*
The tourist information office of the city government runs a private room service as popular as that of Čedok.

PRAGUE SUITES
Through American Hospitality Center, Malé

*náměstí 14 (off Old Town Sq.). Map **4C5***
☎*26 93 84* ⨳*26 61 79. Open daily*
10am–10pm. Metro: Staroměstská.
Fully furnished apartments with hotel
services (24-hour desk clerk, room service, laundry, food-shopping service)

for foreign businessmen or individual
visitors, at prices that range up to
US$180. The American Hospitality Cen-
ter desk also keeps an extensive list of
rooms available in private homes in the
US$15–20 price range.

A SELECTION OF PRIVATE ACCOMMODATION AGENCIES

- **All Tours**   Pod Viktorkou 5, Malešice (Prague 10). Map **2C5** ☎77 10 78.
  Metro: Želivského, or bus 133 from metro Florenc.
- **AR Tour**   Karolíny Světlé 9, Staré město. Map **4D5** ☎ and ⨳235 83 89.
  Open 9am–9pm. Advance booking of better hotels and quality apartments in
  the city. Metro: Národní třída.
- **Arstour**   Na Švihance, Vinohrady (Prague 2). Off map **5D4** ☎275 82 94.
  Metro: Jiřího z Poděbrad. Reservation agency for a range of top hotels.
- **AVE**   In Hlavní nádraží (Central train station). Map **5D7** ☎236 25 60 ⨳236
  29 56. Open May to September 6.30am–2am; October to April 6.30am–
  10.30pm. Metro: Hlavní nádraží.
- **B & B Agentura** 28. října 9, Nové město. Map **5D6** ☎28 82 20 ⨳26 69 79.
  Open 8am–7pm. Metro: Můstek. Cheap lodgings in pensions and student
  dorms.
- **B & B Association**   Legerova 2, Vinohrady (behind the National Museum).
  Map **5E7** ☎54 93 44 ⨳54 78 06. Metro: Muzeum.
- **City of Prague**   Haštalské nám. 13, Staré město. Map **5B6** ☎231 02 02
  ⨳231 40 76. Open 9am–9pm. Metro: nám. Republiky. Large portfolio of
  properties.
- **OK Tours**   Na zámecké 6, Nusle (Prague 6). Map **2D4** ☎43 70 91 ⨳43
  14 39. Metro: Pražského povstáné, then tram 24.
- **Top Tour**   Rybná 3, Staré město. Map **5C6** ☎229 65 26 ⨳232 08 60. Open
  Monday to Friday 9am–8pm, Saturday to Sunday 11am–7pm. Metro: nám.
  Republiky.

CAMPING

Contact Čedok for a complete list of camping sites. All sites provide
simple bungalows for two or four people at very low prices. The best
include the following.

- **Camping Troja**   Trojská 171 (Prague 7). Map **2B4** ☎84 28 33. Near the
  Troja Château in a pleasant garden suburb.
- **Caravancamp**   Plzeňská, Motol (Prague 5). Map **1C2** ☎52 16 32. On the
  western approach route.
- **Na Vlachovce**   Rudé armády, Libeň (Prague 8). Map **2B4** ☎84 12 90. Near
  the northern highway. Unusual accommodation in disused beer barrels. Open
  April through October.
- **Sportcamp**   V podhájí, Podolí (Prague 4). Map **1D3** ☎52 18 02. Near the
  Vltava on the southern approach route. Open March 23 to end October.

Eating and drinking

Dining out

Many of Prague's eating and drinking places are as ancient, cozy and whimsical as the city itself. A Gothic cellar is pretty much *de rigueur*, and any tavern that wasn't a century old when Columbus set sail for the Indies is considered a piffling greenhorn.

The favorite location is under the ground. In the dark decades of communism, these dens supplied the best refuge from the public world of lies, shortages and official pettiness: Praguers who wore a mask of cynicism or indifference all day long turned into the jolliest fellows in the world as soon as they descended into their favorite burrow, where they could drink, sing, revel, philosophize and debate politics with a frankness that would startle the uninitiated foreigner.

A night in the pub was once essential sightseeing in communist Prague, a far more interesting cultural trip than weeks of wandering about the city: it was where a visitor met the "real" Czechoslovakia. Today, economic upheaval has driven eating and pubbing out beyond the means of most Czech wage-earners, and chances are that more than half of your fellow guests at any good mid-town tavern or restaurant will be tourists on the lookout for the "Czech experience." At popular beerhalls like U FLEKŮ and U KALICHA you may find enough roaring Germans to fill a small town. This has brought its advantages (more smiles, less smoking); but for the true cultural experience, the working-class suburbs may be your only choice left.

A *restaurace* (restaurant) is by no means the only place to go dining. A *vinárna* (wine tavern) will usually serve almost as wide a selection of hot dishes as an ordinary restaurant, while a *pivnice* (pub, beerhall; also called *hostinec* or *hospoda*) will have a couple of traditional meat platters to accompany the brew. A *kavárna* (café) specializes in sweet pastries but also carries a few warm meals or sandwiches on the menu. For someone in a hurry, an *automat* (snack bar, cafeteria) will serve fine. Then again, there's McDonald's.

The ubiquitous *U*, incidentally, is Czech for the French *chez* or the German *zu* — it translates awkwardly into English (at? by? at the sign of?). By old Middle European tradition, most inns and taverns (as well as shops and houses, and even some streets) are known by a house sign, which often originates all the way back in the Middle Ages. Thus, you find *U zlaté hrušky* at the sign of the Golden Pear, while *U malířu* translates as *Chez le peintre*.

CZECH CUISINE

Forget yogurt-and-Perrier: the health fad has not yet reached Prague. A decent Czech meal involves a robust piece of pork with much gravy, served with pickled cabbage and the gooey globs of starch known as *knedlíky* (dumplings). Potatoes help; a tankard of beer is essential. You are supposed to leave the table feeling hearty, not healthy. Tasty it generally is, but to call it "varied and imaginative" would be stretching the point.

Best of all are the various cold and stuffed **meats**, a product of the centuries of cohabitation with the Teutonic element. Prague ham *(šunka)* is excellent, and different sorts of sausage *(párek, vuřt, špekáčky)* grace restaurant menus and street vendors' carts. The finest salami *(salám)*, however, comes from Hungary or Romania.

Main courses consist mainly of variations on the theme of a steak (usually pork or beef, less often veal, boar or venison; very exceptionally — for example, at U ZLATÉ STUDNĚ — you may find mutton) topped with sauce and accompanied by dumplings. A characteristic delicacy is the *svíčková*, marinaded beef tenderloin in a sour gravy (not to be confused with *svíčkové řezy*, the same thing minus the marinade and sauce).

Dumplings come in an infinite variety of guises. Some are served as a savory like the ubiquitous sliced *houskové knedlíky* (made from wheat flour and slightly stale bread rolls) or the smaller round *špekové knedlíky* (with bacon), and some as a sweet, filled with fruit or jam, like *bramborové* (grated potato) or *tvarohové* (cottage cheese). Some, like *kynuté* (leavened) or *krupicové* (semolina), can be either savory or sweet. Fruit dumplings *(ovocné knedlíky)* are eaten with sugar, melted butter, and cottage cheese or ground poppy seeds: the sinful *švestkové knedlíky s tvarohem* (plum dumplings with cottage cheese) feature on many tourist menus. How well dumplings are made is what seems to set a good restaurant apart from a mere dump in the eyes of a Prague gourmet, although to a foreigner the distinctions may seem a bit academic.

Seafood remains the underdog of Czech cuisine. Trout *(pstruh)* is usually the only fish available except at Christmas, when enormous quantities of carp *(kapr)* find their way to Prague's tables. Sensing a market slot, a number of Nordic suppliers have lately made a splash by flooding the market with ocean fish, and Prague is probably the only city in the world now besides Reykjavik where Icelandic restaurants are almost as commonplace as Chinese ones.

Soups *(polévky)* are generally excellent, and *dršťková*, or beef tripe soup, one of the best of the lot. A favorite among **snacks** is *bramborák*, a potato pancake laced with garlic. *Smaženy sýr*, or fried cheese, often accompanies your glass of red wine in a *vinárna:* try a bland variety like *eidam* or *hermelín* (a sort of edam and brie, respectively), or go for the malodorous *olomoucké sýrečky* if you like more stimulating sensations.

DRINKS

Beer is the quaff of tradition in Bohemia, the country that brought you the Pilsner and the (real) Budweiser. Drinking beer is subject to elaborate ritual, of which you can read more below under the heading **BEER-HALLS AND PUBS.**

The best **wines** are imported from Moravia and Slovakia, with those originating in the grape-growing regions of Břeclav (South Moravia) and Pezinok (West Slovakia) considered the very best. Bohemia grows some wine too, but with notable exceptions like those of Mělník, they tend to be generally inferior stuff.

Rulandské, also known as Burgundy, is the noblest and driest of the **red wines**. *Vavřinecké* is a ruby-colored red with a velvety flavor that carries a hint of dried plums. **White wines** tend to be excessively sweet even when the label proclaims them as dry as blotting paper. One of the best is *Ryzlink rýnský,* a delicate wine with a faint muscat aroma that goes well with cold entrees and fish. The *Bzenecká lipka* is considered the pinnacle of the Ryzlink family. *Rulandské* (white) is a semi-dry Burgundy with a full-bodied flavor. *Neuburské* sports a full, harmonious, delicately spicy flavor. *Müller-Thurgau* is green when young and yellower in maturity, with a light flavor that goes well with fish and veal. *Veltlínské zelené* is the commonest variety of white wine, with a characteristic light green color and a full flavor that hides a pleasant bite.

The local **sparkling wines** *(sekt)* are extremely cheap and reasonably drinkable. *Burčák,* the freshly fermented wine that is still half grapejuice, makes its appearance on street stands starting in August — beware: it is not as innocent as it looks and tastes! *Becherovka,* a herbs-and-spices **liqueur** that is consumed as a digestive and a hangover cure, is made in the town of Karlovy Vary. *Slivovice,* the Moravian–Slovakian **plum brandy**, and *borovička,* a type of **gin** made of juniper berries, are the favorite hard liquors of a land where Scotch was until a few years ago the exclusive privilege of party moguls and mafia chiefs.

PRICES AND TIPPING

With average monthly wages running at around kc4,000, few Czechs today can afford a restaurant meal. However, despite spectacular price rises that have driven up the real (dollar) cost of a meal fourfold in two years, Prague is still cheapville by Western standards. The following price categories apply to an **average meal for one, including beverage** (wine or beer, where available), **service charge and tips**.

Symbol	Category	Current price	(US dollar amount)
▯	rock bottom	up to kč100	(up to $4)
▯	inexpensive	kč100–250	($4–10)
▯	moderate	kč250–400	($10–16)
▯	expensive	kč400–800	($16–32)
▯	very expensive	kč800 and up	($32 and up)

A tip of 10–15 percent is customary in better restaurants; in others, leaving the small change will do. In most places the bill is added up in front of you and you are expected to tell the waiter or waitress how much you intend to pay *in total,* including the tip.

All of the following establishments are open daily for lunch and dinner unless otherwise noted.

RESTAURANTS — TRADITIONAL

With little more than a hundred restaurants in central Prague to serve a deluge of tourists, you should never count on being able to get a table at the snap of your finger. **Reservations are essential, and best made at least a day in advance.** It would be foolhardy to go out without a booking in the peak season of July and August; you may have luck at other times of the year, but then again you may not, and it is much easier to phone ahead than to have to tackle Prague's trained and merciless restaurant guards.

The service can be smooth and classy in the better restaurants, and you will be treated with a smile so long as you don't go in sneakers, fail to check your coat at the cloakroom, order the wrong wine, pour your beer into another glass (for some reason considered a sacrilege in the case of draft beer), fail to eat your dumplings, etc. Elsewhere old socialist-country habits persist, if to an ever-diminishing extent — in other words, stay calm but firm if you are ignored, forgotten, or asked to revise your order for the third time. Privatization, however, has been breeding customer-friendliness faster than mass tourism can erode it, and very soon the old jokes about Prague waiters will perhaps be as passé as May Day parades and thought police.

We start with our selection of Prague's best traditional restaurants, and follow with a concise listing of other adequate-to-commendable representatives in this category.

BRASSERIE IN THE HOTEL INTER-CONTINENTAL

nám. Curieových 5, Staré město. Map 4B5 ☎280 01 11 ▥ (lunch) ▥ (dinner) AE ⊡ ⊙ ▥ ◁€ *Metro: Staroměstská.*
This is our favorite among the eating establishments offered by the top-notch hotels. The setting is a bright and cheerful hall full of plants, directly above the Vltava. The food: all-you-can-eat breakfast, lunch and dinner buffets of consistently high quality and enormous variety, with a judicious mix of local and international favorites. The service is courteous, and a table can almost always be found without prior reservation. Good value for money despite the high price range. A more formal restaurant exists on the top floor of the hotel. See also INTER-CONTINENTAL on page 126.

LOBKOVICKÁ VINÁRNA

Vlašská 17, Malá strana. Map 3C3 ☎53 01 85 ▥ AE ⊙ ▥ *Metro: Malostranská.*
Polyxena von Lobkowicz brought the Baby Jesus to Prague, Benigna Catharina funded the Loreto sanctuary, and Georg Christian von L. established, about 100 years ago, this princely restaurant/tavern in a corner of his palace to help push wines from the family wineries in Mělník. The palace is now the German Embassy, and a part of the restaurant seems permanently reserved for diplomatic regulars. The fare is traditional gourmet with such classics as *beefsteak à la L.*, which comes under a mountain of tartar sauce, melted cheese and cream, and *pears L.*, which consists of layers of biscuit, ice cream and pears flambé in liqueur.

MYSLIVNA (Forest Hut) ▥

Jagellonská 21, Vinohrady (Prague 3). Map 2C4 ☎27 62 09 AE ⊡ ⊙ ▥ *Metro: Jiřího z Poděbrad or Flora.*
Traditional wild-game restaurant with a kitschy but not unpleasant rustic decor and an ever-jolly atmosphere that can be contagious even if you don't speak the language. On the menu: deer ragout, pheasant in old Bohemian style, wild duck stuffed with apples, hare in cream sauce, quail flambé. Good Moravian wines.

OPERA GRILL
Karoliny světlé 35, Staré město. Map 4D5
☎26 55 08 ▥ Closed Sat–Sun ▣ ▣
▣ ▥ Metro: Národní třída.
An intimate *vinárna*/restaurant of only
24 seats, furnished with comfortable arm-
chairs and decorated with Baroque porcelain and ancient clocks. The gourmet
fare is highly regarded (veal chops with
Cumberland sauce and almonds au gratin,
chicken à la pheasant, delectable pep-
per steaks). Past delectators have included Kim Novak, Yehudi Menuhin
and Shirley Temple Black, who held
here her farewell party as US ambassador in Prague.

U ČERVENÉHO KOLA (Red Wheel) ▥
Anežská 2, Staré město. Map 5B6 ☎231
89 41 ▣ ▥ Metro: Staroměstska.
The ultimate in fashion for the young,
upwardly mobile and trendy in post-
revolution Prague — on a par with wearing Hugo Boss suits in pastel colors,
reading the Czech edition of *Playboy*
and voting for Václav Klaus. The restaurant is set in a charming old house
near the convent of St Agnes. The food
stands out by its quality as well as quan-
tity, and you can order your steaks by
weight. Outdoor section in summer.

U LABUTÍ (Swans)
Hradčanské nám. 11, Hradčany. Map 3C2
☎53 94 76 ▥ to ▥ Bistro 10am–9pm,
Sat–Sun 10am–7pm; restaurant 7pm–1am
▣ ▣ ▣ ▥ Metro: Malostranská, then
tram 22 northbound.
Exclusive restaurant set in a former stable,
with real troughs running through the
middle. The front hall and the bistro–
snackbar are for ordinary mortals who
have just toured the Castle or the National Gallery, while the "Club" is where
you might go if you are dining with a
government minister. Goose liver with
ham and almonds, or deer shank in
madeira sauce, is what the chef recom-
mends, and what better way to end
your meal than an ice cream "Swansong"? Outdoor section in summer.

U MECENÁŠE (Maecenas; Patron)
Malostranské nám. 10, Malá strana. Map
3C3 ☎53 38 84 ▥ Closed Sat ▣ ▣
▣ ▥ Metro: Malostranská.
The invasion of tour groups has introduced imported beer, pushy waiters
and flashy desserts, but this is still a
place to cherish among Prague's old-
style wine taverns. The cellar and two
small rooms are filled with the memorabilia of 400 years in business. One
table is kept for Mydlář the Executioner
(see pages 100–1), who earned a lifetime pass to U Mecenáše for hanging,
drawing, quartering and beheading the
leaders of the 1618 rebellion in the Old
Town Square: see his signature on the
wall, dated 1626. Moravian wines (Pavlovice and Mikulov), and some of the
best steaks in Prague.

U PAVOUKA (Spider)
Celetná 17, Staré město. Map 5C6 ☎231
87 14 ▥ Closed Sun ▣ ▣ ▥ ♪ Metro:
nám. Republiky.
Possibly the coziest of Prague's underground cellar-restaurants. The Gothic
vault seems to date from the 14thC;
before the war, it is said to have housed
the most elegant house of pleasure in
town. Things are more sedate now, re-
volving around five differents sorts of
steak, various duck and veal dishes, and
Moravian wines from Velké Pavlovice.
The bistro upstairs is likely to have seats
when everything else in the Old Town
seems full.

U PĚTI KRÁLŮ (Five Kings)
Vyšehradská 9, Nové město. Map 4F5
☎20 27 27 ▥ ♪ Dinner only. Closed
Sat–Sun. Metro: Karlovo nám. or tram 18,
24.
One of the first private restaurants to
open in Prague, and it has survived the
flood well. The predominantly native
clientele (despite highish prices) is a
sure sign of quality. The English/Czech
menu lists a dozen artful variations on
classic themes (pork tenderloin with apple
and caramel sauce, veal medallions and
chopped onion wrapped in bacon with
green olives and wine sauce), as well as
"meager meals" (a.k.a. vegetarian dishes).
Speedy, unobsequious service, dim lights,
piano music.

U RADNICE (Town Hall)

Malé nám. 2, Staré město (off Old Town Sq.). Map *4C5* AE ⊙ ⊙ VISA Metro: Staroměstská.

It used to be a low-class pub before privatization, dirty, dingy and full of men in workmen's overalls who came in for their morning rum as soon as the place opened at 7am. Privatization has turned it into a rather elegant restaurant with good food and excellent beer, with prices that are reasonable enough to attract Czechs as well as tourists. The location is very central, and it has an attractive garden in summer.

U SCHNELLŮ

Tomášská 4, Malá strana. Map *3C3* ☎*53 20 04* ▥ to ▥ No cards. Metro: Malostranská.

A brewery-pub founded by Mr Schnell in 1787, which served its own brew until a hundred years ago. The house now combines a traditional beerhall (Pilsner Urquell 12°) with a middle-brow restaurant offering hearty portions but no culinary adventures.

U STARÉ SYNAGÓGY (Old Synagogue)

Pařížská 17, Staré město. Map *4C5* ☎*231 85 52* ▥ AE ⊙ ⊙ VISA ⚑ Garden in summer. Metro: Staroměstská.

A tradition-drenched little place in the heart of the Jewish Quarter: it has no culinary pretensions, but huge portions of honest-to-God Bohemian food, old-fashioned service and lots of Pilsner Urquell 12° are served. Tourists now descend on it like a plague of locusts, and no one can guess how much of the old ambience will survive. Live music accompanies dinner.

U TŘÍ PŠTROSŮ (Three Ostriches)

Dražického nám. 12, Malá strana (near Charles Bridge). Map *4C4* ☎*53 22 38* ▥ ⊙ VISA Metro: Malostranská.

This is a small, exclusive restaurant which combines Czech classics (pork chops, sauerkraut, dumplings) with "international" dishes, and serves both wine (from South Moravian Znojmo) and beer (Pilsener Urquell). It is in a lovely location, but is somewhat over-whelmed by tourists. Reservations are essential. See page 128 for the hotel of the same name.

U ZLATÉ HRUŠKY (Golden Pear)

Nový Svět 3, Hradčany. Map *3B2* ☎*53 11 33* ▥ AE ⊙ VISA Metro: Malostranská, then tram 22 northbound.

An "insider's" restaurant quietly tucked away in the most romantic back alley of Hradčany, furnished with cozy old-rustic furniture and famous for its amiably professional staff. The multilingual menu stresses game dishes, including the best deer steaks you are likely to come across in Prague. Other highlights are the goose-liver paté and the duck thighs with rice and peas. Try to leave room for the dessert pancakes (*livance*). Reservations are essential.

U ZLATÉ STUDNĚ (Golden Well)

Karlova 3, Staré město. Map *4C5* ☎*22 05 93* ▥ AE ⊙ ⊙ VISA Metro: Staroměstská.

This is an all-time Prague favorite: a historic townhouse (medieval interior, Renaissance gable and Baroque frills) lying midway between the Charles Bridge and Square, divided into numerous dining rooms that range from intimate to tiny. The menu holds no surprises other than the unusual stress on mutton and the occasional suckling pig on the spit, but the *knedlíky* could almost convince a determined dumpling-hater. It has a commendable selection of wines.

VALDŠTEJNSKÁ HOSPODA

Tomašská 16, Malá strana. Map *3C3* ☎*53 61 95* ▥ AE ⊙ ⊙ VISA Metro: Malostranská.

One of the stars of old-fashioned Czech cuisine, though sadly turning into a tourist attraction full of package groups. The specials may include such delicacies as homemade game paté, wild boar with rosehip sauce, and rabbit in creamy sauce. The name refers to the neighboring palace of Albrecht von Wallenstein, the 17thC warlord who was famous in his day for holding 100-course feasts.

MORE RESTAURANTS — TRADITIONAL

- **Emir Hoffmann TV Věž**   Mahlerovy sady 1, Žižkov (Prague 3). Map **2C4** ☎27 81 25 ▥ ◁€ Metro: Jiřího z Poděbrad. Modern restaurant on top of the futuristic TV tower. Vertiginous view, routine fare, flat beer.

- **Hanavský pavilón**   Letenské sady (Prague 7). Map **4B4** ☎32 57 92 ▥ No cards ◁€ ▤ ♥ from 9pm. Metro: Malostranská. Unexceptional food, but a 1,001 Nights building with a panorama to match. Try their *palačinka Praha*, a pancake coated with chocolate and filled with orange sherbet.

- **Lví dvůr** (Lion's Den)   Pražský hrad, Hradčany (near the Powder Bridge, opposite the palace riding school). Map **3C3** ☎53 53 89 ▥ Metro: Malostranská, then tram 22 northbound. Pleasant old *vinárna*/restaurant with a garden in summer. Reservations necessary.

- **Mucha**   Melantrichova 5, Staré město (off Old Town Sq.). Map **4C5** ▥ to ▥ ▣ ▨ Metro: Staroměstská. Elegant, well-lit space with stained-glass roof and Art Nouveau murals. Traditional menu.

- **Na rybárně** (Fisherman)   Gorazdova 17, Nové město. Map **4F5** ☎29 97 95 ▥ to ▥ Open Monday to Friday 4pm–1am. Metro: Karlovo nám. Regarded as the best seafood restaurant in town and autographed by an amazing roster of rock stars, prime ministers and film actresses. Be warned: prices on the menu are per 100 grams of fish!

- **Nebozízek**   Petřínské sady, Malá strana (at the first stop of the Petřín funicular) ☎53 79 05 ▥ Closed Monday in winter ◁€ Metro: Malostranská, then tram 12 or 22 southbound. The fabulously romantic setting on Petřín Hill more than compensates for the unexceptional selection of dishes on offer. Modern-style interior (reservations essential), summer terrace (no reservations taken), and garden.

- **Obecní dům** (Municipal House)   nám. Republiky 5, Staré město. Map **5C6** ☎231 12 68 ▥ No cards ♪ ♥ Metro: nám. Republiky. Splendid Art Nouveau interior, good steaks, mediocre service. Huge place, so seats are almost always available. Raucous variety show at night. The café of the same name (see page 146) is across the hall.

- **Pelikán**   Na příkopě 7. Map **5C6** ☎22 07 82 ▥ to ▥ ▣ ◑ ◐ ▨ Metro: Můstek. Old-style luxury with crystal chandeliers and real silver cutlery. Three private dining rooms *(separés)* for VIP guests.

- **U čížků**   Karlovo nám. 34, Nové město. Map **4E5** ▥ ☎29 88 91. Metro: Karlovo nám. A new restaurant offering traditional atmosphere plus traditional fare of the highest quality. Their Moravian sampler plate is a good introduction to Czech regional cuisine.

- **U David** (David)   Tržistě 21, Malá strana. Map **3C3** ☎53 93 25 ▥ ▣ Metro: Malostranská, then tram 22, 12 to Malostranské nám. A diminutive restaurant with a cozy atmosphere on a cobblestone street near the US Embassy. A limited menu serves foodstuffs imported from Germany.

- **U Lorety**   Loretánské nám. 8, Hradčany. Map **3C2** ☎53 60 25 ▥ Closed Mon ◐ ▨ Metro: Malostranská, then tram 22 northbound. Elegant restaurant serving tourist groups and employees of the nearby Foreign Ministry in equal measure. Good wine selection. Outdoor section in summer.

- **U pastýřky** (Shepherdess)   Bělehradská 15, Vinohrady (Prague 2). Map **5F7** ☎43 40 93 ▥ Metro: I.P. Pavlova, or tram 6, 11. Slovakian country food, resident gypsy band and free-flowing wine create a very cheery atmosphere in this suburban restaurant. Reservations essential.

- **U Piaristů**   Panská 1. Nové město. Map **5C6** ☎22 36 03 ▥ Closed Sun. Metro: Můstek. *Gemütlich* middle-brow restaurant set in the sacristy of the former Piarist monastery.

- **U sloupů** (Pillars)   Lucemburská 11, Vinohrady (Prague 3). Map 2C4 ☎22 14 57 ▥ Closed Monday lunch ⒶⒺ Metro: Jiřího z Poděbrad. Family-style restaurant in a quiet residential area. Bohemian specialities, good *knedlíky*, Moravian wines, Pilsener beer.
- **U zlatého jelena** (Golden Stag)   Celetná 11, Staré město. Map 5C6 ☎26 85 95 ▥ Closed Saturday to Sunday lunch. Metro: nám. Republiky. Another medieval banqueting hall with excellent steaks, Moravian wines and particularly friendly service.
- **Vikárka** (Vicarage)   Vikářská 6, Hradčany. Map 3B3 ☎53 64 97 ▥ Open Tuesday to Sunday 11am–10pm; Monday 11am–3pm ⒶⒺ ⊙ ▥ Metro: Malostranská, then tram 22 northbound. Part of Prague Castle since 1560: medieval cellar, average food and ambience. Outdoor section in summer.
- **Vltava**   Rašínovo nábřeží, Nové město. Map 4F5 ☎29 49 64 ▥ ⒶⒺ ⇐ Metro: Karlovo nám. Small riverside restaurant with lovely patio and eclectic menu. President Havel lives upstairs.

RESTAURANTS — INTERNATIONAL

The difficulty of procuring imported ingredients stifled most efforts at culinary internationalism under the old regime; the state-owned "foreign" restaurants were little more than glorified nightclubs with an ethnic theme. Since the revolution, foreign food has been all the rave and exotic restaurants have been opening at the rate of one a week. Sorry: our list of favorites is very much "as at the time of writing." We follow it with a selection of other acceptable international-style establishments, though more will be arriving even as we print this edition.

CANADIAN LOBSTER

Husova 15, Staré město. Map 4C5 ☎22 57 24 ▥ to ▥ ⒶⒺ ▥ *Metro: Staroměstská.*

The lobster is flown in twice-monthly from Nova Scotia and costs a fortune. The alternative is shrimp, or you can try the moderately priced lunch special, which consists of soup and pork. "Captain's study" decor with old maps, antique clocks, oil paintings and upholstered chairs.

CHINA RESTAURANT

Francouzská 2, Vinohrady (Prague 2). Map 5E7 ☎25 26 43 ▥ ⒶⒺ ⊙ ⒸⒹ ▥ *Metro: nám. Míru.*

Chinese food (and Indian: see MAYUR) was the height of exoticness in prerevolutionary Prague, and the very few restaurants that offered it, such as the **Chang-čou** (*Janáčkovo nábřeží, Prague 5* ☎54 91 64), belonged to the realm of prodigal luxury. A dozen more have opened since, but prices remain higher than you would expect. This one

(the China Restaurant) is commonly regarded as one of the best.

Others include the **Čínská** (*Vodičkova 19, Nové město* ☎54 91 64 ▥ *metro: Můstek*), the **Zlatý drak** (Golden Dragon) (*Anglická 6, Nové město, map 5E7* ☎235 06 59 ▥ *metro: I.P. Pavlova*), the **Peking** (*at metro station I.P. Pavlova* ☎29 35 31 ▥) and the **Nad Karlovem** (*Legerova 12, Vinohrady, off map 5F7* ☎20 24 95 ▥ *closed Sat-Sun, metro: I.P. Pavlova*).

IL PICCOLO CASTELLO

U sluncové 64, Karlín (Prague 8). Map 2C4 ☎684 66 78 ▥ *Closed Sat–Sun lunch* ⒶⒺ ⊙ ⒸⒹ ▥ *Metro: Invalidovna — but who'd go there by metro?*

The most expensive restaurant in town, Italian-managed, located in everybody's dream of a small European château, in a private park not far from the center. Gastronomic meals cost about US$100 per person, half the monthly salary of an average Czech worker. The clientele, as a result, includes a high proportion of foreign businessmen and diplomats, and the occasional solitary blonde in *very* bold skirt.

MAYUR (Indian)

Štěpánská 61, Nové město. Map **5E6**
☎ *236 99 22* ▦ *Closed Sun. Metro: Muzeum.*

A formerly state-owned restaurant that seems to have made the transition to private ownership well. The North Indian tandoori dishes offer nothing exceptional for a visitor from the British Isles, but the slightly ludicrous elegance of the restaurant is not without its charm.

MOSKVA

Na příkopě 29. Map **5C6** ☎ *26 58 21* ▦
▦ *Metro: Můstek.*

For those who miss the inimitable atmosphere of a fast-vanishing breed, the grand old Soviet restaurant: cavernous hall with Brezhnevite glitz, waitresses who simply vanish, oodles of caviar, shashlik (the inevitable Georgian/Armenian speciality), the whiff of the black-market, the mysterious sobbing woman. A cultural trip for those who have never seen one; a nostalgic experience for those who have. Self-service snack-bar **Arbat** (▦) downstairs.

REYKJAVIK

Karlova 20, Staré město. Map **4C5** ☎ *26 57 76* ▦ ▦ ▦ *Metro: Staroměstská.*

At a very nice location on Karlova, a light and modern menu beckons with a wide selection of ocean fish. No reservations are taken, which means you have a good chance of getting in so long as you don't mind standing in the occasional line at the door.

U MALÍŘŮ (Painter)

Maltézské nám. 11, Malá strana. Map **4C4** ☎ *53 18 83* ▦ *Closed Sun* ▦ ▦ ▦ ▦
Metro: Malostranská, then tram 12 or 22 southbound.

The painter was one Jan Šic, who acquired the house in 1543 and later gave up painting to start a beerhouse. This survived war, plague, pillage and revolution until 1991, when a French firm moved in and turned the house into a

gourmet restaurant with the proud cachet of being the second most expensive place in Prague. Everything now comes from France, including the chef, the waiters, the busboys and the ingredients — even the potatoes, not to mention the 1904 bas-armagnac. The house is a real charmer, with gaily painted Gothic vaults and a quiet setting in one of Prague's most romantic squares.

U ZLATÉHO ROŽNĚ (Golden Roast)

Československé armády 22, Bubeneč (Prague 6). Map **1C3** ☎ *632 10 32* ▦ ▦ ▦ ▦ *Metro: Hradčanská.*

An Icelandic restaurant, which means a lot of fish — but then also Chinese dishes, Czech classics, steaks, roast chicken and delicious fried apples. Modern, friendly and very fashionable.

VINÁRNA V ZÁTIŠÍ

Liliová 1, Betlémské nám., Staré město. Map **4D5** ☎ *26 51 07* ▦ *to* ▦ ▦ ▦ ▦ ▦

One of the best venues for international food in town, owned by an English expat and frequented by the Anglo-American business community. The menu carries a soupçon of the *nouvelle cuisine*, with such specialities as marinated salmon with fresh papaya, grilled pork fillet with fresh fruit sauce, and broiled chicken breast *au camembert*. A good selection of imported wines accompanies the fixed-price menus. Impeccably formal and friendly service. Reservations are essential.

VIOLA

Národní 7, Staré město. Map **4D5** ☎ *235 87 79, 26 67 32* ▦ *Performances Mon–Sat from 8pm. Box office opens Mon–Sat 4pm. Metro: Národní třída.*

Italian restaurant in an elegant Art Nouveau building run amok with Tiffany glass. It consists of several rooms including a bar–pub and a small cabaret, which draws a good cross-section of Prague's bearded intelligensia with its nightly program of poetry readings, drama and jazz. Wide selection of domestic and Italian wines. Reservations are essential.

MORE RESTAURANTS — INTERNATIONAL

- **Alex** *(German)*   Revoluční 11. Map **5**C6 ☎231 44 89 ▥ ▣ ▣ ▥ Metro: nám. Republiky. Pork chops, wurst and sauerkraut — but wasn't that *Czech?*
- **Amigo** *(Mexican)*   Křižíkova 27, Karlín (Prague 8). Map **2**C4 ☎22 62 89 ▥ Metro: Křižíkova. Enchiladas, tacos, Costa Rican beef.
- **Crazy Daisy** *(American)*   Vodičkova 9, Nové město (off Wenceslas Sq.). Map **5**D6 ☎235 00 21 ▥ ▣ Metro: Můstek. Good salads, vegetarian dishes.
- **Faros** *(Greek)*   ▥ Vlašská 32, Malá strana. Map **3**C3 ▣ Metro: Malostranská. Lovely little restaurant in a quiet corner of the Lesser Side.
- **Košer** *(Kosher)*   Maislova 18, Staré město (in the Jewish town hall). Map **4**C5 ☎231 86 64 ▥ Metro: Staroměstská. Fixed menu at a low price.
- **Mikulka's Pizzeria**   Benediktská 16, Staré město. Map **5**C6 ☎231 57 27 ▥ Closed Sunday. Metro: nám. Republiky. Generally recognized as the best pizzeria in town. Also pastas and salads.
- **Obora** *(French)*   Libocká 1, Horní Liboc (Prague 6). Map **1**C2 ☎36 77 79 ▥ Tram 1, 18 from metro Hradčanská, or tram 2 from metro Dejvická. Gourmet cuisine — see page 127 for the hotel of the same name.
- **Principe** *(Italian)*   Anglická 23, Nové město. Map **5**E7 ☎25 96 14 ▥ ▣ Metro: I.P. Pavlova. Excellent food; highly professional Italian staff.
- **Thang Long** *(Vietnamese)*   Šimáčkova 21, Holešovice (Prague 7). Map **2**C4 ☎80 65 41 ▥ Metro: Vltavská. Luxurious decor. Reserve ahead.

WINE TAVERNS *(VINÁRNA)*

Most *vinárny* (pl.) are hoary old cellars located in the womb of medieval, underground Prague. All of them serve some hot dishes; some are practically indistinguishable from your standard *restaurace*, and that is how we have listed such instances above.

Each tavern stocks the wines of a particular grape-growing district, formerly supplied by the local wine-making cooperative, now in the throes of privatization–corporatization. The usual serving unit (0.2 liter; about $\frac{1}{3}$ pint) is about twice the size of the Anglo-American standard, so you should ask for a *deci* (0.1 liter) if you wish to keep within bounds.

U FRANTIŠKÁNŮ (Franciscans)
Jungmannovo nám. 18, Nové město. Map **5***D6. Metro: Můstek.*
A Gothic cellar in the former Franciscan monastery, serving Slovakian wines. Lovely summer garden; live electric-organ music.

U MARKÝZE (Marquis) ▥
Nekázanka 8, Nové město. Map **5***C6 ☎22 42 89 ▥ Closed Sat–Sun* ▣ ▣ ▣ ▥ *Metro: Můstek.*
A tiny winery/restaurant with antique furniture and a lot of style. Wines from South Moravian Mikulov.

U RUDOLFA
Maislova 5, Staré město. Map **4***C5 ☎232*

26 71 ▥ ▣ ▣ ▣ ▥ *Metro: Staroměstská.*
A minuscule modern restaurant/wine bar in the heart of the former Jewish ghetto. You have to fight to get in.

U TŘÍ GRÁCIÍ (Three Graces)
Novotného lávka, Staré město (near Charles Bridge). Map **4***C4 ☎26 54 57 ▥* ◁€
Closed Mon from Oct–Apr. Metro: Staroměstská.
Possibly the loveliest setting for any outdoor eating or drinking spot in Prague: a pedestrian terrace beside the Vltava with a full view of the Charles Bridge and the Castle. A *vinárna* has existed here since 1436, serving Moravian wines from the region of Valtice. Full

range of warm dishes with Moravian specialities like the Pálava fleshpot and the Valtice cheese-and-ham toast.

U TŘÍ HOUSLIČEK (Three Fiddles)
Nerudova 12, Malá strana. Map 3C3 ☎ *53 50 11. Closed Sun; Mon. Metro: Malostranská.*
A delightful little place on one of the most attractive streets in the Lesser Side. The menu is limited to cold snacks, but they include caviar and salted salmon. The wine comes from the South Moravian region of Valtice.

U TŘÍ ZLATÝCH LVŮ (Three Golden Lions)
Uhelný trh 1, Staré město. Map 4D5. Metro: Můstek.
A lively tavern in the Old Town favored by the academic youth.

U ZELENÉ ŽÁBY (Green Frog)
U radnice 8, Staré město (off Old Town Sq.). Map 4C5. Open Sun–Thurs 3–11pm ☎ *26 28 15* ▥ *Metro: Staroměstská.*
The only place in Prague where you can taste the noble *žernoseker* wine short of getting invited to a reception at the Castle. The house dates from the 12thC; the tavern was recorded in existence in the 15th. The name came about as follows:

On the Thursday before Palm Sunday in 1436, a tailor who lived in the house somehow managed to get his legs behind his head while trying an acrobatic number, but could not take them back down. As he was wearing a green suit at the time, the housemaid took him for a monster frog and ran out of the house half mad with fear. Neighbors helped untangle the situation and installed the frog sign in memory of the tailor after his death.

U ZLATÉ KONVICE (Golden Jug)
Melantrichova 20, Staré město. Map 4C5 ☎ *26 01 28* ▥ ▣ ▢ ▢ ▥ ♪ *from Tues–Sat. Metro: Můstek.*
Romany (Gypsy) music in medieval vaults and chambers 7 meters (23 feet) below the ground, in a tavern said to have existed in them at least since 1402. The subterranean network stretches far under the Old Town Square. Historic monument status prevents the management from installing a ventilation shaft, but offers no obstruction to the drunken dancing and revelry that go on until the small hours. Good Moravian wines, a menu of cold plates and three warm ham dishes.

U ZLATÉHO HADA (Golden Snake)
Karlova 18, Staré město. Map 4C5 ☎ *235 87 78* ▥ ▣ ▢ ▥ *Metro: Staroměstská.*
This is where Deodatus the Armenian opened Prague's first coffee-house in the 18thC, but the slick wine bar/café that occupies the house today has little in common with it other than its name. A yuppie sort of place with modern sculptures strewn through the room; good steaks and salads.

PUBS AND BEERHALLS (PIVNICE, HOSTINEC)
Bohemians have been brewing beer since at least the 10thC, and all of the finest pubs in Prague have a history going back the best part of a millenium. Tradition runs as thick as the foam of a properly poured Pilsner. The character of the brew is said to be affected not only by the production process but also by how beer is stored (underground cellars are best), the tapmaster's skill (look for the telltale rings of foam after you down your beer) and the quality of the glass (handles are essential).

Pub tables are always shared (ask, *"Je tady volno?"* to make sure you can sit). Putting a coaster in front of you is the signal that you want beer: you never pull the waiter by the sleeve or you risk all-round wrath — and a Prague publican is nothing if he cannot cuss like a trooper. The moment your empty mug hits the table, you will be brought another beer (to avoid this, pay *before* you finish your beer).

There is usually no menu, but two or three simple dishes — a slab of porker, a goulash, a sausage platter — which the maître will announce when serving your beer. When you want to pay, you try to catch the man with the oversize wallet and say, *"Platit, prosím."* A 5–10 percent tip will make him smile.

In the past, most beerhalls in Prague brewed their own liquor, as one (**U FLEKŮ**) still does today. The Pilsner was invented in 1842 in the Bohemian town of Plzeň (German *Pilsen*) and took the country — and the world — by storm. One by one Czech pubs gave up their brewing privileges and began serving the blond newcomer. Other popular beers include Kozel and the locally brewed Smíchov. The superb Budvar/Budweiser beer is relatively rare outside its home town of České Budějovice (German *Budweis*).

Beer is also categorized by degree: 8° is light, 12° is standard and 14° is for buffs. Contrary to general belief, the numbers do not represent alcohol content but the level of sugar added in brewing, which in turn determines the amount of alcohol in the final product.

U FLEKŮ ▥

Křemencova 11, Nové město. Map 4E5
☎29 32 46 ▦ 🆎 ⊙ ⊡ ▨ *Garden* ♫
Metro: Národní třída.

A must on every tourist's program — and as a result filled with as many as 1,000 Germans at a time, relieving homesickness and turning merry to the tunes of an oompah band. The brewery/tavern has existed continuously since 1499, and keeps carefully preserved bits of lore in each of its several halls ("Knight's Hall," "Academy," "The Pits") and huge garden. It is the only brewery left in Prague that still serves its own beer — a strong, creamy 13° dark — in-house. An entrance fee is payable; pub food is served.

U KALICHA (Chalice)

Na bojišti 12–14, Nové město. Map 5F6
☎29 19 45 ▦ *No cards* ♫ *Metro: I.P. Pavlova.*

A legend for the fans of the Good Soldier Švejk, Jaroslav Hašek's World War I anti-hero. The story has Švejk nabbed as a draft dodger at the Chalice on the first day of the war, and Palivec the pub-keeper gets into trouble for hanging a picture of Franz Joseph that has been fouled by the flies. The walls are now covered with tasteful illustrations of Švejk's adventures, and instead of deadbeat dog-thieves the place is filled

with tour groups paying US$2 for a glass of beer that costs 50 cents everywhere else. A lot of atmosphere, however — and no one will believe you have been to Prague until you have seen the Chalice. Pilsner Urquell 12°.

U KOCOURA (Tomcat)

Nerudova 2, Malá strana. Map 3C3 ☎53 *89 62* ▦ *Closed Sat–Sun. Metro: Malostranská.*

Famous old pub in the heart of the Lesser Side, renowned for serving the best Pilsner in town. Reports say it has taken the low road of commercialization since it was bought by the Friends of Beer Party, a political group that contested the 1990 elections on a platform promising to guard the quality of the nation's beer; but this may be a temporary blip. The house in which it is located dates from the 16thC and served until 1888 as the royal apothecary.

U PINKASŮ

Jungmannovo nám. 15, Nové město. Map 5D6 ☎26 18 04 ▦ *Metro: Můstek.*

An old pub that holds the honor of serving the first Pilsner in Prague (in 1843) and thereby setting off the worldwide success story of that particular brew. Privatization has worked wonders, and U Pinkasů distinguishes itself with fast and friendly service and excellent pub food. There are five rooms, one of which (on the left as you enter) is reserved for nonsmokers — a rare treat for a Prague pub.

U SV. TOMÁŠE (St Thomas)
Letenská 12, Malá strana. Map 4C4 ☎*53 00 64* ▥ ▤ *Metro: Malostranská.*
Three quaint medieval halls painted with scenes of Bohemian history (defenestration at the Castle; the murder of Wallenstein) and a garden that adjoins Wallenstein's palace are the setting for this tavern where the Augustinian monks ran a brewery from 1358 until they were kicked out of town by Joseph II in 1784. Unlike most other establishments of this type, St Thomas also serves a full range of meals, including

meats from an open-air grill in summer. The beer is Braník (12˚ light or 14˚ dark).

U ZLATÉHO TYGRA (Golden Tiger)
Husova 17, Staré město (off Karlova ul.). Map 4C5 ☎*26 52 19* ▥ *Closed Sun. Metro: Staroměstská.*
Bohumil Hrabal and his clique of Prague intellectuals meet nightly at the Tiger amid the smoke and din of long wooden benches packed with (nearly all-male) regulars. Havel used to be a frequent visitor in the past and returns for private parties after closing time. The waiters, understandably, try to keep tourists out, but with a bit of persistence you can get yourself into a corner of a communal table. The back room is reserved for the VIPs.

MORE PUBS AND BEERHALLS
Each of the following has a few hundred years of history behind it.

- **U černého vola** (Black Bull)   Loretánské nám. 1, Hradčany. Map **3C2** ☎53 86 37 ▥ Metro: Malostranská, then tram 22 northbound. Attractive old building with stained-glass windows; excellent Kozel beer.
- **U dvou koček** (Two Cats)   Uhelný trh 10, Staré město. Map 4D5 ☎26 77 29 ▥ Has withstood the tourist flood with much of its integrity and traditions intact, continuing to attract a loyal clientele of native revelers, including many regulars from the Charles University. Pilsner Urquell 12˚.
- **U krála Brabantského** (King of Brabant)   Thunovská 15, Malá strana. Map 3C3 ☎53 99 75 ▥ Closed Sunday. Metro: Malostranská. Charming little tavern in the Lesser Side that claims to have served King Wenceslas IV in the 14thC.
- **U medvídků** (Bearlets)   Na perštýně 7, Staré město. Map 4D5 ☎23 58 90 ▥ Closed Sunday. Metro: Národní třída. Old pub founded in 1464 but now mostly a tourist trap. Only place in central Prague serving Budvar (Budweiser) beer.
- **Ve skořepce**   Skořepka, Staré město. Map 4D5 ☎22 80 81 ▥ to ▥ Closed Saturday dinner; Sunday. Metro: Národní třída. Enormous tankards of Gambrinus 12˚ light or Black Special, and big roasted pork knees.
- **V korunní**   Korunní 39, Vinohrady (Prague 3). Map 2C4 ▥ Closed Saturday. Metro: Jiřího z Poděbrad. Pleasantly unassuming pub with wholly local clientele.

FAST FOOD AND SNACKS
Prague now has two branches of **McDonald's** within hailing distance of each other on and near Wenceslas Square, and enough **Pizza Huts**, **Kentucky Fried Chickens**, **Wienerwalds**, **Nordsees** and **Tschibos** to keep everyone happy. The local equivalent is usually called an *automat* (i.e., serve-yourself cafeteria). You can find dozens of them along Wen-

ceslas Square and Na příkopě, in the streets behind the National Museum and around nám. Republiky. We can recommend the following.

DŮM POTRAVIN
Václavské nám. 59 (corner of Wenceslas Sq. and Washingtonova). Map 5D7 ▢ to ▥ Open Mon–Fri 8am–8pm; Sat 8am–1pm. Metro: Muzeum.
Supermarket, take-out deli, coffee house and classy restaurant in one. Good open sandwiches, salads.

FRIONOR
Vodičkova 34, Nové město (near Wenceslas Sq.). Map 5D6 ☎26 02 23 ▢ ▢ Open Mon–Fri 9.30am–10pm. Metro: Můstek.
Very pleasant little place with a huge list of seafood choices, which you can consume at a table or a counter or take out.

KORUNA AUTOMAT
Na Příkopě 1 (corner of Wenceslas Sq.). Map 5D6 ▢ to ▢ Open Mon–Sat 8.30am–11pm; Sun 8am–6pm. Metro: Můstek.
The best known of all *automats:* lots of choice, fresh food, quick service — and they are always there when all restaurants are booked solid.

SATE GRILL
Pohořelec 3, Hradčany. Map 3C2 ☎53 21 13 ▢ Metro: Malostranská, then tram 22 northbound.
Altogether tasty Indonesian and semi-Indonesian food; a few tables, stand-up counters and take-out.

U GOVINDY
Na hrázi 5, Libeň (Prague 8). Map 2B4 ☎82 14 38 ▢ Open Mon–Fri 11am–5pm. Metro: Palmovka.
A mecca for Prague's vegetarians, operated by the disciples of Hare Krishna, who grow most of what they serve in a communal farm outside Prague. Until recently you could eat here for free, but now there's a set fee of kč25.

VEGETARKA
Celetná 3, Staré město. Map 5C6 ▢ Open for lunch only. Metro: nám. Republiky.
Vegetarian dishes, which make a welcome change from Prague's pork chops and dumplings.

CAFÉS *(KAVÁRNA)*
One of the most civilized legacies of the 300 years of Austrian rule was the implantation of the Viennese café/*Konditorei* in the Bohemian soil. Once you have ordered your obligatory cup of *presso, vídeňská* (Viennese) or *turecká* (Turkish), you can sit as long as you wish, read newspapers, write immortal prose, sort out defunct love affairs or interview prospective actresses.

Each *kavárna* has its lore: here Kafka used to meet Einstein, there André Breton invented some forgotten variant of Surrealism, elsewhere Jaroslav Seifert used to sip his afternoon coffee. Mostly irrelevant — you will see some young people debating politics, a few old ladies in funny hats, and throngs of tourists clutching their maps and guides. The food selection consists of the inevitable strudel and *Sachertorte*, a few sandwiches and usually some hot dishes.

You can find a half dozen *kavárny* (pl.) on the Old Town Square and as many more on and around Wenceslas Square. Here are a few others that are worth seeking out.

ADRIA
Národní 40, Nové město (on Jungmannovo nám.). Map 4D5 ☎26 05 55 ▣ Open 4pm–midnight. Metro: Můstek.
Strong on ambience and location: a posh 1920s decor and a terrace that overlooks one of Prague's liveliest squares.

ARCO

Hybernská 16, Nové město. Map 5C7
☎ *236 19 03. Open 7am–11pm. Metro:*
nám. Republiky.

Sad relic of a literary *belle époque*, the former haunt of Kafka, Franz Werfel, Max Brod, E.E. Kisch, Karl Kraus and other "arconauts." In miserable shape today, but the restoration squad must be waiting somewhere out there.

EVROPA

Václavské nám. 27, Nové město. Map 5D6.
Open 7am–11.30pm. Metro: Můstek.

Part of the hotel EVROPA, this is a pinnacle of Art Nouveau elegance gone to seed. There is even an entrance charge now, which does not prevent tourists from flocking there at all hours of the day. The Palm Court Quartet plays syrupy teatime music Wednesday to Sunday.

OBECNÍ DŮM

nám. Republiky 5, Staré město. Map 5C6.
Open 7am–11pm. Metro: nám. Republiky.

Very popular café in an environment of faded *fin-de-siècle* elegance. Across the hall is the restaurant and variety hall of the same name (see page 138).

SAVOY

Vitěžná 1, Malá Strana (near most Legii).
Map 4D4. Open 1am–10pm. Metro:
Národní třída.

Stunning decor, splendidly restored, of murals and carved wood. Jazz plays in the background. This is an ideal place to spend an afternoon doing nothing in particular.

SLAVIA

Národní 1, Prague 1. Map 4D5 ☎ *26 12*
50 🆎 *Open 8am–9pm. Metro: Národní*
třída.

The most famous of Prague's cafés, the chief haunt of nationalist intellectuals in the 19thC and of dissidents before 1989. Past regulars include the composer Smetana and the playwright Havel. Closed for restoration at the time of writing.

U KISCHE

Celetná 14, Staré město. Map 5C6 ☎ *236*
79 80. Open 10am–10pm. Metro: nám.
Republiky.

A new café has been established in the birth house of the legendary journalist-essayist and café-goer Egon Erwin Kisch.

Entertainments

Prague by night

Organized fun is not yet the high-powered industry in Prague that it is in the West, but it's all the more lively, accessible, fresh, joyful and creative for that. On a warm summer night, the entire stretch from the Castle to the Wenceslas Monument looks and feels like one huge outdoor party where street strummers compete for attention with church concerts and underground rock clubs. It is remarkably free from the sleaze and commercialism that one has come to take for granted in cities farther west. And when all else fails, there is always the alternative of a night of beer-drinking and red-faced singing at the local *pivnice* (see page 142).

The change since 1989 has been dazzling. The old regime frowned upon (and occasionally criminalized) independent theater, pop, jazz, cabaret, and anything else that smacked of creative fun. The authorities' own idea of entertainment ranged from wholesome "cultural" yawns to a bit of Čedok-chaperoned topless variety show.

Since the liberation, theater has seen a renaissance under the moral example of a playwright-president. Pop and jazz clubs proliferate, while classical music broadens its already substantial field with new festivals, new performing groups and new concert venues. Avant-garde groups have taken over cultural bodies formerly under the thumb of bureaucrats, and flood the city with a barrage of street concerts, clown and puppet shows, revived medieval crafts, multimedia experiments and hyper-modern "events."

A huge reservoir of young talent goes into the performing arts — partly because of the underdeveloped status of many of the other channels (say, management, finance, dog-food design) into which creative talent naturally flows in other countries, and partly encouraged by the inflow of tourism, which provides the largest source of cash in an economically depressed country. The outcome of all this energy can occasionally be naive or over-earnest, but it rarely lacks the creative spark.

The underside of the night, meanwhile, has also expanded mightily, with an explosive growth in organized gambling, professional sex and related activities.

INFORMATION
A typical Prague night will offer a dozen or more classical concerts, twice as many live jazz and pop venues, a variety of plays — including

some in English or multilingual — puppet, mime and clown shows, and some unique forms of spectacle like the Laterna Magica and Laterna Animata multimedia dramas.

The English-language periodicals, *Prague Post* and *Prognosis*, carry extensive listings. To make sure you miss nothing, check also the posters and flyers at the information offices of PIS and Pragotur (see page 42), as well as the American Hospitality Center. If you wish to delve deeper into Prague's art world than the average visitor, you can also try to squeeze sense out of the listings in the monthly *Přehled kulturních pořadů v Praze* (Summary of Cultural Programs in Prague), available at news kiosks during the first few days of each month.

TICKET AGENCIES

As a foreigner, you are expected to pay a whopping surcharge on most state-sponsored performances — *if* you know where to buy the tickets. One way of getting around this is to send in a Czech decoy; another way, if it suits you to be diddled at, say, 50 percent rather than 200 percent, is to buy through one of the ticket agencies. These proliferate around Wenceslas Square. **Čedok** is sole agent for a number of performances · including those of the Prague June festival and the Laterna Animata multimedia show.

Bohemia Ticket International   • Na příkopě 16. Map **5**C6 ☎22 87 38. • Václavské nám. 25. Map **5**D6 ☎26 03 33. • Salvatorská 6, Nové město. Map **4**C5 ☎26 18 89 Fx231 22 71.
Čedok   Na příkopě 18. Map **5**C6 ☎212 71 11 Fx232 16 56. • Václavské nám. 24. Map **5**D6 ☎234 89 43. • Bílkova 6, Staré město. Map **4**B5 ☎ and Fx231 97 44. Also in hotels ATRIUM (see page 126) and Panorama.
PIS (Prague Information Service)   Staroměstské nám. 22. Map **4**C5 ☎22 44 53. • Na příkopě 20. Map **5**C6 ☎22 18 60.

Performing arts

SPECTACLE

Laterna Magica, Prague's longest-running show, combines theater, film, mime, music, dance and technical wizardry to dramatize scenes of Bohemian history for a broad audience. Among the original creators of the concept in 1958 was young Miloš Forman, who would later sail to international stardom with hits like *Hair, One Flew over the Cuckoo's Nest* and *Amadeus*. Having (perhaps temporarily) lost its regular home at Národní 40, Laterna Magica now leads a nomadic existence between the National Theater's New Scene (Nová scena) and the multipurpose Palace of Culture (Palác kultury). An offshoot called **Laterna Animata**, based on the Faust story, was the hit of the 1992 season.

The first magic lantern to hit Prague was that of Rabbi Loew (see page 29). The rabbi was commissioned by Rudolf II to call up the Old Testament patriarchs for a seance with the emperor. The court gathered in a darkened hall of the Castle; an oven glowed and puffed smoke; and voilà, *there was Abraham parading ahead of Isaac, Jacob and his twelve sons.*

Then, however, things went disastrously wrong. Naphtali, one of the twelve, began wriggling uncontrollably. Rudolf found this hilarious and let out a snort; the patriarchs vanished in a huff, and the courtlings had that sinking feeling — slowly, the entire Castle had begun to cave in over their heads. Rabbi Loew averted catastrophe by uttering the magic word at the last minute, but the show had to fold after only one run.

- **Laterna Animata**   Výstaviště, Prague 7. Map **1**C3. Metro: Nádraží Holešovice, then on foot or tram 12, 14. Tickets at all Čedok offices, travel agents and hotels. Reservations ☎212 76 39, 212 73 64.
- **Nová scena**   Národní 4, Prague 1. Map **4**D5. Metro: Národní třída ☎20 62 60. Performances Monday to Friday 8pm, Saturday to Sunday 5pm and 8pm. Box office opens daily, except Sunday, 3–6pm and half hour before show.
- **Palác kultury**   5. května 65, Nusle (Prague 4). Map **2**D4. Metro: Vyšehrad. Performances at 5pm.

THEATER, OPERA, PUPPET THEATER

Independent theater has experienced a marvelous boom since 1989. Although most performances are in Czech, a foreigner may still want to try it for the sheer excitement of sharing with a nation that takes its theater seriously. Some companies stage various combinations of drama, music and song for a specifically foreign audience. Also worth keeping an eye for are one-offs like the lavish 1992 production of *A Midsummer Night's Dream* in German in the Výstaviště fairgrounds, which drew rapturous reviews in the Western press.

What Praguers call the "stone theaters" — the historic halls of the **Estates Theater**, **National Theater** and **National Opera** — present an overlapping repertoire of opera, ballet, operetta and the occasional

Shakespeare or Chekhov. The dazzlingly renovated ESTATES THEATER, in particular, deserves a visit for its architectural merit alone (see page 83).

Finally, nothing quite captures the magic spirit of Prague better than the **Marionette Theater**, an enchanting and virtuoso concoction of imagination, humor, drama and music.

DIVADLO NA ZÁBRADLÍ
Anenské nám., Staré město (near the Charles Bridge). Map 4D5 ☎*236 04 49. Metro: Staroměstská.*
One of the consistently excellent smaller theaters, where Václav Havel cut his teeth in the 1960s as stage-hand, actor and playwright.

DIVADLO U ITALŮ
Italian Cultural Center, Vlašská 34, Malá strana. Map 3C2. Performances usually Fri–Sat only. Tickets through CS-Tour, Senovážná 6, Nové město (off nám. Republiky), map 5C6 ☎*236 86 80.*
Alfred Story, a collage of Jewish anecdotes and songs in three languages, has proven a successful recipe and is likely to go on running for seasons to come.

DIVADLO ZA BRANOU II
Adria Palace, Jungmannova 31, Nové město. Map 5D6. Metro: Můstek.
The **Black Light Theater** of Jiří Smec is billed as a bolder alternative to the Laterna Magica.

ESTATES THEATER (Stavovské divadlo)
Ovocný trh 6, Staré město. Map 5C6 ☎*22 86 58. Metro: Můstek.*
See the main entry on page 83 for a theater that is one of Prague's wonders in its own right. Simultaneous English translation is available for most plays at the Estates: just get a headphone at the box office for a refundable deposit. Tickets are absurdly cheap — *if* you can find them. The average opera seat goes for kč60–90, and standing room is always available for kč20–30.

NATIONAL MARIONETTE THEATER
(Říše loutek)
Žatecká 1, Staré město. Map 4C5 ☎*232 34 29. Advance booking* ☎*538 045. Metro: Staroměstská.*
A tiny stage to delight child and grown-up alike. Their puppet performance of

Mozart's *Don Giovanni* has been voted the opera event of Prague for several seasons in a row.

NATIONAL THEATER (Národní divadlo)
Národní 2, Prague 1. Map 4D5 ☎*20 53 64. Metro: Národní třída. Performances usually 7pm. Box office open Mon–Fri 10am–6pm; Sat–Sun noon–6pm; half hour before performances. Tickets kč12–250.*
See the main entry on page 96 for this monument of 19thC Czech national architecture. The repertoire centers on light opera (usually in Czech) and ballet.

OPERA MOZART
Novotného lávka 1, Staré město (near the Old Town end of Charles Bridge). Map 4C4 ☎*26 53 71. Advance booking hotline* ☎*53 80 45. Metro: Staroměstská.*
Half spoof and half avant-garde reinterpretation based on clips from Mozart's operas, performed by a star cast of young directors, singers and choreographers. The location is a lovely nook on the bank of the Vltava, and there is an outdoor café/bar and open-air dance floor associated with the company.

REALISTICKÉ DIVADLO
Štefánikova 57, Smíchov (Prague 5). Map 1D3 ☎*54 50 27. Metro: Anděl or tram 6, 9, 12.*
A small theater that regularly comes up with some of the most provocative new plays: their staging of Tabori's *Mein Kampf* was the scandal of the 1991–92 season.

STATE OPERA HOUSE (Statní opera Praha)
Wilsonova 4, Nové město. Map 5D7 ☎*26 97 48. Performances usually 7pm. Box office open Mon–Fri 10am–6pm; Sat–Sun noon–6pm; half hour before performances. Tickets from kč16–450. Metro: Muzeum.*
Prague's main opera house. Formerly the Deutsche Opera, then the Smetana Opera until it was re-renamed in 1992.

CLASSICAL MUSIC

A flourishing concert scene greets the visitor in a city that was at or near the forefront of European music from the 14th through to the end of the 18thC. Six annual festivals enriched the musical menu at the last count, and several more were in preparation.

The **Prague Spring**, which starts traditionally on Smetana's birthday on May 12, is the oldest and most solid of the lot. The **Prague June, Prague Autumn** (September 11–20) and the generically-named **Prague Festival** (September 20 to October 4), all inaugurated since 1990, stretch the festival season practically through the summer. A new Austrian–French–Italian joint sponsorship called **Prague/Europe Music** (Praha/Evropa Hudba, September 12–27) puts strong emphasis on the history of music, with exciting and little-known works, unusual interpretations and startling juxtapositions. The widely-heralded **Mozart Open** made a somewhat shaky start in 1992.

The well-known **Czech Philharmonic Orchestra** performs regularly in the newly renovated Rudolfinum and occasionally in the Smetana Hall of the Municipal Building (Obecní dům). Perhaps more exciting are the plethora of chamber and solo concerts that usually take place in historic surroundings, which have benefited immensely from the proliferation of private concert agencies.

Some popular concert venues:

BERTRAMKA (Mozart Museum)
Mozartova 2, Smíchov (Prague 5). Map 1D3
☎*54 38 93. Metro: Anděl.*
Regular chamber concerts in addition to *A Night with Mozart*, a play in period costumes with arias from famous operas by Mozart performed by star soloists, in Wolfgang's favorite Prague home (see page 64).

DOMINICAN CHURCH (St Giles; sv. Jiljí)
Husova 8, Staré město. Map 4D5. Metro: Staroměstská.
The splendid 18thC organ is used frequently for recitals, but the real treat is a garden concert in the cloisters of the neighboring Dominican abbey, one of the most romantic spaces in Prague.

OBECNÍ DŮM / SMETANOVA SÍŇ
nám. Republiky 5, Staré město. Map 5C6
☎*232 58 58. Metro: nám. Republiky.*
Periodic concerts by the Czech Philharmonic Orchestra in an elegant Art Nouveau ambience.

NOSTIC PALACE (Nostický palác)
Maltézské nám. 1, Malá strana. Map 4C4. Metro: Malostranská, then tram 12 or 22
southbound. Regular concerts every Tues, Thurs, Sat at 5pm.
The first public concerts in Prague were given in 1808 under the auspices of Count Franz Anton Nostitz (or František Antonín Nostic) in the ballroom of his palace. The same room, renovated, now serves for regular chamber concerts, which frequently feature unpublished works from the Nostitz family library.

RUDOLFINUM / DŮM UMĚLCŮ (Artists' House)
nám. Jana Palacha 1, Staré město. Map 4C5 ☎*231 91 64. Box office open Mon–Fri 1am–6pm and 1hr before concerts. Metro: Staroměstská.*
Recently restored 1880s concert hall, for regular Czech Philharmonic Orchestra performances.

ST NICHOLAS'S CHURCH (Kostel svatého Mikuláše)
Staroměstské nám. (Old Town Sq.). Map 4C5. Metro: Staroměstská.
Four (rival) organizations present chamber music concerts, sometimes two a day, in this little Baroque gem on Prague's central square. (See also page 104.)

VILLA AMERIKA (Dvořák Museum)
Ke Karlovu 20, Nové město. Map **5F6**
☎ *29 82 14. Metro: I.P. Pavlova.*
A costumed and staged pastiche of Dvořák's vocal works is performed twice-weekly in the attractive 18thC mansion that serves as his museum. (See main entry on page 120.)

Additional historic halls where classical music is played on a more or less regular basis include the following. Most of them are described at greater length in SIGHTS A TO Z.

- **CHURCHES AND MONASTERIES:** Loreto, Convent of St Agnes, St George's Basilica *(in the Castle)*, St James, Strahov Abbey.
- **PALACES:** Kaunitz Palace, Kunštát and Poděbrady Palace, Lobkovic Palace *(in the Castle)*, Martinic Palace, Pálffy Palace, Schwarzenberg Palace, Spanish Hall *(in the Castle)*, Star Castle, Troja Château, Riding Hall of Wallenstein Palace.
- **OTHER HALLS:** Mirror Room of the Clementinum *(Zrcadlova síň Klementina)*, Bartok Hall *(Rytířská 27, Staré město, map 4D5)*, Shostakovich Hall *(Rytířská 31, Staré město, map 4D5)*, Stone Bell House.

CINEMA

Prague's cinemas are awash with the latest American films, which now arrive almost as soon as they are released in the West. One reason for the haste is to undercut the pirate video-cassette industry, which flourished after 1989. Films are generally shown in the original language with Czech subtitles. Check the *Prague Post* for a complete listing, with critical commentary.

The collapse of communism has been a disaster for the Czech film industry, which once produced such classics as Jiří Menzel's *Closely Observed Trains* (1966). The censors are gone, but so have state subsidies, cozy monopolies and protectionist laws limiting the number of foreign movies that can be shown, and feature-film production is down to less than a third of what it was before 1989. Prague's Barrandov studios, the biggest in the old Eastern Europe, were privatized in 1992.

JAZZ

A small but sparkling circuit of jazz used to be one of the privileged sanctums of the dissident intelligentsia under the old regime, and it has remained so even after many of its members became ministers, company directors and media gurus under the new one. President Havel set an example to the nation by taking Frank Zappa and Lou Reed on a club-hopping tour in 1990.

- **Agharta Jazz Center** Krakovská 5, Nové město. Map **5E6** ☎ 22 45 58. Daily from 9pm. Jazz café and jazz shop Mon–Fri 1pm–2am; Sat–Sun 7pm–2am. Metro: Muzeum. One of Prague's most exciting jazz haunts celebrated its first anniversary in September 1992.
- **Reduta** Národní 20, Prague 1. Map **4D5** ☎ 20 38 25. Daily from 9.30pm. Closed Sun. Cover from kč70. Metro: Můstek. A small and cozy place, which doesn't seem to have seen a redecorator since its foundation in 1958, and is

all the more charming for that. Books some of the best jazz acts in town and features the largest number of goateed poets and Havel buddies.

- **Viola** Národní 7, Prague 1. Map 4D5 ☎235 87 79, 26 67 32. Performances Mon–Sat from 8pm. Box office open Mon–Sat 4pm. Metro: Národní třída. Restaurant/pub/theater/arts center that often presents first-rate jazz acts; see under RESTAURANTS — INTERNATIONAL for more.
- Other jazz venues: • **Jazz Art Club** *(in Radiopalác, Vinohradská 40, Prague 2 ☎25 76 54, closed Mon).* • **Luxor** *(Václavské nám. 41, map 5D6 ☎26 40 65).* • **Press Jazz Club** *(Pařížská 9, Staré město, map 4C5 ☎22 47 23).*

ROCK, POP, ETC.

Rock is nothing if it is not political in a country where it was regarded as bourgeois decadence until the day before yesterday. Police action against a rock band called Plastic People of the Universe (they're still around) was the immediate cause of the protest movement that culminated with the Charter 77 declaration, which in turn catapulted Václav Havel to the opposition leadership. A high point of the 1989 revolution was when the banned singer Karel Kryl sang for the crowds on Wenceslas Square. Michal Kocáb, a rock musician and friend of Havel, became a leading member of parliament after the revolution.

Big concerts generally take place: at the **Sportovní hala** in the Výstaviště exhibition grounds in Holešovice *(map 2 C4; metro: Nádraží Holešovice).* The following are some of the hottest of the rock venues that have emerged since 1989.

BUNKR

Lodecká 2, Nové město. Map 5B7 ☎231 07 35. Club daily 6pm–5am (bands start at 9pm); café 8pm–5am. Metro: nám. Republiky.

The star of 1992 among the young (i.e., teen and just a bit over), the hip, the drunk, and possibly the stoned-out. The venue alone is worth braving all that horrendous waiting in line: a (formerly) secret underground bunker apparently built for the Central Committee to sit out the Third World War. It came to light after the revolution and was turned into a disco, which seemed on the verge of eviction at the time of this writing. Assuming it survives, it is *the* place for heavy rock and metal fans. For a somewhat quieter atmosphere, try the café upstairs.

MALOSTRANSKÁ BESEDA

Malostranské nám. 21, Malá strana. Map 3C3 ☎53 90 24. Mon–Fri from 8pm; Sat from 9pm. Closed Sun. Metro: Malostranská.

Big hall, lots of beer. The music ranges from jazz to rock to bluegrass, and quite randomly too, so check listings before you go if you are choosy.

PEKLO (Hell)

In Strahov Abbey, Strahovské nádvoří 1, Hradčany. Map 3C1 ☎53 32 77. Daily 10am–4pm. Metro: Malostranská, then tram 22 northbound.

A fantastic new addition to Prague's night scene: a cavernous catacomb carved out of the rock below one of the Strahov monastery buildings. The music is more disco than rock, and the dancers include as many tourists as Czech yuppies. Adjacent restaurant, expensive drinks.

REGGAE SOUND SYSTEM

Hybernská 10, Nové město. Map 5C7 ☎26 35 46. Daily 9pm–5am. Metro: nám. Republiky.

The newest place in town as of this writing, located in the basement of a communist-era club. Specializes in black music and African DJs, and this is the only place in Prague where you'll meet the occasional Rastafarian. "Rocking 60s" on Tuesdays.

ROCK CAFÉ

Národní 22, Prague 1. Map 4D5 ☎ *20 66 56. Mon–Fri 10am–3am, Sat–Sun noon–3am; live music from 10pm. Disco Sun, Tues. Metro: Národní třída.*

An old favorite, for consistently good if faintly unadventurous rock bands. Even on days that the club advertises "disco" nights, rock is the dominant music. Industrial decor with black walls and linoleum floor. The building also houses the famous jazz club **Reduta**, as well as an art gallery and music store.

STRAHOV 007

Across from Spartakiádní stadium. Map 3D2. Daily from 7pm. Bus 218 from Anděl to 2nd stadium stop.

Young crowd from the student dorms nearby, and hellish acoustics, but features some of the best new local bands, and the beer is cheap, *and* you get the kc2 bottle deposit back . . . . Punk is in, and wearing black is the cool thing to do.

UBIQUITY

Na příkopě 22, Prague 1. Map 5C6. Daily from 9pm. Metro: nám. Republiky.

The most talked-about nightspot of post-1989 Prague. The owner is John-Bruce Shoemaker, an American whose imagination runs to things like bubble machines, a naked woman riding around the dance floor on a Harley-Davidson, large circus animals, and six-foot-eight African men clad in rubber clothes. Great Mexican food, a separate reggae room, and uninhibited shadow-dancers.

ÚJEZD

Újezd 18, Malá strana. Map 3D3 Mon–Sat from 8pm. Closed Sun. Metro: Malostranská, then tram 12 or 22 southbound.

Terribly smoky and with the looks of a cheap dive, but this is very much *en vogue* (at least as of 1992) among the young and hip, and often full of all sorts of (intellectually and sexually) adventurous types. Most nights you will have to beg before you are allowed in. There is even a medieval cellar.

Nightlife

NIGHTCLUBS AND DISCOS

Wenceslas Square is where you normally must go if you want to find a place to dance, or to watch more or less dressed girls dancing. If you are without a partner, you'll have a good chance of finding one in-house, particularly if you pay your bill in hard currency. Most top hotels — such as the DIPLOMAT, ESPLANADE, INTER-CONTINENTAL, INTERNATIONAL, JALTA and PARKHOTEL — own a nightclub–disco; that of the AMBASSADOR is the most famous and the most strategically located. Other favorite places to go dancing are the botels (floating hotels) **Admiral** and **ALBATROS**.

All of the following establishments feature a dance floor.

ALHAMBRA

In Hotel Ambassador, Václavské nám. 5
☎ *22 04 67* ☙ *Closed Sun; Mon. Metro: Můstek.*
An evening at Prague's best-known variety-cabaret show can be reserved through any hotel. After the show, you can move on to the video club/disco, which stays open till 2am.

EDEN PALLADIUM

U slavie 1 (corner of Vršovická), Vršovice (Prague 10). Map 2D4 ☎ *74 32 92. Thurs–Sun 8.30pm–2am. Metro: Strašnicka, then tram 7; or nám. Míru, then tram 4, 22.*
The biggest dance hall in Prague, occupying the second-floor auditorium of a former cultural center. The music is pure disco with a heavy preference for Madonna, and this is the only establishment listed in this section where you will see considerably more Czechs than tourists. At least the DJ is American.

HANAVSKÝ PAVILÓN

Letenské sady (Prague 7). Map 4B4 ☎ *32 57 92. Metro: Malostranská.*
See under LETNÁ GARDENS (page 95) and RESTAURANTS — TRADITIONAL (page 138). Floor show and dancing from 9pm.

KONÍČEK

Staroměstské nám. 20, Staré město (Old Town Sq.). Map 4C5 ☎ *235 89 27. Tues–Sat 9pm–2am. Metro: Staroměstská.*
Tremendous, dank Romanesque cellar with vaulted ceilings and massive piers and a Felliniesque procession of prostitutes, black marketeers, undercover cops and bewildered tourists lurking in its dark corners. You have to stand in line to get in, and you cannot wear tennis shoes. Huge dance floor.

LUCERNA / BOHEMIAN FANTASY

Lucerna Ballroom, Vodičkova 36, Nové město (off Wenceslas Sq.). Map 5D6 ☎ *235 0909* ⊟ *Performances Mon, Wed, Fri, Sat 9pm. Metro: Můstek. Buffet dinner 7pm. Box office 10am–6pm, until showtime on performance days.*
Music, ballet, folk dance, pantomime and technical gee-whizzery hosted by famous Czech stage-and-TV stars. The venue is one of Prague's most venerable ballrooms — designed, incidentally, by Václav Havel Sr., grandfather of the president. Price includes dinner, and you can move on to the dance floor once the show is over.

OBECNÍ DŮM

nám. Republiky 5, Staré město. Map 5C6 ☎ *23 12 68* ⊟ *Metro: nám. Republiky.*
See main entry under RESTAURANTS — TRADITIONAL (page 138). Sedate variety show; disco dancing.

SLOVANSKÝ DŮM

Na příkopě 22. Map 5C6 ☎ *22 48 51* ⊟ ☙ *Metro: nám. Republiky or Můstek.*
This is the legendary Café Continental of yore, the haunt of 1930s Sudeten-German separatists, Nazi officers and Gestapo toughs. It is now a maze of eating and drinking places, including a late-night cocktail bar on the top floor and a nightclub with floor show and striptease.

U NOVÁKŮ
Vodičkova 30, Nové město. Map 5D6. For
Varieté Praga ☎*235 08 61; for restaurant*
☎*22 31 43. Metro: Můstek.*
Sprawling and sleazy entertainment
complex off Wenceslas Square, the
nearest you can get in Prague to the
spirit of 42nd Street or Soho. Restaurant,
poker-machine arcade, lowbrow **Var-
iete Praga** with leggy floor show, disco
Korag (to 4am) and late-night bar **Admiral** (to 6am).

SEX
It is not quite Bangkok, nor even Bucharest, but the combination of
economic upheaval and tourist boom is said to have brought zest to
Prague's formerly mediocre sex market. A law permitting licensed pros-
titution was adopted around the time of this writing to bring some
order to a chaotic business. What actual effect it will have is anybody's
guess. Meanwhile, the bars of the top hotels are where lonely foreign
males go looking. Ads in tourist brochures supply further tips.

GAY CLUBS
Suppressed under the old regime, overt homosexuality has been one of
the great discoveries of post-revolutionary Prague. Fads come and go,
but at the time of writing the following four were the popular hangouts
for gay men and women.

- **America**   Petřínská 5, Malá strana (near Most legií). Map 4E4 ☎53 49 09.
  Open daily from 8.30pm. Metro: Anděl, then tram 12 northbound. Basement
  dance club opened by an American. Only a tiny US flag marks the entrance.
- **T-Club**   Jungmannovo nám. 17, Nové město. Map 5D6 ☎236 98 77. Metro:
  Národní třída. Heavy leather.
- **U Rožmberka**   Na bělidle 40 ☎53 75 31. Open Tues–Sun from 9pm.
  Closed Mon. Waiters in pink shirts.
- **Valdek**   nám. Míru 1, Vinohrady (Prague 2). Map 5E7 ☎25 93 70. Open
  daily 9pm–8am. Metro: nám. Míru. Popular café/dance club, mainly for gay men.

GAMBLING
That a gambling casino should open in the Palace of Culture, once the
proudest symbol of the cultural achievements of People's Czechoslovakia, was a symbol of the times; turning an 18thC Rococo palace into Las
Vegas followed logically. Gambling parlors also exist in the hotels AM-
BASSADOR, ATRIUM, FORUM and PALACE. More will have opened before
you read this. The usual dress code (tie and jacket obligatory for men,
no blue jeans, no sneakers) applies.

- **Casino Admiral**   Palác Kultury, 5. května 65, Pankrác (Prague 4). Map 2D4
  ☎417 11 11. Metro: Pankrác. Slot machines from 9am, roulette and blackjack
  from 6pm.
- **Palais Savarin**   Na příkopě 10, Prague 1. Map 5C6. Metro: Můstek. Classical grand casino in the Rococo palace otherwise known as the Sylva-Taroucca
  Palace. Opened in 1992 after thorough remodeling, which restored the
  interior to its original princely splendor.

Shopping

Where and what to buy

Things have improved a whole lot since 1989, although Prague is still a long way from a shopper's paradise. Prices are low by Western standards. But so too are quality and variety, and one hears too many woeful tales of would-be bargain hunters who end up with wads of unspent *koruns* in their pockets.

Nevertheless, the pace of change has been miraculous. Nearly all of Prague's small and medium businesses, 97 percent of them state-owned in 1989, are now private. Larger firms are set to go next, most likely by way of direct or indirect sale to big Western capital. The more enterprising ones among Prague's horde of street vendors have been rapidly upgrading themselves from market-stall to kiosk to fixed shop to chain-store. However, the most successful retail propositions are all Western imports, which are unlikely to be of much interest to a foreign visitor.

Most tourists enjoy shopping for **crystal** and **cut-glass** items, a historic Bohemian industry whose products have shown a marked improvement since their all-time nadir in the 1980s. **Antiques** and **art** are obvious areas of interest in a country with a long and superb tradition of artistry. A less well-known but equally distinguished field of craftsmanship is children's **toys**, in which Czech artists have traditionally created some of the world's most original, poetic and humorous products. Semiprecious **gems**, which come mostly from the northern Bohemian town of Turnov, also have their devotees.

For **shop opening hours**, see page 43. Department stores generally open 8am–7pm on weekdays and until 2pm on Saturdays. You can never know with private shops, but it is safe to assume that most will be closed after 6pm.

ANTIQUES

If you are in the market for a nice Picasso or Lucas Cranach, ex-Czechoslovakia is your place and now is your time. It is of course strictly illegal, but thousands of historic properties and art collections are being restituted to their old owners, and not all of the restituees are nobly indifferent to a bit of ready cash .... In 1991, more than a thousand Czechoslovak castles, churches and museums were reported looted, with some 20,000 paintings and art objects lost. In many cases museum authorities seem to have been directly involved.

Antique dealers and "art agencies" in Prague can direct you to the right addresses — but beware: trying to export any pre-1945 art work from the Czech Republic is a criminal offence, and controls can at times be strict. Even if you merely buy contemporary art, it pays to be very careful with the paperwork to avoid unpleasant surprises at the customs.

Back on the straight and narrow, Prague has a slew of antiquarian stores full of old objects, books and prints as wonderful and fascinating as the city itself. The best congregate on **Karlova ul.** in the Old Town and **Pohořelec** in Hradčany.

ATELIER KAVKA
Vězeňská 4, Staré město. Map 4C5 ☎*232 08 47. Open daily 10am–6pm.*
Wonderful old shop in the Jewish Quarter containing an amazing variety of strange and beautiful objects, as well as a contemporary art gallery.

MERCATOR
Pohořelec 26, Hradčany. Map 3C2.
A tiny shop with a most astonishing collection of beautiful old maps, prints and books, perhaps remaindered from the monks' library in the STRAHOV ABBEY, across the street.

U KARLOVA MOSTU
Karlova 2, Staré město (near Charles Bridge). Map 4C5 ☎*26 56 72.*
Excellent range of old books and prints, as well as selected current magazines from the West (e.g., the *New York Review*).

VLADIMÍR ANDRLE
Branches at Křížovnická 1 (Staré město), map 4C5; Karlova 8 (Staré město), map 4C5; and Pohořelec 7 (Hradčany), map 3C2.
Prague's top purveyor of antiques and collector's pieces, for a mainly foreign clientele. Wide selection of antique glassware.

ART GALLERIES
Art galleries range from private and strictly commercial ones (all opened since 1989) to the more prestigious exhibition halls, which formerly stood under the party-approved thumb of the Union of Artists but have now been taken over by various independent cultural-cum-commercial groups. The following are some of the galleries that dominated the reviews at the time of writing. As new ones continue to open, close and change hands at head-spinning speed, there can be no guarantee that any of this will have any practical validity in a year's time, but at least it will give you a flavor.

FRONTA
Spálená 53, Nové město. Map 4D5 ☎*29 65 08. Closed Mon. Metro: Národní třída.*
One of Prague's most attractive galleries belongs to the communist party youth organization, metamorphosed into a successful private enterprise. Mladá fronta, their publishing house, is virtually the only one in the Czech Republic that can still afford to publish "good" literature alongside the usual junk.

HOLLAR
Smetanovo nábř. 6, Staré město (near National Theater). Map 4D4. Open Tues–Sun 10am–1pm, 2–6pm. Closed Mon. Metro: Národní třída.
The most prestigious gallery for contemporary graphic arts. The attractive rooms overlook the Vltava embankment.

MÁNES
Masarykovo nábř. 2, Nové město. Map 4D4 ☎*29 55 77. Open Tues–Sun 10am–6pm. Closed Mon. Metro: Národní třída.*
The seat of the Union of Artists, and its principal gallery. The building, in Con-

structivist style, was designed in 1930 by O. Novotny. The attached garden café provides a pleasant retreat in summer.

PEITHNER-LICHTENFELS
Michalská 12, Staré město. Map 4C5 ☎*26 14 24. Open 10am–7pm. Metro: Národní třída.*
The Prague branch of the prestigious Viennese gallery of the same name. Two tiny Gothic halls in the Golden Melon House (U zlatého melouna) host high-powered exhibitions stressing the artistic affinities of the former Habsburg lands. Those with lots of money can take the paintings home.

STŘEDOČESKÁ (Central Bohemian Gallery)
Husova 19–21, Staré město. Map 4C5 ☎*236 07 00. Open Tues–Sun 10am–noon, 1–6pm. Closed Mon. Metro: Staroměstská.*
Gallery and publishing house owned by a public body. It possesses possibly the most comprehensive collection of contemporary (post-1960) Czech art, which director Jiří Kohoutek says will form the core of an as yet unrealized Museum of Modern Art.

U LORETY
Loretánská 23, Hradčany. Map 3C2 ☎*531 98 21. Open 10am–6pm. Metro: Malostranská, then tram 22 northbound.*
The best place for a beginner's course in contemporary Czech art, with works by well-known artists like Jiří Anderle, Adolf Born, Karel Demel and Šerých. Don't let the tourist-filled ambience distract you from some of the genuinely good stuff.

Other art galleries to look for include:

- **Art Forum**   In the Pálffy Palace, Valdštejnská 14, Malá strana. Map 4B4. Closed Monday. Metro: Malostranská.
- **Behemot**   Elišky Krásnohorské 6, Staré město (near Hotel Inter-Continental). Map 4B5 ☎231 78 29. Open 10am–7pm. Metro: Staroměstská.
- **Lukas**   Národní třída 21, Prague 1. Map 4D5. Metro: Národní třída.
- **MXM**   Nosticova 6, Malá strana. Map 4D4. Open Tuesday to Sunday 10am–7pm. Closed Monday. Metro: Národní třída.
- **Nová síň**   Voršilská 3, Nové město (off Národní). Map 4D5. Metro: Národní třída.
- **U černého orla**   Mostecká 11, Malá strana. Map 3C3 ☎53 75 78. Open Monday to Friday 2–7pm; Saturday to Sunday 9am–6pm. Metro: Malostranská.
- **U řečických**   Vodičkova 10, Nové město. Map 5D6 ☎22 59 02. Open Tuesday to Sunday 10am–1pm, 2–6pm. Closed Monday. Metro: Můstek.
- **U zlatého koníčka**   Husova 18, Staré město ☎216 65 22. Open 10am–6pm. Metro: Staroměstská.
- **Via Art**   Resslova 6, Nové město. Map 4E5. Metro: Karlovo nám.

DEPARTMENT STORES
The biggest department stores congregate along Wenceslas Square, Národní třída, Na příkopě and nám. Republiky. Most of them are still owned by the state and awaiting suitors, so whatever comments we might make here (they'd mostly be scathing) are unlikely to remain valid for long. As it is, you might be reduced to tears just trying to catch the attention of a shop attendant.

- **BATA**   Václavské nám. 6. Map 5D6 ☎235 45 65. The former Dům obuvi (House of the Shoe) was transformed in 1992 into the new flagship store of Bata, a worldwide shoe empire that had its origins in prewar Czechoslovakia (see page 115). Western flair and excellent value.

Other leading stores include:

- **Bílá labuť** (White Swan)   Na poříčí 3 (off nám. Republiky). Map 5C6 ☎232 06 22. The second-largest department store in the land (the biggest is Kotva — see below). It carries a surprisingly good (and cheap) range of fabrics.
- **Dětský dům** (Children's House)   Na příkopě 15. Map 5C6 ☎235 10 80. Children's things.
- **Družba** (Friendship)   Václavské nám. 21. Map 5D6 ☎26 38 42. General department store.
- **Dům módy** (House of Fashion)   Václavské nám. 58. Map 5D6. Clothing and accessories.
- **Dům potravin** (House of Edibles)   Václavské nám. 50. Map 5D6. Food and drink.
- **Dům sportu** (House of Sport)   Jungmannova 28. Map 5D6. Sport articles.
- **Kotva** (Anchor)   nám. Republiky 8. Map 5C6. Vast department store. Reasonable food department in the basement, and while-u-wait shoe repairs.
- **Máj** (May)   Národní 26. Map 4D5 ☎26 38 42. General department store.

GLASS, CRYSTAL AND PORCELAIN

Cut glass and crystal have been associated with Bohemia ever since Venetian masters brought the art here in the 14thC. They still constitute by far the most popular item on most tourists' shopping list: some tour operators even supply special shopping carts for carrying glass, to each person who participates in their walking tours. The traditional items (tableware, chandeliers) have by and large been reduced to kitsch, but one does occasionally spot a heart-quickening piece among the modern designs.

Shops selling the standard range of glass and crystal items are thick on the ground along the main tourist routes, and there is little point in trying to list them all. Here are a couple of major stores and some art gallery/shops that exhibit and sell highly original, individually signed works of art in glass or porcelain.

ARS BOHEMICA
Řetězová 3, Staré město. Map 4C5. Open 10am–6pm. Metro: Staroměstská or Můstek.
Modern art applied to Karlsbad porcelains, exhibited and sold in the eerie setting of the subterranean medieval palace of the Lords of Kunštát and Poděbrady.

BÖHM
Anglická 1, Vinohrady (Prague 2). Map 5E7. Open Mon–Fri 2pm–6pm; Sat–Sun 10am–3pm ☎236 20 16. Metro: I.P. Pavlova.
Contemporary glass gallery.

ČESKÝ PORCELÁN
Perlová 1, Staré město (corner of Národní).

Map 4D5 ☎22 12 95. Open 9.30am–6pm. Metro: Můstek or Národní třída.
Sole factory outlet for classic cobalt-blue Bohemian porcelain with the characteristic "onion" design (*cibulák* in Czech, *Zwiebelmuster* in German), produced only here and in Meissen.

GALERIE JUSTITZ
Národní 25, Prague 1. Map 4D5 ☎26 20 81. Open Mon–Fri 10am–6.30pm; Sat 10am–2pm. Closed Sun. Metro: Národní třída.
Modern applied arts.

LUNA
Na příkopě 16, Prague 1. Map 5C6. Metro: Národní třída.

Crystal chandeliers, traditional and modern.

MOSER
Na příkopě 12. Map 5C6 ☎ *22 91 57.*
Oak-paneled sales rooms and elegant ambience. Will ship abroad.

ROB VAN DER DOEL
Janský vršek 15, Malá strana (off Nerudova). Map 3C3. Metro: Malostranská.
Contemporary glass art.

FLEA MARKETS
There is a big flea market every Saturday in the former slaughterhouse in Holešovice (Prague 7), and one on Sunday mornings in the cultural center of the metal workers' union (Dům kultury kovoprůmyslu) in Arbesovo nám., Smíchov (Prague 5).

MUSIC
The state recording company **Supraphon** produces fairly creditable CDs (classical, jazz and pop), which are sold at a quarter of comparable Western prices in every souvenir shop and pedlar's stand in Prague. The catch is the extremely limited range of choice, with the identical set of Dvořáks and cheap Mozarts at each one of a hundred points of sale. They are so cheap you cannot resist buying, and seven out of ten turn out to be an acceptable purchase. Supraphon's own retail chain seems to have closed down pending a reorganization.

STAMPS
Profil, a new stamp collectors' center at Na příkopě 24 (in the arcade), provides a range of philatelists' services including export permits and customs formalities *(map 5 C6* ☎ *22 33 27, open Mon-Fri 10am-6pm, metro: Můstek, nám. Republiky).*

TOYS
Prague's craftsmen excel in wooden toys and doodads of great originality, as well as marionettes, dolls and Punch-and-Judy figures in the tradition of Jiří Trnka, the "Czech Walt Disney." You can find some of these in department stores, notably the **Dětský dům** (Children's Store) on Na příkopě (see DEPARTMENT STORES).

But for truly fascinating pieces, try the little shops on Nerudova ul. and Pohořelec — above all the **Obchod se vším možným** at Nerudova 45 *(map 3 C3)*, a magical treasury of strange and beautiful things. Another good shop is the **U zlatého koníčka** at Husova 18, Staré město *(map 4 C5).*

The **Albatros** store at Na perštýně 1, Staré město *(map 4 D5)* stocks children's books of excellent quality.

Recreation

Sports and leisure

Slavia and Sparta are the top soccer teams of the capital, and Martina Navratilova and Ivan Lendl only two of the tennis greats who sailed to international stardom from Prague's courts. The traditional Czech preoccupation with physical fitness has filled the city with many publicly supported fitness centers, providing swimming pool, sauna, gym and ping-pong tables for a nominal fee. One among many is the **Fit Centrum Dlabačov** *(Bělohorská 24, Břevnov, Prague 6, map 1 C3, open Sun-Fri 1-9pm, closed Sat).*

- Several hotels have gym/fitness facilities and/or swimming pools for use by their guests: look for the ⚕ and ≋ symbols in our hotel listings.

BOWLING
The most popular place to bowl is in the **Hotel Forum**, Kongresová 2, Nusle (Prague 4), map **2**D4 ☎419 01 11.

GOLF
The **Karlstein Golf Club**, the first 18-hole course in Prague, is currently being developed by a Swiss group. Contact their information bureau at Na příkopě 20, Prague 1, map **5**C6 ☎26 40 18 ⓕⓧ26 40 23. The **Golf Hotel** in Motol, Prague 5 *(map 1 B2 ☎55572)* offers a 9-hole course.

For minigolf, try the **International Hotel** in Dejvice *(Prague 6, map 1 C3 ☎32 10 51)* and the **Výstaviště** exhibition grounds in Holešovice *(Prague 7, map 2 C4 ☎37 73 41).*

RIDING
The city's racecourse is at **Velká Chuchle** in Prague 5, a 15-minute bus journey from metro Smíchovské nádraží *(map 1 E3).* The nearest place where you can go for riding is the **Konopiště castle**, 44km (27 miles) SE of the city. For information ☎(0301) 21366.

SQUASH
The only squash courts in Prague are at the **Forum** hotel and the **Club Hotel Průhonice**. See WHERE TO STAY, pages 126 and 128.

SWIMMING
The best place to go swimming is **Podolí** *(Podolská 74, Prague 4, map 1 D3 ☎42 73 84),* which offers a 50-meter (165-foot) indoor pool, an outdoor pool in an attractive park, saunas and steam bath. Take tram 3

(from Wenceslas Sq./Charles Sq.) or tram 17 (from the right riverbank). Open 6am–10pm on weekdays, 8am–8pm Saturday, Sunday, holidays.

The **Šeberák lake** in Prague 4 *(map 2 D5, a 10min bus journey from metro Chodov)* is reserved for naturists.

TENNIS
There are indoor and outdoor courts on **Štvanice Island** *(Prague 7, map 5 A7-B7)*, which can be rented by the hour *(☎ 231 63 23 for reservations)*. Further public courts exist in the **Letná Gardens** *(map 4 A5 ☎ 37 36 83)*.

Ideas for children

A city of 500 towers — most of them climbable — with crazily painted matchbox houses, gargoyles and statues leaping from every house-front, and mysterious underground cellars is bound to delight any child who has a sense of the wonderful.

Begin to impress them with a visit to the **astronomical clock** of the Old Town Hall (page 105). Visit, next, any of a number of **toy stores** (page 161), where they may sell replicas of the clock's marionette figures. A toy museum is rumored to be in the works in Hradčany; if it is not yet there, divert to the **Prague City Museum** (page 121), where a historic model of Prague will rivet child and parent alike. Then consider a tour of the model coalmine at the **National Technical Museum** (page 121).

How you go is as important as where you go: excite them with a ride in a **horse-drawn buggy** (Old Town Square), or one of Prague's clanking, groaning **trams**.

Take the **Petřín funicular** (page 107) into the park, where there is a planetarium, an observatory *(open Tues-Sun 2-7pm, 9-11pm, closed Mon)* and a mirror maze to provide hours of fun.

The skeletons and fossils of the **National Museum** (page 113) are rather dull, and the **zoo** in Troja (page 111) somewhat mediocre except for its stable of wild Przewalski horses. Not so, however, the old **Botanical Garden** at Na slupi 18, Nové město *(near Karlovo nám., off map 4 F5)*, featuring the *Victoria regia*, the world's largest flower; nor the wonderful 1891 **Výstaviště Fairgrounds** (page 123) in Stromovka.

Nightlife? Obviously the **National Marionette Theater** (page 150), where it will impress your kid for life that Mozart is actually a lot more fun than Michael Jackson or whatsisname.

When you have had enough, then the **Dům dětí** (Children's House) in Prague Castle will help. Their friendly staff take care of children between ages one and 15 for a few hours while you romp around Prague. They have toys, computer games and a weekly children's theater every Wednesday at 3pm, and it is all free of charge. Address: Jiřská ul, in the Castle; open daily except Monday, 10am–5pm.

There is even a new babysitter service for tourists. The **Martina Agency** *(Post Box 12, Prague 9 ☎ 859 14 27)* provides babysitters who speak 16 languages and will come to your hotel room or house.

Excursions

Day trips from Prague

Few countries in Europe can boast as many quaint towns and old villages and castles per square mile as the Czech Republic, and a large number of these lie within a couple of hours' drive from Prague. The country is hilly and pleasant; forests alternate with sown fields, and there are, as of this writing, very few billboards, shopping malls, discount palaces, gas station chains, drive-in facilities, park-and-ride pools, car showrooms, holiday parks, industrial estates, satellite towns and clover-leaf intersections cluttering the landscape. In short, a delightful place to go driving around.

Listing all the nice places that can be reached on a day's trip from Prague would be beyond the scope of this book. However, this chapter offers a few route suggestions and highlights.

WHERE TO GO
If you have at least a day and a half to spend outside Prague, we think the best you could do is to head west toward **KARLOVY VARY** and **MARIÁNSKÉ LÁZNĚ**, the grand 19thC spas better known by their German names, Karlsbad and Marienbad. Exploring each takes the better part of a day, and adjusting to their peculiar lazy charm may demand a little longer. The one-hour drive between the two towns runs across some of the most attractive countryside in western Bohemia.

Where to stay? Karlovy Vary has the more pleasant site, Mariánské Lázne the more unrestrained architecture, but to our mind nothing matches the decadent pleasure of a night in Karlovy Vary's venerable **Grand Hotel**.

If you want to keep nearer to the capital, there are a dozen castles, a medieval wonder-town and a lot of beautiful nature to sample within an hour's radius of Prague, the best of them lying in a southerly half-circle. Start at the village of **Lány** (40km/25 miles W of Prague). Visit the medieval castle of **KŘIVOKLÁT** and the stalactite caves of **Koněprusy**, then proceed to **KARLŠTEJN**, one of Central Europe's most impressive castles, and enjoy the natural scenery of the **SLAPY** lakes.

Visit, next, Archduke Franz Ferdinand's Wilhelmine extravaganza at the **KONOPIŠTĚ** castle. Drive past the medieval **SÁZAVA** monastery and the **Český Šternberk** castle, and end your day in the delightfully preserved Gothic mining town of **KUTNÁ HORA**, 70km (43 miles) E of Prague.

Trying to squeeze all this into a day may prove hectic: adjust as you wish, but be sure to keep Kutná Hora on the itinerary. Karlštejn is another

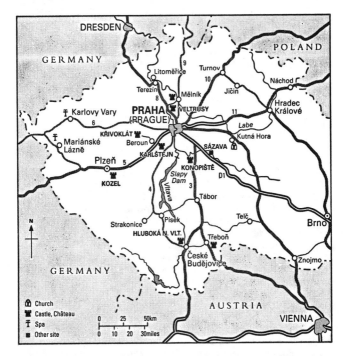

must, except that its most interesting parts may be off-limits for a while.

The Nazi concentration camp at **TEREZÍN** is an interesting excursion for most people, not least for its model-town architecture, which is a fascinating example of 18thC rationalism at its most extreme. You could combine a tour of Terezín with a visit to the Baroque château of **VELTRUSY** and a stroll through the historic town of **Litoměřice**. On the way back, stop in **MĚLNÍK** to admire its vineyards and perhaps taste some of their product in the castle wine cellars.

CASTLES AND STATELY HOMES

The official handbook of the Czech Ministry of Culture lists 163 visitable castles and country estates in Bohemia and Moravia. A number of these are currently at some stage or another of being restituted to their former owners. So a castle that was a tourist attraction last year may very well have in the meanwhile turned into somebody's private home, or be padlocked pending a court decision, or be scaffolded-up pending conversion into a hotel.

You are more or less free to wander around Karlštejn, but in other castles you must wait to join one of the guided tours, which are usually once-hourly, and not always "on the hour." Further, some castles — both private and public — can only be toured by prior arrangement. Consult Čedok or an information office in Prague before you depart if you don't want to leave anything to chance.

Many castles and stately homes outside Prague are closed in winter (November through March inclusive), and operate on a restricted schedule in the months of April and October. Virtually all of them are closed on Mondays and days following official holidays. Some observe a midday pause from noon to 1pm.

TRANSPORT

It is a pleasure to drive through the winding country lanes and sleepy villages of Bohemia, so a car is worth investing in if you plan to travel out of Prague. See pages 40 and 41 for details on driving and car rental.

Trains are frequent, punctual, very cheap and serve just about every town and large village in the country. Addresses of the main train stations are given on page 38. The bus network is nearly as extensive as the train, and faster too. The main bus terminal, **Florenc**, is located at Křižíkova 5, Prague 8 *(map 5B7, metro: Florenc)*. Timetable information is available in English on ☎ 22 14 40.

There are additional long-distance bus stations in the suburbs of **Smíchov** *(metro: Anděl)*, **Holešovice** *(metro: Nádr. Holešovice)* and **Roztyly** *(metro: Roztyly)*. (Locate these outlying stations via the metro map at the back of the book.)

BOAT EXCURSIONS

Another enjoyable way to get out of Prague is to join one of the river excursions that depart daily in summer (April to September) from the right (w) bank of the **Palacký Bridge** (Palackého most) *(map 4F4, metro: Karlovo nám.)*. Information and tickets are available at **Hořejší nábř. 17, Prague 5** *(off map 4F4* ☎ *54 35 45, 29 38 03)*.

The northbound (downstream) boats leave daily at 8.30am, 9.30am, 1.30pm and 3pm on the short jaunt to the park at STROMOVKA (see page 123) and TROJA CHÂTEAU (see page 110). On Saturday and Sunday, the 8.30am boat continues on to **Roztoky**, a hilly riverside town with a Renaissance château housing a museum of local history. From Roztoky, you can take the boat, train or bus back to Prague.

The southbound (upstream) excursion departs daily at 9am for the 3-hour journey to SLAPY DAM, sailing through country that becomes greener, hillier and wilder as you follow the Vltava. From Slapy, you can follow a marked hiking trail on the west bank of the river through valleys and rocky gorges to the village of **Štěchovice** (8km/5 miles), where you can catch a bus to Prague or wait for the boat on its return trip.

Excursions A to Z

ČESKÉ BUDĚJOVICE (Budweis) ☆
*140km (87 miles) s of Prague. **By car** via Písek (Rte4 s from Smíchov) or Tábor (D1 motorway from 5. května, exit at km 26). **Trains** from Prague-Central and Prague-Smíchov.*

A charming historic town in a deep southern Bohemian province, with a splendid **central square** (Nám. Přemysla Otakara II) fringed by arcaded Renaissance and Baroque houses and dominated by the 16thC **Black Tower**, a symbol of the town. The back streets are sadly dilapidated, in lively contrast with Prague's all-fresh coat of paint. There is a particularly old and attractive area around the Gothic Piarist Church.

The town was founded in the 13thC by King Ottokar II. The superb Budvar (Budweiser) beer, undeservedly overshadowed by the Pilsner, has been brewed in it since 1531. There is no better place to enjoy it than the **Masné krámy**, an ever-crowded and jolly beer arcade, which has been documented as existing since the Middle Ages *(at Krajinská 13, off the main square ☎ (038) 326 52)*.

☞ **Zvon** *(on main square ☎ (038) 353 61 ✉ (038) 236 08 ▥ no cards ⇰). A historic inn in business since 1533, though the interior is ruined by modernization. Most rooms are without bath.

Vicinity
The medieval castle of **Hluboká nad Vltavou** (☆), 10km (6 miles) N of Budějovice, was rebuilt by the Schwarzenbergs in the 19thC English (or Windsor) Gothic style. It houses valuable collections of Flemish tapestry, armor and period furniture, and can be visited from March to October inclusive *(☎ (038) 96 50 45)*.

Situated in an attractive area of lakes and peat bogs 25km (15 miles) E of Budějovice is the walled medieval town of **Třeboň** (☆), with a population of 5,000, a castle and 14thC brewery. The town was the seat of the powerful Rožmberg family of counts until the 17thC. It was later acquired by the Schwarzenbergs, whose family mausoleum is located a short distance outside the town.

☞ ⇰ and lakeshore **campsite**.

KARLOVY VARY (Karlsbad) ☆
*130km (80 miles) w of Prague. **By car** via Rte6/E48 (from Milady Horákové, behind Letná Park). Regular **buses** from Florenc station (map 5B7). **Trains** (3hrs) from Prague-Central. Daily **air service** in summer. For **i** (spa information) ☎ (017) 20 35 69 ✉ (017) 246 67.*

"Taking the waters" at Karlsbad was what the elegant people of Europe did for their holidays before the coming of mass tourism — in that age of transition in which the upper classes had begun to travel for leisure, and people who could travel affected the manners and titles of the upper classes.

The heyday of the West Bohemian spa was from the mid-1700s to the eve of the World War in 1914. Goethe and Beethoven spent a few seasons in Karlsbad; Karl Marx went three times (hence the unremoved bust on Petra Velikého ul.); Czar Nicholas II and the future King Edward VII each spent time there. Russian aristocrats came to teach "Europe" to their sons and daughters, Viennese fops to get away from their lovers, Victorian gentlemen to nurse a gout.

From that period, especially the last decades of the 19thC, Karlovy Vary (as Karlsbad is now called) inherits one of Europe's most astonishing concentrations of Romantic architecture, which 40 years of socialist mediocrity have chipped at the edges but failed to spoil.

The cures

The therapeutic properties of Vary's warm springs were already noted in the Middle Ages, before Charles IV transformed the little settlement on the Teplá by granting it in 1370 a charter to dispense medical treatment. There are 12 springs in all, which boil up from hot rocks 2,000 meters (over 6,500 feet) underground and reach the surface at temperatures ranging from 30° (86°F) to 72°C (162°F). Their composition, properties, history and medical effects are subject to intense and serious disquisition. Most people come to town on a medically prescribed cure, which involves drinking from various combinations of the springs according to a closely monitored schedule, as well as subjection to hot baths, massages, electrical shocks, inhalation, pneumopuncture, moorpacks and other obscure procedures.

An essential, if unofficial, part of the treatment seems to be the consumption of large amounts of Becherovka, a digestive liqueur that is sometimes called "the 13th spring of Karlsbad." Another Karlsbad perennial, the sweetened wafers called *oplátky*, helps to neutralize the foul taste of the waters.

Medical care and bathing in Karlovy Vary

- Various treatment programs can be booked in Prague through **Čedok** or **Balnea** *(Pařížská 11, Staré město, map 4C5* ☎ *232 37 67)*, and on-site through the spa administration, which is located next to the Vřídlo *(Mlýnské nábřeží 7* ☎ *(017) 20 35 69* [Fx]*(017) 246 67)*.
- The **Bath I** *(Lázně I)* opposite the Grand Hotel Pupp is usually the only place where you can get treatment without having made a prior reservation *(* ☎ *(017) 285 15, open Mon-Fri 6.45am-3pm, Sat 6.45am-noon)*.
- The **Hotel Thermal** at I.P. Pavlova 11 *(* ☎ *(017) 283 91)* has a public swimming pool of warm water.

What to see

The historic district stretches along the wooded valley of the River Teplá for two enchanting kilometers of cream-cake palaces and Proustian nostalgia.

The heart of the spa is the **Mill Promenade** (Mlýnská kolonáda ✮), a Corinthian colonnade of the 1870s where people gather gravely all day long, pacing up and down and sipping from the nozzled porcelain mugs designed to keep water at a constant temperature. Nearby, the main spring of Karlovy Vary, the **Vřídlo** (German: *Sprudel*), bursts temperamentally in the glass-and-concrete case built for it by the communists. The discovery of this fountain by Charles IV, who is said to have been led to it by a deer, proved to be the event that set Karlovy Vary on the path to fame and fortune.

The **Church of Mary Magdalen** (kostel sv. Maří Magdalény), which raises a dainty Baroque facade on Divadelní náměstí (Theater Square), is a work by K.I. Dienzenhofer dating from 1731-37. The sumptuous **Vítězslav Nezval Theater**, which gives the square its name, features a curtain painted by the young Gustav Klimt. The gold-bulbed **Russian Orthodox Church** (✫) hides at the edge of the hill on the left bank. It was built in 1893-98 in imitation of the church of Ostankino near Moscow, and commemorates Peter the Great's visit to the spa in 1711.

A beautiful row of *fin de siècle* architectural gallantries lie along **Sadova ul.** (✫). Nearly all of them were turned into state-owned guesthouses — *lázeňský dům* — under the socialist regime, one of whose few genuine successes was the promise of free and universal spa-care for every Czechoslovak worker and pensioner. The street leads up to the most exclusive part of old Karlsbad along **Petra Velikého ul.** (✫), from where a forest path climbs up to the rock of the **Deer Leap** (Jelení skok ◀❧). A funicular railway *(lánovka)* takes you down from the peak to the neighborhood of the **Grand Hotel Pupp** (✫), the sprawling Baroque and Neo-Baroque mansion which has been the heart of Karlsbad's social life since 1701.

❧   All but one of Karlovy Vary's hotels were still state-owned at the time of writing, which in practice meant a more or less dramatic gap between outward splendor and inward shabbiness. If "atmosphere" is the measure, then the **Grand Hotel Pupp** has no peer. A large number of private pensions and small hotels have recently opened in the immediate vicinity of the town.

It may be difficult to find a hotel room during the summer high season. In low season, conversely, prices are slashed by at least half. **Our price categories apply to summer rates.**

❧ GRAND HOTEL PUPP

Mírové nám. 2 ☎*(017) 20 91 11* 🖷*(017) 240 32* 🎞 *270 rms* 🆎 ⊙ 💳 🃏 *Two* 🍽 *Cafeteria. Pub* 📺 ⚽ ☐ *Gambling casino.*
Once one of Europe's grandest hotels, reduced to formica-paneled penury under the name of "Grand Hotel Moskva," reviving (very) slowly since it got its name back in 1990. The rooms may have 5-meter-high ceilings and crystal chandeliers, but that's no guarantee your TV set will work. Insist on a room in the main wing, as opposed to the modern extension. Goethe, Schiller and Beethoven stayed there.

❧ DVOŘÁK

Nová louka 11 ☎*(017) 241 45* 🖷*(017) 228 14* 🎞 *87 rms* 🆎 ⊙ 💳 🔲 ⚽ ♨ ⚑ ☕ *Garden. For golf reservations* ☎ *or* 🖷*(017) 240 11.*
The first post-socialist hotel in Karlovy Vary, in a historic building rebuilt and managed impeccably by an Austrian team. For the ultimate treat, seek a room in the satellite called **Villa Margareta**, a 19thC dream mansion 10km (6 miles) NE of town, with attached 18-hole golf course.

❧ PUŠKIN

Tržiště 37 ☎(017) 226 46 ▢ *No cards* ☰
A splendid turn-of-the-century building gone to seed, a delight if you don't mind the linoleum and the mildew.

☰ The **Francouzský** restaurant of the Grand Hotel Pupp (▥) is where people dine for status, although both service and cuisine leave room for improvement. For rustic charm and good food, try a country restaurant in the villages neighboring Karlovy Vary, such as the **Svatý Linhart** *(in Doubí ☎ 234 90* ▥ *open Wed–Sun 9am-6pm).*
Among cafés, the **Elefant** *(Stará louka 30, near the Grand Hotel Pupp* ▢*)* is a leftover from the *belle époque*, which awaits the return of better times.

CAMPING **Hájovna** *(in Březová, 3km/2 miles s of the center ☎ (017) 251 01 ☰),* a motel (75 beds) and campsite in the lovely natural surroundings of the Teplá valley.

KARLŠTEJN CASTLE (Karlstein) ☆
28km (17 miles) sw of Prague. By car via Beroun (Rte5 toward Plzeň) or Černošice-Dobřichovice (Rte4 toward Strakonice). Trains (35mins) every half hour from Prague-Smíchov. For numerous organized tours ☎ and ⊠(0311) 942 11 ▨ *Open June-Aug 8am-6pm; Sept-Oct and Apr-May 9am-5pm; Nov-Mar 9am-4pm. Closed Mon.*
• *NOTE: The Chapel of the Holy Cross, the most outstanding feature of the castle, has been closed for restoration since 1981 and is unlikely to reopen until the mid-1990s. Inquire about the latest position at an information bureau in Prague before you set off on this excursion.*

The most celebrated of Bohemian castles was built by Charles IV to safeguard the crown jewels of the Holy Roman Empire and the emperor's own collection of sacred relics; it also served as a royal safehouse in times of danger. Matthew of Arras, the first architect of St Vitus's Cathedral, constructed Karlštejn in the remarkably short span of nine years (1348-57). It was restored and in part rebuilt in 1888-1904 by Friedrich Schmidt and Josef Mocker, the leading theorists of the Neo-Gothic movement in Bohemia.

What to see

A steep path of 1.5km (1 mile) leads through the wine-growing village of Karlštejn (population 1,200) to the castle, whose three building blocks are said to represent a symbolic ascent from the worldly (the royal quarters) to the celestial (the treasure chapel).

At the lowest level is the **Palace of Charles IV**, in part preserved in its original wood paneling; it houses a permanent exhibition of the emperor's life and times. **St Mary's Tower** (Mariánská věž), the intermediary stage, is centered on the chapel of the Virgin, with a series of portraits (c.1357) which are among the earliest in European art. The adjoining **chapel of St Catherine** (kaple sv. Kateřina ☆) was reserved for the private prayers of the emperor; it has walls faced with large slabs of semiprecious stone and a fresco showing Charles kneeling alongside one of his wives, Anna of Schweidnitz.

The **Great Tower** (Velká věž) culminates the ascent to Heaven with a mighty bastion of walls 5.5 meters (18 feet) thick. In its upper story, accessible by a narrow stairway, is the **Chapel of the Holy Cross** (kaple sv. kříže ★), a pinnacle of the Gothic decorator's art. The low, vaulted ceilings of the chapel are entirely gilded and set with hundreds of glass stars, a sun and a moon. A row of 127 wood panels, painted with saints and angels by Master Theodoric (see page 19), cover the niches that once held Charles' astounding collection of sacred relics (highlights include a segment of the True Cross, thorns of the Passion, and a piece of the vinegar-soaked sponge). In an alcove behind the main altar, the imperial jewels (now in the Vienna Hofburg) and the Bohemian royal insignia (now in the treasury chamber of St Vitus in Prague) used to be kept.

Having deteriorated badly over the years, the chapel is currently closed to visitors for restoration. (See note opposite.)

Mlýn (☎ *(0311) 942 08* 🇫🇽 *(0311) 943 09* ▥ ➡ *)*, an attractive building in the woods, with restaurant, beer garden, and boats for hire.

➡ Numerous little cafés can be found along the road to the castle.

Vicinity

11km (7 miles) sw of Karlštejn, in the direction of Beroun, are the **Koněprusy caves** *(Koněpruské jeskyně)*, the largest stalactite caves in the country. They were (re)discovered in 1950, although explorations have revealed traces of earlier human presence, including a forgers' workshop from the 15thC (☎ *open Apr-Sept 8am-4pm)*.

KONOPIŠTĚ CASTLE ☆

44km (27 miles) sw of Prague (2km/1¼ miles nw of Benešov). **By car** *via Benešov (D1 highway toward Brno, exit toward Tábor).* **Trains** *from Prague-Central and Prague-Smíchov. Numerous organized* **tours.** *For castle ☎ and* ⌧*(0301) 213 66* ✗ *Apr-Oct daily, except Mon, 9am to 3, 4, 5 or 6pm.* **Closed** *on days following a public holiday.*

The Renaissance château of Konopiště was reconstructed at the end of the 19thC as a residence for Archduke Franz Ferdinand, the heir to the Austro-Hungarian throne, whose assassination in Sarajevo was to be the immediate cause of World War I. The splendidly decorated interior holds three memorable exhibitions: the **historic armor collection** of the d'Este dukes of Modena, which Franz Ferdinand inherited through his paternal grandmother; a unique collection of **pictures and statues** of the dragon-slaying St George; and the **trophies** of the archduke's own hunting career, which seems to have amounted to a small genocide.

> *Franz Ferdinand d'Este, a nephew of Franz Joseph I, became heir to the Habsburg throne after the emperor's only son, the intelligent and liberal Rudolf, committed suicide at Mayerling in 1887. He was a narrow-minded bigot and a militarist who shared with Germany's Kaiser Wilhelm II a "Wagnerian" infatuation with medieval chivalric lore. His fatal tour of Bosnia in 1914 was a deliberate provocation of the Serbian nationalists, who claimed that Austrian-occupied province as their own.*

The castle is surrounded by a magnificent park offering opportunities for swimming and horseback-riding. The Baroque outer gate holds sculptures by Matthias Braun (1725).

✑ **Motel Konopiště** *(* ☎ *(0301) 250 71* ▥ *bungalows* ⇶ ⚑ *minigolf, garden),* a branch of Prague's Panorama Hotel in an attractive country setting.

KŘIVOKLÁT CASTLE ☆

40km (25 miles) w of Prague. **By car** *via Beroun (Plzeň road) or Lány (Karlovy Vary road).* **Buses** *in summer (1½ hrs) from Dejvice station (metro: Hradčanská, map 3A3). Numerous organized* **tours.** *For castle* ☎*(0313) 981 20* 🖃 **Open** *Feb-Dec 9am to 5 or 6pm except Mon.* **Closed** *Jan and on days following a national holiday.*

One of the oldest and finest medieval castles in Bohemia rises in a compact mass of turrets, towers and battlements from a vast forest, formerly a hunting preserve of the Bohemian kings.

Already mentioned in the 12thC, Křivoklát was extended to its present scope under Vladislav II at the end of the 15thC (hence the architectural similarities with Prague's Vladislav Hall). Rudolf II used it as a hunting retreat and a jail: among the castle's prize exhibits are six skeletons of starved prisoners that were found in a cellar during a later restoration. The castle passed into private hands in the 17thC. It was eventually acquired by the Fürstenberg counts, who carried out repairs early in this century.

The architectural highlight of the castle is the **chapel** (✯), a Gothic gem with a sumptuous winged altar of carved wood. Other displays include an excellent collection of Late Gothic sculpture and painting, the library and portrait gallery of the Fürstenbergs, hunting trophies, historic carriages and torture instruments. Concerts occasionally take place in the castle grounds in the summer months.

Vicinity

An attractive drive along the Berounka river leads SW of Křivoklát to the ruined castle of **Týřov** (12km/7 miles).

The castle of **Lány**, approximately 17km (10 miles) to the N, serves as a presidential residence. In its graveyard is the modest tomb of Tomáš Masaryk, the founder of Czechoslovakia. President Havel does regular broadcasts of a philosophical nature from here, entitled *Conversations from Lány*.

KUTNÁ HORA (Kuttenberg) ★

*68km (42 miles) E of Prague. **By car** via Rte 333 (from Vinohradská). **Trains** from Masarykovo or Prague-Central (some with a change in Kolín). **Buses** ($1\frac{1}{2}$ hrs) from Florenc station (map **5B7**) **i** on Main Square. **St Barbara, Italian Court, Sedlec ossuary** open daily (except Mon) 8am-5pm (summer), 9am-4pm (winter). **Ursuline Convent** and **Castle/Mining Museum** open daily (except Mon) 8am-5pm (summer), Sat-Sun only in Apr, Oct; closed in winter.*

Kutná Hora ("Mine Hill") was built on a silver boom that began in the late 13thC with the discovery of Europe's largest silver deposits in a hill near the town. King Ottokar II used the proceeds to finance Bohemia's rise to medieval greatness. The town soon grew larger than Prague, and even served as a royal residence for some years after 1400, when Wenceslas IV was compelled to leave his capital.

The ore ran out in the 16thC. Very little was built in Kutná Hora after that apart from some Jesuit-inspired institutions and Rococo townhouses of the 18thC. Filled with the monuments of its prosperous era, the town easily qualifies as the most picturesque in Bohemia.

What to see

All but one of the town's chief points of interest lie within short walking distance of **Palackého náměstí** (Main Square).

The church of **St Barbara** (chrám svaté Barbory ★) ranks among the most splendid Gothic churches in Europe. Dedicated to the patron saint of miners and financed wholly by miners' contributions, the church was begun in 1388 under the baton of Peter Parler. Benedict Ried added the spectacular flowers and stars of the nave's vaulting shortly after he had completed the ceiling of Prague's Vladislav Hall in 1500. The Jesuits, who took the church over in the 17thC, contributed two Baroque chapels dedicated to St Francis Xavier and St Ignatius of Loyola. They also built the Baroque **Jesuit College** neighboring the church on Barborská ul.

The 15thC **Castle** (Hrádek), at the end of Barborská, possesses a chapel and Gothic wall-paintings, but its main attraction is a **Mining**

Museum (✭), which gives access to an enormous subterranean network of disused mine shafts and tunnels.

The **Italian Court** (Vlašský dvůr ✭) was Kutná Hora's mint during its 14thC boom. It is named after the Florentine coin-makers who arrived in c.1300; they designed the *groschen*, which was to remain the most popular silver currency in continental Europe for many centuries. (The rival *taler* originated from another silver town, the West Bohemian Joachimstal/Jáchymov, and formed a model for the American dollar; the building's museum has examples of both.) In 1400 the compound was converted into the residence of Wenceslas IV, who signed here the famous Decrees of Kutná Hora, authorizing the Hussite takeover of Prague's university (see page 65).

The former **Ursuline Convent** dominates the main square with its elegant Baroque façade designed by K.I. Dienzenhofer (1733-43); it houses a museum of local history. Other sights in the center include the Gothic church of **St James** (sv. Jakuba, 1330-1420), with an 82-meter (270-foot) tower and splendid 17thC altar, the Baroque church of **St John Nepomuk** (1734-54), built by F.M. Kaňka, and a 16thC fountain on attractive **Rejskovo náměstí**.

Outskirts

The bizarre ossuary of **Sedlec** (✭) is located at the edge of the town in the former Cistercian monastery of the same name *(2km/1¹⁄₄ miles from center; buses from Masarykovo ul.)*. The monastery church, a Gothic edifice (c.1320) with 18thC vaulting by Santini-Aichl, is worth a visit in its own right. More unusual, however, are the extraordinary compositions (cherubs, a chandelier, the Schwarzenberg coat-of-arms) which a local artist by the name of František Rint fashioned out of human bones in the crypt of the small graveyard chapel. The monastery had been a popular place of burial since the 13thC after having been strewn with earth from Golgotha, and Rint, working in the 1870s, had 40,000 neatly stacked skeletons from which to choose.

MARIÁNSKÉ LÁZNĚ (Marienbad) ✭
*162km (101 miles) w of Prague (48km/30 miles s of Karlovy Vary). **By car** as for Karlovy Vary, but turn off at Bochov for Toužim-Teplá.*

The second most famous Bohemian spa (population 15,000) surpasses Karlovy Vary in both the extravagance of its *fin de siècle* architecture and in stylistic harmony, nearly undisturbed by any building newer than the 1920s. The town occupies a beautiful site on a richly wooded hillside. A vast *Kurpark* lies in the middle, with boulevards running along its sides, lined with resort houses and hotels that seem to lose touch with reality the farther you climb toward the central area around the **Main Colonnade** (✭) and **Goethovo náměstí** (Goethe Square).

The former, built of cast iron, dates from 1889; the latter commemorates the poet, who fell in love with the 17-year-old Ulrike von Levetzow during a visit in 1823 — when he was 74 — and composed the *Marienbad Elegies* in response to this experience. He stayed at the **Hotel Kavkaz** (✭)

(formerly the Weimar, and before that the Klebelsberg), whose caryatids and trumpet-blowing angels now mask a tired interior of peeling walls and morose clerks; also here, King Edward VII met the Russian foreign minister in 1907 to carve Asia into spheres of influence.

The **New Bath** (Nové lázně) of 1893-96 features a spectacular Art Nouveau bathing hall, which is reserved for men or women during different parts of the day. The **Wagner** house on Karlovarská ul. takes its name from the composer, an avid fan of Marienbad. Mark Twain is remembered in the **Sofia** — formerly the English Court — on the main boulevard (Hlavní třída). At the **Balmoral-Osborne**, Franz Kafka spent the summer of 1916.

A recently installed monument honors the US Army, which freed Mariánské Lázně from the Germans in May 1945 (the Soviets took over, five months later).

☞ There are 13 hotels, and a number of sanatoria which act more or less like hotels, each with its own satellite residences. Service, professional attitude and inner decor have only just begun to adapt to the new times. The **Carlton**, **Kavkaz** and **Pacifik** are the most impressive outwardly, **Excelsior** the most comfortable inside. Some private pensions exist in the lower town, but none near the center.

• **Carlton** at Chopinova 383 ☎(0165) 2796, no cards ⊒ᵈ • **Excelsior** at Hlavní třída 121 ☎(0165) 2705 ᴱˣ5346 Ⅲ 56 rms 🆎 💿 💿 💳 ⊒ᵈ ♈ ♔ • **Kavkaz** at Goethovo nám. 9 ☎(0165) 3141 Ⅲ no cards ⊒ᵈ 🎿 • **Pacifik** at Mírové nám. 84 ☎(0165) 3006 Ⅲ 💿 💿 💳 ⊒ᵈ

Vicinity

The Premonstratensian monastery at **Teplá** (✰) was established in 1193 by Blessed Hroznata and restyled in Baroque by Christoph Dienzenhofer in the early 18thC. Its library contains many rare manuscripts (☎*(0169) 922 64; mass on Sat 2.30pm).*

The spa of **Kynžvart** (Königswart ✰) deserves a visit less for its baths than for the magnificent residence of Prince Metternich, which once hosted such illustrious figures as Goethe, Beethoven and the naturalist Alexander von Humboldt. Following restorations, it was reopened to visitors in 1993 (☎*(0165) 912 69).*

MĚLNÍK
36km (22 miles) N of Prague. By car via Rte8/E55 (from Horňátocká, N of Holešovice): look for the marked turnoff on either Rte9 or Rte16. Buses from Florenc station (map 5B7). Trains from Prague-Central or Masarykovo, involving two changes. For castle ☎(0206) 2421.

The town (population 20,000) and **castle** (✰) stand at the strategic junction where the Vltava joins the Elbe. The castle had historically been the endowment of Bohemian queens; Charles IV is credited with planting (or improving) its famous vineyards, which produce the St Ludmila wine. The present Renaissance structure is the work of the counts (later princes) Lobkowicz, who acquired the estate in the 16thC. They are now again in possession, since 1991, operating a delightful *vinárna*/restaurant where visitors can taste the local wine.

Vicinity

The 18thC castle of **Liběchov**, 7km (4$\frac{1}{4}$ miles) N of Mělník, houses the East Asian collections of Prague's NÁPRSTEK MUSEUM (see page 120). An attractive 8km (5-mile) hiking path leads from the castle through a landscape of strange rock formations, some of them fashioned into beasts, imaginary creatures or historical scenes by 19thC sculptor V. Levy.

PLZEŇ (Pilsen)

*88km (55 miles) sw of Prague. **By car** via D5/E50 (follow Plzeňská from Smíchov). **Trains** (1$\frac{1}{2}$ hrs) from Prague-Central and Prague-Smíchov.*

The second city of Bohemia, famous for the beer-making method that bears its name, is a dreary industrial waste, centered on the huge Škoda armament works which provide its economic backbone. At its center lies a rather attractive **main square** (náměstí Republiky), said to be one of the largest medieval squares in Europe, with the Gothic church of St Bartholomew and an impressive 16thC Town Hall sadly in need of restoration.

The **Pilsner Urquell** brewery (Plzeňský prazdroj), where the first Pilsner beer came on tap in 1842, can be seen on the left as you leave the city in the direction of Prague. Reduced to a sad state under state ownership, it is now privatized and poised for a takeover by foreign (i.e., German) capital. Guided tours start at the main gate, (usually) on every hour. There is also an interesting **Brewery Museum** on Veleslavínova ul., near the main square.

Vicinity

The Baroque château and hunting lodge of **Kozel** is located 14km (8 miles) SE of Plzeň, near the village of Šťáhlavy. It has a magnificent interior, which holds collections of armor and 18thC Meissen porcelain, and wonderful formal gardens with views over Šťáhlavy (☎ *(019) 96 92 13* 🖾 *open May-Sept daily except Mon; Apr and Oct only open Sat-Sun).*

PRŮHONICE GARDENS

*16km (10 miles) SE of Prague. Map 2E5. **By car**, take second exit on the D1/E14 motorway to Brno/Vienna. **Metro:** Družby, then hourly bus to Průhonice-Dobřejovice or Průhonice-Říčany. **Gardens open** Apr-Oct 7am-7pm.*

One of the most magnificent botanical parks in the Czech Republic, indeed in Europe, lies on the southeastern outskirts of Prague within the boundaries of the former aristocratic estate of Průhonice.

The park was laid out in the 1890s by Count Ernest Sylva-Taroucca, who imported a variety of exotic plants from around the world and arranged them in a pleasant combination of gardens and wooded areas. The historic **château** was rebuilt around the same time as a pastiche of various historic styles; it is currently closed to the public. A small 12thC **church** stands near the park entrance. A modern country hotel has recently opened nearby (see CLUB HOTEL PRŮHONICE, page 128).

SÁZAVA MONASTERY ★
*45km (28 miles) SE of Prague. **By car,** drive to the monastery from the Mirošovice exit on the D1 motorway, or drive to the village from the Ostředek exit and take the river ferry ☎(0328) 911 77 ▨ **Open** May-Sept 8am-5pm daily except Mon; Apr, Oct Sat-Sun only 9am-4pm ✗ available.*

The famous Benedictine abbey of Sázava, the only Bohemian monastery devoted to the Old Slavonic liturgy, was founded in the 11thC by the abbot Prokop, whose statue, by Brokoff, stands on Prague's Charles Bridge (see page 80). The monastery was dissolved by Joseph II in the 18thC and subsequently converted into an aristocratic residence. The Gothic architectural core is overlaid with splendid Baroque additions, and the site on the Sázava river is one of great natural beauty.

Vicinity
Český Šternberk, a medieval castle built above a steep rock on the bank of the Sázava, was owned by the Sternberg family from the 13thC up to 1949, and has been in their possession again since 1991. The 6km (4-mile) distance from the monastery is easily negotiable on foot or by train, but the drive involves a disproportionately long detour over the D1 motorway. No tour of the castle interior is possible at present.

SLAPY DAM *(Slapská přehradní nádrž)*
*From 24km (15 miles) to 105km (66 miles) s of Prague. **By boat:** see BOAT EXCURSIONS, page 166. **By car** via Zbraslav-Štěchovice or via Rte4 (Strakonice road) to Orlík. It is no longer possible to drive across the dam to Rabyně. **Buses** from Smíchovo nádraží.*

The favorite summer weekend destination of Praguers is a 44km-long (27-mile), 1,400-hectare (3,500-acre) reservoir created by a series of dams built on the Vltava between 1948 and 1954. The artificial lake is surrounded by woods dotted with bungalows and resort colonies, and offers ample scope for various water sports, fishing and boating.

The village of **Štěchovice** has several attractive restaurants and pubs. In **Hrazany** there are archeological traces of a Celtic settlement of the 1stC BC. The tiny village of **Nová Rabyně** features an attractive restaurant with good views. A panoramic road leads from here to the castle of KONOPIŠTĚ.

TEREZÍN *(Theresienstadt)* ★
*64km (40 miles) N of Prague. Frequent morning **buses** from Florenc station (map **5B7**). Organized **tours** from Prague's Old Town Hall every Sunday morning. **Trains** from Prague-Central and Masarykovo go to Litoměřice, with a change at Lysá nad Labem. **Lesser Fort** ▨ open daily 8am-6.30pm (summer), 8am-3.30pm (winter). **Crematorium** ▨ open Apr-Oct daily (except Mon) 10am-5pm.*

The Nazi terror apparatus at Terezín consisted of two separate units: a "model town" for Jewish deportees from different parts of the Protectorate, and a prison fortress whose inmates were mostly non-Jewish political offenders or war captives. The physical setup dates from an earlier age of ideological hubris, and is frighteningly elegant in design.

The fortified **town** (★) of Theresienstadt/Terezín (population 2,700) was built in 1780 on purely scientific principles of planning laid down by Joseph II, who named the town after his mother Maria Theresa.

The Nazis began transporting Jews to Theresienstadt in 1941, and evacuated the last of the town's Czech inhabitants the following year (they returned after the war). Technically, it was meant to be a self-governing ghetto for Jews rather than an extermination camp like Auschwitz. The inmates were allowed their own currency, a printing press, a theater, even a jazz band, as the town's newly opened **museum** records in painful detail. Of the 140,000 deportees who went to Terezín, 87,000 were eventually sent to die at Auschwitz and another 30,000 died of various causes while in the town. A **crematorium** located outside the town walls disposed of their bodies.

The **Lesser Fort** (Malá pevnost ★), a military compound situated 2km ($1\frac{1}{4}$ miles) s of the town, served as a Habsburg prison from the early 19thC. Its inmates included Gavrilo Princip, the assassin of Sarajevo, who spent four years shackled to his cell wall before expiring in 1918, and other heroes of sundry Balkan national struggles.

The Nazis turned the fortress into a concentration camp, which has been preserved exactly as it was. The presentation is admirably free of false pathos and conveys the horror with shattering directness. Visitors are handed a detailed plan and allowed to wander alone among the ghastly wards, starvation cells, underground passages, torture chambers and mass graves.

Vicinity

The pretty, historic town of **Litoměřice** (population 24,000), 3km (2 miles) to the N, helps to reinforce the sense of tragedy conveyed by the camp. Leitmeritz (as it used to be called) was a cultural and economic center in German Sudetenland until the expulsion of its inhabitants after the war. Today it wears the wretched look of a town in terminal decline.

There are various beautiful and crumbling monuments, including a medieval bell tower, a Gothic parish church with an altarpiece by Lucas Cranach, a Renaissance town hall and a Baroque Dominican church.

The most arresting of all, however, is the former **Jesuit church** (★), a Baroque masterpiece (1704-31) now reduced to shambles through neglect or vandalism. The church is filled with half-destroyed sculptures of Baroque ecstasy and pain, which obtain an almost abstract intensity in the midst of the wreckage surrounding them. A group of young artists exhibit beside them their own quasi-Surrealist sculptures, to startling effect. A much-needed restoration project is under way.

Schlosshotel Hubertus *(10km/6 miles E of Litoměřice: 6km/4 miles in the direction of Česká Lípa, then left 4km/2½ miles in the direction of Ploškovice* ☎ *and* Fx *(0416) 9535* ▥ AE VISA ➾ Ⴤ *garden)* is a historic mansion recently converted into a hotel, under German management.

VELTRUSY

27km (17 miles) N of Prague ☎*(0205) 812 07* 📧 **Open** *May-Sept daily except Mon; Apr and Oct only open Sat-Sun.*

The Baroque château of the Chotek family (early 18thC) houses a rich collection of Eastern Asian porcelains. The main attraction of the estate is a large park in English style littered with mostly late 18thC pleasantries: canals, bridges, artificial ruins, a church in the French Empire style, a Swiss lodge and a Neo-Gothic mill.

A short distance from Veltrusy is the attractive village of **Nelahozeves**, the birthplace of the composer Dvořák. The house in which he was born is a museum.

ZBRASLAV

Zbraslav nad Vltavou, Prague 5 (10km/6 miles s of center). Map 1E3 ☎*59 11 88.* **Bus** *129, 241, 243 or 255 from metro Smíchovské nádraží.*

The former monastery and château of Zbraslav, one of the finest Baroque ensembles in the environs of Prague, houses the permanent exhibition of modern (19th and early 20thC) Czech sculpture of the National Gallery (Národní galerie).

The compound has had an eventful history. Originally a royal hunting lodge under Ottokar II, it was rebuilt as a Cistercian monastery under Wenceslas II, who added the important Early Gothic Church of the Virgin Mary. It was demolished during the Hussite and Thirty Years' wars. The architect Santini-Aichl redesigned it in its present form in 1709-27. Deconsecrated and converted into a sugar factory under Joseph II, it was restored as a private estate in 1833, and finally nationalized in 1948. The last two kings of the Přemysl line, Wenceslas II and III, are buried in the church.

The **sculpture gallery** contains a number of outstanding works by, among others, Stanislav Sucharda, František Bílek, Otto Gutfreund and Bohumil Kafka, and receives far fewer visitors than it deserves.

Czech in a nutshell

Czech is a member of the Western Slavic languages, which also include Slovak (a closely related language) and Polish. Modern literary Czech was created in the 19thC on the basis of Old Czech, which had disappeared from literary use after the Middle Ages. The spoken language contains many German loan-words.

PRONUNCIATION

Czech vowels are either short or long. A long vowel is indicated with an accent (´) (in the case of *u*, also the sign ˚), whose effect can be best approximated by putting an imaginary English *h* after the vowel sound. *Y* is considered a vowel and for all practical purposes sounds like an *i*. The stress is almost always on the first syllable of a word.

vinárna	pron. VI-nahr-na
palác	pron. PA-lahtz
náměstí	pron. NAH-mnye-steeh
nábřeží	pron. NAH-br(zh)e-zeeh
křižovnické	pron. KR(zh)I-zhov-nitz-keh

A *háček* (˘) above a letter "softens" its sound.

č	ch	as in *chip*
ď	dy	as in *video*
ě	ie	as in *fiesta*
ň	ny	as in *new*
š	sh	as in *ship*
ž	zh	as in French *journal*
ř		is a sound between *r* and *zh*, unlike anything in English, e.g., *Dvořák* (the composer), pron. DVOR-zhahk.
ť	ty	as in *tube*

Other consonants are as in English except:

c	ts	as in *gets*
ch	kh	as in Scottish *loch*
g	g	always hard as in *go*
j	y	as in *yes*

Note that *ch* is treated as a separate letter of the alphabet that comes between h and i. The haček'ed letters also count as separate letters and follow their respective straight versions. The letters q, w and x are not native characters of the Czech alphabet, though they appear in Czech words derived from other languages, such as *luxusní* (luxury/-ious).

BASIC COMMUNICATION

Good morning	*dobrý den*	Thank you (very much)	*děkuji*
Good evening	*dobrý večer*	(*moc*)	
Goodbye	*na shledanou*	Excuse me	*promiňte*
My name is . . .	*jmenuji se . . .*	Hello, bye (informal)	*Ahoj*
Please, you're welcome	*prosím*	I don't understand	*nerozumím*

Do you speak English/
  Czech? *Mluvíte anglicky/česky?*
  German/French *německy/*
  francouzsky
Help me please *pomozte mi*
  prosím.
Who? *kdo?*
What? *co?*
Where (is)? *kde (je)?*
From where? *odkud?*
When? *kdy?*
Why? *proč?*
How much/many? *kolik?*
Is there . . . ? *máte . . . ?*
Yes/no *ano/ne*
Help! *pomoc!*
Right *vpravo*
Left *vlevo*
Straight *přímo*

Here *zde, tady*
There *tam*
Up *nahoru*
Down *dolů*
Back *zpět*
From *od*
To *do*
For *pro*
Much *hodně*
Little (amount) *málo*
Nothing *nic*
Good *dobrý* (m), *dobrá* (f),
  dobré (n)
Bad *špatný* (m), *špatná* (f),
  špatné (n)
Small, little *malý* (m), *malá* (f),
  malé (n)
Large, great *velký* (m), *velká* (f),
  velké (n)

NUMBERS

1 *jeden/jedna/jedno*
2 *dva*
3 *tři*
4 *čtyři*
5 *pět*
6 *šest*
7 *sedm*
8 *osm*
9 *devět*
10 *deset*

20 *dvacet*
30 *třicet*
40 *čtyřicet*
50 *padesát*
100 *sto*
500 *pět set*
1000 *tisíc*
Zero *nula*
Half *půl*
Quarter *čtvrt*

333 silver sprinklers sprinkled over 333 silver roofs
Třistatřiatřicet stříbrných stříkaček stříkalo přes třistatřiatřicet stříbrných střech.

TIME

What time is it? *Kolik je*
  hodin?
Minute *minuta*
Hour *hodina*
Day/today *dnes*
Tomorrow *zítra*
Yesterday *včera*
Morning *ráno*
Evening *večer*

Night *noc*
Week *týden*
Month *měsíc*
Year *rok*
Century *století*
Now *teď*
Later *později*
Before *před*
After *po*

MONTHS AND SEASONS

January *leden*
February *únor*
March *březen*
April *duben*
May *květen*
June *červen*
July *červenec*
August *srpen*

September *září*
October *říjen*
November *listopad*
December *prosinec*
Spring *jaro*
Summer *léto*
Fall, autumn *podzim*
Winter *zima*

DAYS OF THE WEEK

Monday   *pondělí*
Tuesday   *úterý*
Wednesday   *středa*
Thursday   *čtvrtek*

Friday   *pátek*
Saturday   *sobota*
Sunday   *neděle*

COLORS

Black   *černý*
Blue   *modrý*
Brown   *hnědý*
Golden   *zlatý*
Green   *zelený*

Red   *červený*
Violet   *fialový*
White   *bílý*
Yellow   *žlutý*

TRAVEL

Airport   *letiště*
(Train) station   *nádraží*

Bus station   *autobusové nádraží*

SIGHTSEEING

Bridge   *most*
Castle   *hrad, hrádek*
Chapel   *kaple*
Château   *letohrádek, zámek*
Church   *kostel, chrám*
Hill   *hora*
Monastery/abbey   *klášter*
Palace   *palác*
Tower   *věž*
Open/closed   *otevřeno/zavřeno*

When are you open?   *Jak máte otevřeno?*
Two tickets for . . .   *dva lístky na . . .*
Where is . . . ?   *Kde je . . . ?*
How do I get to . . . ?   *Jak se dostanu na . . . ?*
When does it leave?   *Kdy odjíždí?*
• See also NOTE ON STREET NAMES, page 47.

AT THE HOTEL

Room   *pokoj*
Single/double   *pro jednu osobu/pro dva*
May I pay by credit card?   *Mohu platit kreditní kartou?*

Do you have a free room?   *Máte volný pokoj?*
How much does it cost?   *Kolik to stojí?*

AT THE RESTAURANT

Food, meal   *jídlo*
Breakfast   *snídaně*
Lunch   *oběd*
Dinner   *večeře*
Kitchen   *kuchyně*
Menu   *jídelní lístek*
Meatless dish   *bezmasé jídlo*

Do you have a table?   *Máte volný stůl?*
. . . for one/two   *. . . pro jednoho/dva*
Could I make a reservation?   *Mohu reservovat?*
May I order?   *Mohu si objednat?*
Bon appetit!   *Dobrou chuť!*

FOODS

Appetizer   *předkrm*
Beer   *pivo*
Bread   *chléb*
Bread (buns)   *rohlík*
Butter   *máslo*
Cheese   *sýr*
Chips (American)   *brambůrky*
Chips (British)   *hranolky*
Coffee   *káva*

with whipped cream   *šlehačka*
with milk   *s mlékem*
Cream   *smetana*
Delicatessen   *lahůdky*
Dessert   *moučník*
Drink   *nápoj*
Dumplings   *knedlíky*
Eggs   *vajíčka*
French fries   *hranolky*

Fruit	*ovoce*	Rice	*rýže*
Honey	*med*	Salt	*sůl*
Ice cream	*zmrzlina*	Sauce	*omáčka*
Jam	*džem*	Soup	*polévka*
Milk	*mléko*	Sugar	*cukr*
Mineral water	*minerálka*	Tea	*čaj*
Orange	*pomeranč*	Vegetable	*zelenina*
Pancake	*palačinka*	Water	*voda*
Pepper	*pepř*	Wine (white, red)	*víno (bílé,*
Potatoes	*brambory*		*červené)*

MEAT, FISH, POULTRY

Beef	*hovězí*	Liver	*játra*
Boiled	*vařené*	Meat	*maso*
Charcuterie	*uzeniny*	Pork	*vepřové*
Chicken	*kuře, slepičí*	Rabbit	*králík*
Duck	*kachna*	Roast	*pečené*
Fish	*ryba*	Sausage	*párek*
Fried	*smažené*	Shrimp	*krevety*
Goose	*husa*	Steak	*biftek* (not necessarily beef)
Grilled	*na rožni*	Turkey	*krocan*
Ham	*šunka*	Veal	*telecí*

SHOP SIGNS

Cukrárna	pastry shop, sweets	*Obuv*	shoes
Dárky	gifts	*Oděv*	clothing
Hostinec	pub/restaurant	*Pivnice*	pub, beerhall, bar
Kavárna	coffee shop	*Potraviny*	groceries
Klenoty	jewelry	*Restaurace*	restaurant
Květiny	flowers	*Samoobsluha*	supermarket (lit.
Lahůdky	delicatessen		self-service)
Lékárna	pharmacy	*Sklo*	glass
Maso uzeniny	charcuterie	*Starožitnost*	antiques
Noviny	newspapers	*Tabák*	tobacco
Občerstvení	snack bar	*Vinárna*	wine tavern/restaurant

SIGN DECODER

Cena	price	*Sem*	pull
Dámy	ladies (WC)	*Směnárna*	exchange
Muži	men	*Směr*	direction
Nekuřte	don't smoke	*Směr prohlídky*	this way
Neparkovat	no parking	*Tam*	push
Objížďka	detour	*Vchod*	entrance, way in
Obsazeno	occupied	*Vstup*	entrance (boarding)
Odjezd	departure	*Východ*	exit, way out
Otevřeno	open	*Výjezd*	driveway, car exit
Páni	gents (WC)	*Výstup*	exit
Pokladna	cashier	*Zadáno*	reserved
Pozor	attention	*Zakázáno*	prohibited
Přestup	transfer, way through	*Zákaz kouření*	no smoking
Příjezd	arrival	*Zastávka*	(bus) stop
Prodej	sale	*Zavřeno*	closed
Pronájem	rent	*Ženy*	ladies, women

TONGUE TWISTERS
Strč prst skrz krk.   Stick a finger into your throat.

Index

- Place names are generally given in English.
- Page numbers in **bold** indicate main entries.
- *Italic* page numbers indicate illustrations and maps.
- See also LIST OF STREET NAMES on page 194.

List of street names

- All streets mentioned in the text that fall within the area covered by our maps **3** to **5** are listed below.
- Map numbers are printed in **bold** type. Some smaller streets are not named on the map, but the map reference given below will help you locate the correct neighborhood.

Pražský hrad, **3**C3

Rašínovo, nábř., **4**E5–F5
Republiky, nám., **5**C6
Resslova, **4**E5
Řetězova, **4**C5
Revoluční, **5**B6–C6
28. října, **5**D5–D6
Rybná, **5**C6
Rytířská, **4**D5–6

Salvátorská, **4**C5
Senovážná, **5**C6
Skořepka, **4**D5
Smetanovo, nábř., **4**C5–D5
Sněmovni, **3**C3
Spálená, **4**D5–E5

Staroměstské, nám., **4**C5
Štěpánská, **5**E6–D6
Strahovské nádvoří, **3**C1
Štupartská, **5**C6

Těšnov, **5**B7
Thunovská, **3**C3
Tomašská, **3**C3
Tržistě, **3**C3

Uhelný, trh, **4**D5
Újezd, **3**D3
U milosrdných, **5**B5–6
U obecního domu, **5**C6
U radnice, **4**C5

Václavské, nám., **5**D6

Valdštejnské, nám., **3**C3
Valdštejnská, **3**C3–**4**B4
Vězeňská, **4**C5–B6
Vlašská, **3**C2–3
Vikářská, **3**B3
Viničná, **5**F6
Vitěžná, **3**D3–**4**D4
Vodičkova, **5**E6–D6
Voršilská, **4**D5
Vyšehradská, **4**F5

Washingtonova, **5**D7–C7
Wilsonova, **5**D7–B7

Žatecká, **4**C5
Železná, **4**C5–6
Žitná, **5**E5–6

KEY TO MAP PAGES

KEY TO MAP SYMBOLS

Metropolitan Map

- ■ Place of Interest
- Built-up Area
- Wood or Park
- Motorway
- Motorway (under construction)
- Main Road
- Secondary Road
- Other Road
- Road Number
- Railway
- Airport

City Map

- Place of Interest or Important Building
- Built-up Area
- Park
- Cemetery
- † Church
- ✡ Synagogue
- Hospital
- *i* Information Office
- ⊠ Post Office
- Garage / Parking Lot
- Stepped Street
- No Entry
- Ⓜ Metro Station
- Funicular Railway
- Adjoining Page No.

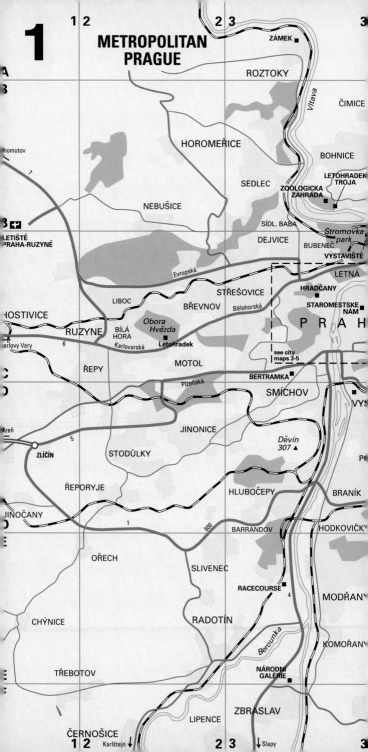

1

METROPOLITAN PRAGUE

ZÁMEK

ROZTOKY

Vltava

ČIMICE

HOROMĚŘICE

BOHNICE

SEDLEC

LETOHRADEK
TROJA

NEBUŠICE

ZOOLOGICKA
ZAHRADA

SÍDL. BABA

Stromovka
park

LETIŠTĚ
PRAHA-RUZYNĚ

DEJVICE

BUBENEČ

VÝSTAVIŠTĚ

Evropská

LETNÁ

STŘEŠOVICE

HRADČANY

LIBOC

BŘEVNOV

Bělohorská

STAROMĚSTSKE
NÁM

HOSTIVICE

RUZYNE

BÍLÁ
HORA

Obora
Hvězda

P R A H

Karlovarská

Letohradek

Karlovy Vary

6

ŘEPY

MOTOL

see city
maps 3–5

Plzeňská

BERTRAMKA

SMÍCHOV

VY

Plzeň

JINONICE

Děvín
307 ▲

ZLÍČÍN

5

STODŮLKY

P

ŘEPORYJE

HLUBOČEPY

BRANÍK

JINOČANY

1

600

BARRANDOV

HODKOVIČK

OŘECH

SLIVENEC

RACECOURSE

4

MODŘAN

CHÝNICE

RADOTÍN

Berounka

KOMOŘAN

TŘEBOTOV

NÁRODNÍ
GALÉRIE

ZBRASLAV

ČERNOŠICE

LIPENCE

Karlštejn ↓

↓ Slapy

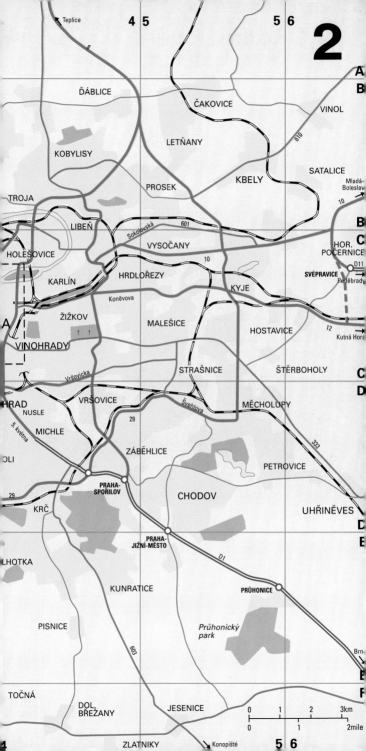

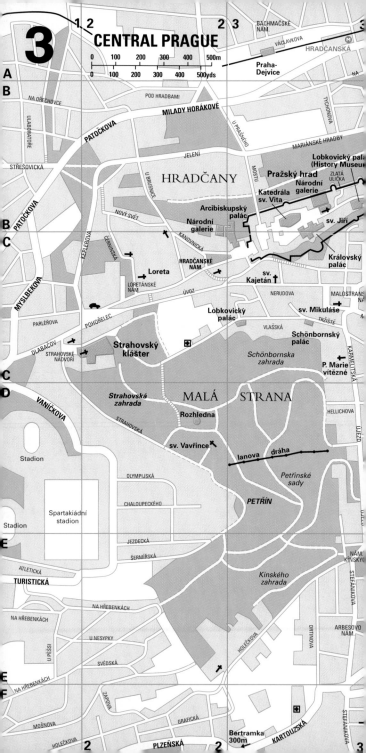

3 CENTRAL PRAGUE

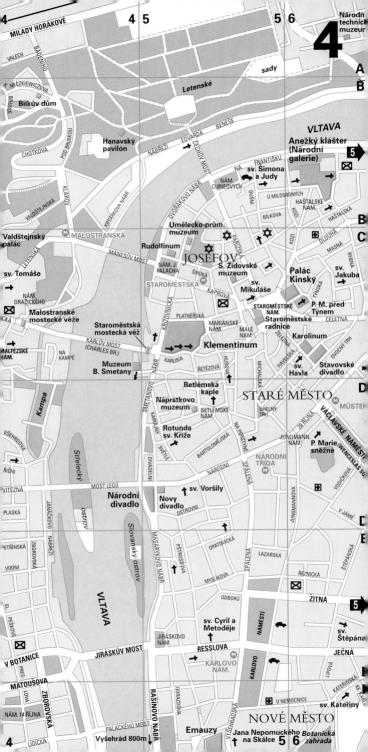

VALECH

BÁDENTHO

MICKIEWICZOVA

BRUSCE

Bílkův dům

CHOTKOVA

POD BRUSKOU

KLAROV

VALDŠTEJNSKÁ

Valdštejnský
palác

sv. Tomáše

NÁM.
DRAŽICKÉHO

Malostranské
mostecké věže

MALTÉZSKÉ
NÁM.

NA
KAMPĚ

Kampa

VŠEHRDOVA

ŘÍČNÍ

VÍTĚZNÁ

PLASKÁ

PETŘÍNSKÁ

VODNÍ

EL.

PEŠKOVÉ

V BOTANICE

MATOUSOVA

ZBOROVSKÁ

NÁM. 14 ŘÍJNA

LIDICKÁ

Letenské

sady

A

B

Hanavský
pavilón

EDVARDA

NÁBŘEŽÍ

ČECHŮV MOST

BENEŠE

VLTAVA

Anežký klášter
(Národní
galerie)

NA
FRANTIŠKU

sv. Simona
a Judy

NÁM
CURIEOVYCH

DUŠNÍ

U MILOSRDNÝCH

HAŠTALSKÉ
NÁM.

KOŽNÁ

HAŠTALSKÁ

B

DVOŘÁKOVO NÁBŘ.

KOŠÍRKOVA NÁBŘ.

Umělecko-prům.
muzeum

BÍLKOVA

PAŘÍŽSKÁ

KOŽÍ

DLOUHÁ

MASNÁ

MALOSTRANSKÁ

Rudolfinum

NÁM. J.
PALACHA

JOSEFOV

ŠIROKÁ

S. Židovské
muzeum

sv.
Mikuláše

Palác
Kinský

RYBNÁ

sv.
Jakuba

C

MÁNESŮV MOST

STAROMĚSTSKÁ

KAPROVA

TÝNSKÁ

P. M. před
Týnem

KŘIŽOVNICKÁ

PLATNÉŘSKÁ

MARIÁNSKÉ
NÁM.

MALÉ
NÁM.

STAROMĚSTSKÉ
NÁM.

Staroměstské
radnice

CELETNÁ

Karolinum

OVOCNÝ TRH

Staroměstská
mostecká věž

KARLŮV MOST
(CHARLES BR.)

KARLOVA

ŘETĚZOVÁ

HUSOVA

MICHALSKÁ

ŽELEZNÁ

HAVELSKÁ

sv.
Havla

Stavovské
divadlo

MŮSTEI

Klementinum

Muzeum
B. Smetany

SMETANOVO

Betlémská
kaple

Náprstkovo
muzeum

BETLÉMSKÉ
NÁM.

NA PERŠTÝNĚ

UHELNÝ
TRH

STARÉ MĚSTO

VÁCLAVSKÉ NÁMĚSTÍ (WENCESLAS SQ.)

28 ŘÍJNA

D

KAROLINY

DIVADELNÍ

Rotunda
sv. Kříže

SVĚTLÉ

BARTOLOMĚJSKÁ

JUNGMANN.
NÁM.

JUNGMANNOVA

P. Marie
sněžné

Strelecký

OSTROV

MOST LEGIÍ

Národní
divadlo

Slovanský ostrov

MASARYKOVO NÁBŘ.

sv. Voršily

Novy
divadlo

OSTROVNÍ

NÁRODNÍ
TŘÍDA

SPÁLENÁ

NÁRODNÍ

C

V JÁMĚ

E

PŠTROSSOVA

OPATOVICKÁ

LAZARSKÁ

ŠTĚPÁNSKÁ

VLTAVA

JANÁČKOVO NÁBŘEŽÍ

MYSLÍKOVA

ODBORŮ

ŘEZNICKÁ

ŽITNÁ

5

JIRÁSKŮV MOST

JIRÁSKOVO
NÁM.

sv. Cyril a
Metoděje

RESSLOVA

NÁMĚSTÍ

KARLOVO

sv.
Štěpána

JEČNÁ

LIPOVÁ

PRES.

LOVA

GORAZDOVA

VYŠEHRADSKÁ

KARLOVO
NÁM.

U NEMOCNICE

sv. Kateřiny

KATEŘINSKÁ

NA BOJIŠTI

NOVÉ MĚSTO

PALACKÉHO MOST

RAŠÍNOVO NÁBŘ.

Vyšehrad 800m

Emauzy

Jana Nepomuckého
na Skálce

5 6

Botanická
zahrada

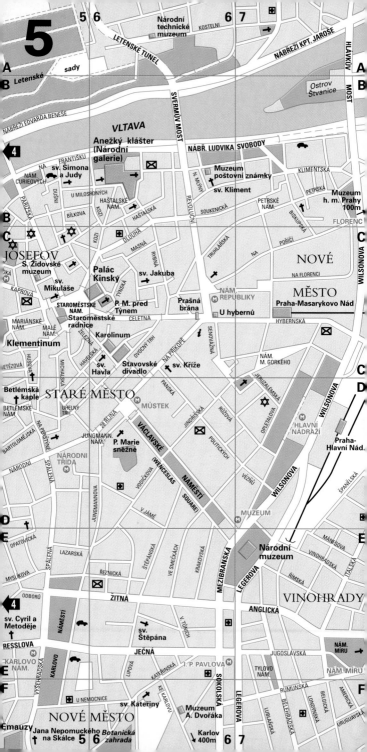

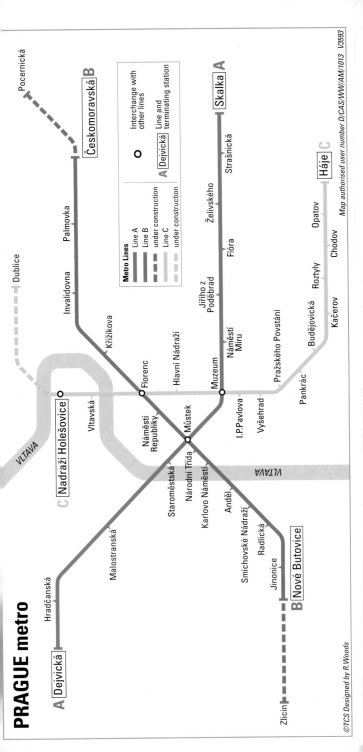

PRAGUE metro

A Dejvická

Hradčanská

Malostranská

C Nadraží Holešovice

Vltavská

VLTAVA

Náměstí Republiky

Staroměstská

Národni Třida

Karlovo Náměstí

Anděl

Smíchovské Nádraží

Radlická

Jinonice

B Nové Butovice

Zličin

Florenc

Křižíkova

Invalidovna

Palmovka

Dublice

Českomoravská B

Pocernická

Hlavní Nádraží

Müstek

Muzeum

I.P.Pavlova

Vyšehrad

VLTAVA

Pankrác

Pražského Povstání

Náměstí Miru

Jiřího z Poděbrad

Flóra

Želivského

Strašnická

Skalka A

Budějovická

Roztyly

Opatov

Kačerov

Chodov

Háje C

Metro Lines
Line A
Line B
under construction
Line C
under construction

○ Interchange with other lines

A Dejvická Line and terminating station

©TCS Designed by R.Woods

Map authorised user number D/CAS/WW/AM/1013 V3593

CONVERSION FORMULAE

To convert	Multiply by
Inches to Centimeters	2.540
Centimeters to Inches	0.39370
Feet to Meters	0.3048
Meters to feet	3.2808
Yards to Meters	0.9144
Meters to Yards	1.09361
Miles to Kilometers	1.60934
Kilometers to Miles	0.621371
Sq Meters to Sq Feet	10.7638
Sq Feet to Sq Meters	0.092903
Sq Yards to Sq Meters	0.83612
Sq Meters to Sq Yards	1.19599
Sq Miles to Sq Kilometers	2.5899
Sq Kilometers to Sq Miles	0.386103
Acres to Hectares	0.40468
Hectares to Acres	2.47105
Gallons to Liters	4.545
Liters to Gallons	0.22
Ounces to Grams	28.3495
Grams to Ounces	0.03528
Pounds to Grams	453.592
Grams to Pounds	0.00220
Pounds to Kilograms	0.4536
Kilograms to Pounds	2.2046
Tons (UK) to Kilograms	1016.05
Kilograms to Tons (UK)	0.0009842
Tons (US) to Kilograms	746.483
Kilograms to Tons (US)	0.0013396

Quick conversions

Kilometers to Miles	Divide by 8, multiply by 5
Miles to Kilometers	Divide by 5, multiply by 8
1 meter =	Approximately 3 feet 3 inches
2 centimeters =	Approximately 1 inch
1 pound (weight) =	475 grams (nearly $\frac{1}{2}$ kilogram)
Celsius to Fahrenheit	Divide by 5, multiply by 9, add 32
Fahrenheit to Celsius	Subtract 32, divide by 9, multiply by 5

What the papers say:

• "The expertly edited American Express series has the knack of pinpointing precisely the details you need to know, and doing it concisely and intelligently." **(*The Washington Post*)**

• "*(Venice)* . . . the best guide book I have ever used." **(*The Standard* — London)**

• "Amid the welter of guides to individual countries, American Express stands out . . . . " **(*Time*)**

• "Possibly the best . . . guides on the market, they come close to the oft-claimed 'all you need to know' comprehensiveness, with much original experience, research and opinions." **(*Sunday Telegraph* — London)**

• "The most useful general guide was *American Express New York* by Herbert Bailey Livesey. It also has the best street and subway maps." **(*Daily Telegraph* — London)**

• " . . . in the flood of travel guides, the *American Express* guides come closest to the needs of traveling managers with little time." **(*Die Zeit* — Germany)**

What the experts say:

• "We only used one guide book, Sheila Hale's *AmEx Venice,* for which she and the editors deserve a Nobel Prize." **(travel writer Eric Newby, London)**

• "Congratulations to you and your staff for putting out the best guide book of *any* size *(Barcelona & Madrid)*. I'm recommending it to everyone." **(travel writer Barnaby Conrad, Santa Barbara, California)**

• "If you're only buying one guide book, we recommend American Express . . . . " **(*Which?* — Britain's leading consumer magazine)**

• "The judges selected *American Express London* as the best guide book of the past decade — it won the competition in 1983. [The guide] was praised for being 'concise, well presented, up-to-date, with unusual information.' " **(News release from the London Tourist Board and Convention Bureau)**

What readers from all over the world say:

• "We could never have had the wonderful time that we did without your guide to *Paris*. The compactness was very convenient, your maps were all we needed, but it was your restaurant guide that truly made our stay special . . . . We have learned first-hand: *American Express — don't leave home without it.*" (A. R., Virginia Beach, Va., USA)

• Of Sheila Hale's *Florence and Tuscany:* "I hope you don't mind my calling you by your first name, but during our recent trip to Florence and Siena [we] said on innumerable occasions, 'What does Sheila say about that?' " (H.G., Buckhurst Hill, Essex, England)

• "I have visited Mexico most years since 1979 . . . Of the many guides I have consulted during this time, by far the best has been James Tickell's *Mexico,* of which I've bought each edition." (J.H., Mexico City)

• "We have heartily recommended these books to all our friends who have plans to travel abroad." (A.S. and J.C., New York, USA)

• "Much of our enjoyment came from the way your book *(Venice)* sent us off scurrying around the interesting streets and off to the right places at the right times". (Lord H., London, England)

• "It *(Paris)* was my constant companion and totally dependable . . . . " (V. N., Johannesburg, South Africa)

• "We found *Amsterdam, Rotterdam & The Hague* invaluable . . . probably the best of its kind we have ever used. It transformed our stay from an ordinary one into something really memorable . . . . " (S.W., Canterbury, England)

• "Despite many previous visits to Italy, I wish I had had your guide *(Florence and Tuscany)* ages ago. I love the author's crisp, literate writing and her devotion to her subject." (M. B-K., Denver, Colorado, USA)

• "We became almost a club as we found people sitting at tables all around, consulting their little blue books!" (F.C., Glasgow, Scotland)

• "I have just concluded a tour . . . using your comprehensive *Cities of Australia* as my personal guide. Thank you for your magnificent, clear and precise book." (Dr. S.G., Singapore)

• "We never made a restaurant reservation without checking your book *(Venice)*. The recommendations were excellent, and the historical and artistic text got us through the sights beautifully." (L.S., Boston, Ma., USA)

• "The book *(Hong Kong, Singapore & Bangkok)* was written in such a personal way that I feel as if you were actually writing this book for me." (L.Z., Orange, Conn., USA)

• "I feel as if you have been a silent friend shadowing my time in Tuscany." (T.G., Washington, DC, USA)

American Express Travel Guides

spanning the globe....

EUROPE

Amsterdam, Rotterdam
& The Hague
Athens and the
Classical Sites ‡
Barcelona, Madrid &
Seville
Berlin, Potsdam &
Dresden ‡
Brussels
Dublin
Florence and Tuscany
London
Moscow &
St Petersburg ‡
Paris
Prague
Provence and the
Côte d'Azur ‡
Rome
Venice ‡
Vienna & Budapest

NORTH AMERICA

Boston and New
England ‡
Florida ‡
Los Angeles & San
Diego
Mexico
New York
San Francisco and
the Wine Regions
Toronto, Montréal &
Québec City
Washington, DC

THE PACIFIC

Cities of
Australia
Hong Kong
& Taiwan
Singapore &
Bangkok ‡
Tokyo

‡   Titles in preparation.

Clarity and quality of information, combined with outstanding maps — the ultimate in travelers' guides